How to Get
Happily Published

How to Get Happily Published

FIFTH EDITION

❖   ❖   ❖

Judith Appelbaum

HarperPerennial
A Division of HarperCollins*Publishers*

HarperCollins books may be purchased for educational, business, or sales promotional use. For information, please call or write: Special Markets Department, HarperCollins Publishers, Inc., 10 East 53rd Street, New York, NY 10022. Telephone: (212) 207-7528; Fax: (212) 207-7222.

First Edition

Library of Congress Cataloging-in-Publication Data

Appelbaum, Judith.
  How to get happily published/Judith Appelbaum.—5th ed.
    p. cm.
  Includes bibliographical references and index.
  ISBN 0-06-273509-8
  1. Authorship—Marketing. 2. Authors and publishers. 3. Publishers and publishing. I. Title.
PN155.A67 1998   97-41128
070.5'2—dc21   CIP

98 99 00 01 02 ❖/RRD 10 9 8 7 6 5 4 3 2 1

*For writers everywhere
who could use encouragement,
and for Alan,
who specializes in that.*

Contents

The Sale and Its Sequels

Endnote

Resources

Acknowledgments

Hundreds of people in and around publishing provided valuable information and advice for this book. My warmest thanks go both to those who are mentioned in the pages that follow and to those whose contributions the book reflects indirectly, including:

Bob Adelman, Alfred H. Allen, Carolyn Anthony, Robert E. Baensch, Nicholas Bakalar, Ann Banks, Virginia Barber, Marvin G. Barrett, John Baskin, Walter L. Bateman, Bob Bender, Sheila Berger, Susan Bergholz, Louise Bernikow, Meredith Bernstein, John Berry, Janice Blaufox, Georges Borchardt, Ruth Brengel, Richard P. Brickner, Donna Brodie, Selma Brody and Diana Brown.

And Robert Cassidy, Carol Cohen, Janet Coleman, Faith Conlon, Gay Courter, Page Cuddy, Ginger Curwen, Joann Davis, Kenneth C. Davis, Julia della Croce, John P. Dessauer, Paula Diamond, Paul D. Doebler, Arnold Dolin, Jane Dystel, Robert J. Egan, Lisel Eisenheimer, Martha Fairchild, Paul Fargis, Jenny Feder, Cheri Fein, Jean Feiwel, John Fischer, Zelda Fischer, Joan Foster, Lawrence B. Friedman and Len Fulton.

And Jonathan Galassi, Elizabeth Geiser, John Gilbertson, Susan Ginsburg, David Glotzer, Elizabeth Gordon, Annette Grant, Judith Grossman, Hannelore Hahn, Elise Hancock, Stuart Harris, James B. Heacock, Bill Henderson, Mildred Hird, Susan Hirschman, Lois Hjelmstad, Berenice Hoffman, Elaine Hughes, Hayes Jacobs, Alison Jahncke, Sylvia Johnson, Tony Jones, Joan

Kahn, Irwin Karp, Laura Katz, Mimi Kayden, Evelyn Kaye, Ralph Keyes, Rhoda Koenig, Diane Kruchkow, Mary and Robert Lane, Georgie Lee, Bill Leigh, Tom Lewis, Leslie Li and Lydia Link.

And Tom Loven, Nick Lyons, Miriam Madfis, Rich Marchione, Richard Marek, Elaine Markson, Peter McCabe, Ken McCormick, May McLaughlin, Karin McQuillan, Walter Meade, Kate Medina, Patricia Medved, Lisa Merrill, Robert R. Miles, Tom Montag, Joseph Montebello, Helen Moore, Richard Morris, William Morris, Adam Moss, Jennifer Moyer, Julian Muller and Raymond Mungo.

And Jean Naggar, Victor Navasky, Kenneth P. Norwick, William Novak, Carol Ohmann, Don Passer, Christina Paterniti, Molly Peacock, Sam Perelson, Jean Peters, Ryan Petty, Bob Pilpel, Christine Pisaro, Terry Pristin, Alice Quinn, Eleanor Rawson, Carl Mark Raymond, Eric L. Reiss, Evie Righter, Stephen F. Roth, Pat Rotter, Deborah Rust, Marc Sacerdote, Richard Sandomir, Karl Schumacher, Eleanor Shatzkin, Leonard Shatzkin, Mike Shatzkin, Robert Shnayerson, Albert Simmonds, Maggy Simony, Louise Smith, Ruth Sonsky, Sybil Steinberg and Miriam Steinert.

And Helen A. Stephenson, Patsy Sweely, Cindy Taylor, Carl Thorgerson, Linda Triegel, Carll Tucker, Joseph Vergara, Sharon Villines, Scott Walker, Lois Wallace, Maron Waxman, Michael Weber, Florence Weiner, Richard Weiner, Sally Williams, Lydia Wills, Stephanie Winston, Marianne Woolfe, Susan Zakin, Suzanne Zavrian, Mel Zerman and Charlotte Zolotow.

So Young Park's invaluable contributions to this new edition included research, reporting and database management. And, as always, Alan Appelbaum kept me on track and opened my eyes to new trails. To them, to the rest of my family and to Florence Janovic, my partner in providing Sensible Solutions, I owe an enormous debt of gratitude, which it's a pleasure to express here.

Thank you all.

Connections, or Welcome to the 20th-Anniversary Edition

The right image might be a spreading freeform shape like liquid from a tipped bottle, or (more structure! more drama!) a luminous cone reaching out into the darkness from a floodlight. Or maybe it's a network of limbs and leaves sprouting from a seed. But for sure this book's history follows some sort of expansive pattern with powerful built-in imperatives.

In the beginning, the goal seemed nice and narrow: Help people who have valuable things to say get them into print, even if those people aren't professional writers or aren't professional writers yet. But that meant addressing some readers who wrote articles, some who wrote stories or poems and some with material that belonged in books. Clearly, advice for them had to focus on selling to magazines, newspapers, newsletters, book publishing companies and other media as they developed. In short, it turned out, the nice narrow goal entailed covering publishers of every kind.

Selling to publishers, it then became apparent, was only half the battle, at best. In candid, often anguished conversations, people who were professional writers—accomplished, acclaimed professional writers—testified that the valuable things they had to say reached pitifully small audiences and that their editors weren't surprised. What they needed was help in dealing with that problem. So the mission of this book expanded to include demystifying the publishing process and explaining where and how a writer can make it work better.

Once writers understood how publishing works, the idea was, they'd fix many of the short circuits in it. Once they'd done that, however, many of them figured to wonder what else they might be able to do. Since successful self-publishers showed that they could, in some cases, do everything, self-publishing strategies and techniques would have to be included. So the design broadened once more, to cover all paths between writers and readers.

Continuing to focus on these three broad and overlapping arenas of author activity, this edition reflects expansion in each one. You'll find material on new buyers for written work (including publishers on the Internet and thousands of small, growing firms), new tactics for interacting with publishers (taking account of current procedures and expectations), new opportunities for self-publishers (as well as major challenges) and a huge new array of resources (including hundreds of helpful books, groups, services and Web sites).

You may want to access the information just as it's served up, focusing first on what attracts publishers, second on how to work with publishers and third on how to be a publisher for a particular project or projects. Alternatively, you may want to read "Initiation" and then jump around from section to section. New writers might start by concentrating on the "Foot in the Door" chapters, refer back to "Getting the Words Right" for help with content and style or leap forward to "Money" and its "Resources" to fund writing projects. Professional writers might begin with "The Sale and Its Sequels" section, pick up marketing ideas from the chapter on "Managing Sales" in "The Self-Publishing Option" section and consult "Resources" not only for those sections but also for "A Foot in the Door" when it's time to start promoting books scheduled for publication.

Preparing this edition for its publication, I found that the facts, figures, illustrations and observations in it were coalescing as a panoramic picture of the writer's world today, and this picture then suggested another expansive image, one that reflects what's happening to and for writers in general.

As the summary above suggests—and despite the perpetual flow of new constraints and complications—authors keep widening their sphere of influence. They have more alternatives, more autonomy, more ability to control what happens to their work. Individually and collectively, they are the prime movers and the ongoing energy behind an amazingly intricate sort of web—a web far bigger than the vast World Wide Web it incorporates, an ever-expanding network that can connect them with everyone out there who will benefit from their words.

In my mind's eye now, I sometimes envision the story of this book as a portion of the written-word web and imagine its filaments branching toward areas each of you have created, which generate filaments of their own, of course, extending out in all directions. For me, the happiest part of getting published is seeing where those threads are headed, so I will look forward to a new crop of reports on your publishing projects and, when quick answers might help, to a new crop of questions too.

Judith Appelbaum
P.O. Box 204
Katonah, NY 10536

How to Get
Happily Published

Initiation

TO BEGIN WITH, an announcement for professional writers, would-be writers and people who have important things to say from time to time and want to say them in print: It is largely within your power to determine whether your work will get published and whether the public will buy it once it's released.

That having been said, two questions naturally arise: Why do so many people fail to get their articles, stories, poems and books into print? And why do so many people who succeed in getting articles, stories, poems and books into print then find that their work never attracts a sizable audience?

The answer is surprisingly simple. Failures abound because hardly anybody treats getting published as if it were a rational, manageable activity—like practicing law or laying bricks—in which knowledge coupled with skill and application can lead to success. Instead, almost everybody approaches the phases of the publishing process, which have to do with finding (or, in some cases, becoming) a publisher and then attracting an audience, by trusting exclusively to luck, to merit, to formulas or to somebody else.

Such behavior is thoroughly counterproductive, but it's entirely understandable at the same time, and on several grounds.

In the first place, just like everybody else, people who write are reluctant to risk ridicule by asking questions. Seeking information is an intimidating task. Since knowledge is power, as we've all been raised to believe, ignorance must be impotence, and it's shameful, therefore, to admit it when there's something we don't know.

And in the second place, we tend to proceed on the assumption that mastery of any field is the exclusive province of specialists and experts. The lay public, so the theory goes, can't expect to understand how to fix a leaky pipe, let alone how to get a manuscript from writer to reader, so people who aren't prevented from inquiring by the fear of looking silly are hindered by the fear that the information they'll receive will be unintelligible anyway. But even those who are brave and energetic enough to go in search of knowledge about getting published have not, in many cases, found the effort worthwhile.

What all authors really need is an experienced editor who has the time and the inclination to sit down with them and show them how the industry actually works. What writers have, however, is an oppressively large canon of works on selling to established publishing houses (which usually tell only parts of the truth and may not tell the truth at all), a growing body of guides to self-publishing (some of which make pie-in-the-sky promises) and a few books about publishing in general (which tend to explain the way the business works without focusing on the flesh-and-blood men and women who run it and who inevitably alter the rules to fit personal and practical demands).

This book is a substitute for the friendly, experienced editor. It offers a full and frank description of the contemporary publishing picture—complete with fallible human beings in the foreground and annotated guides to hundreds of helpful resources at the back. Anyone who reads it intelligently should come away with a good idea of the way the publishing process normally works, valuable information on the ingenious tactics writers have devised to make it work best for them, and easy access to additional information about the full range of publishing options, which together give you everything you'll need to create effective publishing strategies for particular projects.

Decades of personal experience in editing books, magazines,

newspapers and newsletters have gone into the advice you'll find here about getting through the publishing labyrinth. And so have myriad experiences other publishing professionals shared, all of which help explain each phase, introduce the people in charge, define the unfamiliar terms, set forth the basic unwritten rules that govern progress and tell you how to discover more about whichever aspects of getting published interest you.

But at every step the main focus of attention will be on you—what you want, what you need, what you'll have to contend with to get it, how wide your options are, and how you can reach your goals most expeditiously.

This book, in other words, is designed to facilitate writing careers and writing projects, and its overriding purpose is to help you improve your improvisational skills so that you'll be able to switch gears when you need to, no matter what the rulebook experts say. The idea is that once you understand why your novel got just half a page in the catalog (for example), you'll take steps to improve its image. Similarly, once you see how queries work in context, you'll choose to use them for books as well as articles, and once you've gained the confidence to obey other people's dictates only when they fit your situation, you'll refuse to rely on a manuscript speaking for itself and craft strong covering letters, making sure that the one for the editor at *New Woman* is quite different in tone—and maybe even in content—from the one you're sending *New Age.*

New Woman may return your material, of course, and so may *New Age Journal* and Random House and Moyer Bell, but please don't let yourself be discouraged if getting what you want involves a few false starts. To keep your spirits up on darker days, you may find it useful to dwell on four important facts:

❖ *Publishers need you at least as much as you need them.* Despite widespread suspicions of conspiracy, there's little truth in the theory that an elite circle of editors and writers concentrated in Manhattan and doing business on the cocktail-party circuit reserves every printed page for itself.

Editors do, no doubt, know established writers, and established writers do, no doubt, know editors, and, unquestionably, a lot of assignments are given out at New York cocktail parties and New York publishing lunches as well (they do exist, those lunches, and they're worth angling for if you find yourself with a big-city publisher interested in you).

On the other hand, (a) even the deputed leaders of the New York Literary Establishment are wary of accepting too much material from fellow NYLE members; in spite of long and liquid lunch hours, editors are always aware of the dangers of provincialism; and (b) no matter how many authors editors know, they never have enough first-rate material. In publishing firms on both coasts and in between, the quest for new ideas and new writers is considered so vital that editors-in-chief frequently chide—and sometimes threaten—their junior colleagues about it. "Unless you have three projects to propose, don't come to the editorial meeting this week; and if you miss three meetings, don't come back to work," a particularly stern taskmaster is in the habit of telling his staff.

Thanks to the constant search for new manuscripts, authors sometimes find publishers wooing them. "Out of the blue," Dava Sobel reports, George Gibson called from Walker & Company to suggest that her article about the struggle to measure distances at sea had the makings of book. And so it did. Sobel's *Longitude* went on to become a bestseller, and three huge houses bid on her next book, a study of the planets, which Penguin USA bought, reportedly for an advance in seven figures.

Sobel happened to get a break because Gibson saw a piece she'd done for an alumni magazine, but editors doggedly scan publications of all sorts looking for promising material. And of course they spend hours each day paging through the manuscripts and outlines and proposals that arrive on their desks in the hope of discovering a new writer who will boost their status with their colleagues and improve their employer's standing in the marketplace.

❖ *Editors make mistakes.* By actual count, 121 publishers said "No thanks" to *Zen and the Art of Motorcycle Maintenance.* John Grisham's *A Time to Kill,* Roger Tory Peterson's *Field Guide to the Birds* and Harriet Goldhar's *The Dance of Anger* were turned down too, again and again. *The Clan of the Cave Bear, The Spy Who Came in From the Cold, The Peter Principle, Watership Down, The First Wives Club*—rejected, every one. And John Fischer, for many years head of the trade (i.e., general) book department at Harper, used to tell—with the aplomb made possible by his otherwise admirable record—of the time he confidently spurned a book that went on to make publishing history.

"I hate to remember," Fischer confessed in *Harper's Magazine,* "when James R. Newman first told me his scheme for a history of mathematics.... He wanted to gather all the basic documents of mathematical thought and arrange them into an anthology which would trace the development of the science in the words of the masters themselves. It would be a big book—perhaps five hundred pages. What did I think of it?

"I told him it was impossible. Nobody would buy it; its subject was too specialized—in fact, to most people (including me), downright repellent—and it would be far too costly to manufacture."

Newman's *The World of Mathematics* was subsequently issued by Simon & Schuster, having grown to four volumes from the originally contemplated one, and Fischer noted dryly that before long the publisher had sold over 120,000 sets, in addition to those distributed by two book clubs. Microsoft Press did an edition as well, releasing it with considerable fanfare and a $75,000 advertising and promotion budget.

The point, clearly and comfortingly, is that a rejection (which in any case is directed to your work and not to you as a person) may well reflect more unfavorably on the editor's ability than on yours.

❖ *Perseverance pays.* Outlets for writing are multiplying rapidly nowadays, as new technology makes small publishing ventures economically feasible. In the aggregate, editorial tastes are so varied that there should be an editor somewhere who's looking for what you have to offer, and who's eager, maybe desperate to find it.

"It's really exciting to find something new, somebody that nobody's ever published before that we think is really wonderful," according to Shelly Shapiro, executive editor at Del Rey Books. When you're "playing the grim reaper with a stack of proposals," Nick Lyons of The Lyons Press finds, the underlying goal is to spot a project you want to take on. Fourteen or fifteen manuscripts had come and gone as he worked his way through a pile of submissions not long ago, Lyons recalls. Then he got to the last one, a book "on a subject on which I am fairly expert. I had never heard of the author and I follow the literature of the field closely . . . The title was a cliché. I'd make short shrift of this one. But I didn't. It drew me in and I smiled and traveled with the man and found—from the first paragraph on to the end—a person of intelligence and wit, a happy capacity for simple joys, a shrewd eye for the natural world . . . and I grabbed it."

Lyons, who loves fishing and publishes lots of books on the subject, says reading submissions offers the same sort of pleasure. "I don't know what's down there, but I'd certainly like to have something come up," he explains, adding that it's "enormously exciting to find a work that just rings with originality and freshness. I like that more than anything else about publishing."

Precisely because so many people inside publishing companies want to get valuable pieces of writing the attention they deserve, it makes sense for an author to persevere even after the acceptance stage. In fact, a wise writer will shepherd written work all the way through production and distribution until finally it reaches its readers, realizing that when the pros are prepared to do their part, it would be a shame to have a project fizzle and die because the person who created it didn't pitch in.

Please understand: There's no need for a writer to actually perform every publishing chore, but authors who make it their business to know what should be done to give their work its best shot—and when it should be done and why and by whom and how they themselves can participate—stand by far the strongest chance of winning attention from the critics and purchase money from the public. Moreover, they figure to escape the frustrations that so often arise to plague people who rely on the specialists in a big and busy organization to handle important matters for them.

❖ *No matter how much publishers need you, you may not need them at all.* For much-published authors and beginners alike, self-publishing is an increasingly viable option. Some people decide to become their own publishers because they're tired of getting rejection slips. Others choose self-publishing for a variety of positive reasons: to get a book or periodical out more quickly, for instance, or to market it better or to keep more of the money it earns.

It's the second group that's growing fastest. Writers who would have been insulted if you suggested self-publishing a few years ago ("I've sold dozens of articles and 11 books; I'll sell this too in time, thank you very much") are making it their first-choice option now ("Why should I wait and wait and wait for some publisher to agree to buy this and then have to knock myself out on promotion and lose the lion's share of the profits?").

Given the rising count of self-publishers and the fact that small publishers are multiplying too, it's no surprise to see new companies selling publishing goods and services. Need an editor, a designer, a printer, a marketer? Plenty of them are out there, so you can hire help where you need it and can afford it.

There's only one kind of help you shouldn't hire: a vanity press (see "Danger: Dead Ends" in "Openings"), because their imprints will stigmatize your work.

Won't your own imprint do that too, you may be wondering. No, it won't. This is partly because self-publishing has a long and distinguished past (featuring luminaries such as Blake, Poe, Joyce and Nin) and a star-studded present (featuring blockbusters big houses competed to pick up). But it's also because media people, librarians, wholesalers and retailers have learned from experience that self-published books and periodicals fill needs and please readers. Thousands of these titles are out there. Chances are you even own some, though if they're professionally produced and marketed (as yours would be, of course) you—and everyone else—probably can't tell.

Needless to say, becoming your own publisher doesn't guarantee success any more than having a publisher does. And in any event *success in publishing,* as in any other field, is a term that does, and should, mean different things to different people.

But if you assess all your options carefully, set your goals wisely and learn to understand the framework that surrounds their realization, you can find a good measure of fulfillment in getting published, and you will encounter serendipitous pleasures at several points, for using your own wits and your own energies provides an especially satisfying way to ensure that the profoundly personal act that writing constitutes comes finally to fruition.

Getting the
Words Right

❖   ❖   ❖

What the Pros Know

A GREAT MANY successful authors have never taken a writing course or read a writing manual, and they wouldn't want to. Instead, they rely on commonsense measures to improve their writing skills. Realizing, for example, that reading offers one good way to learn about using words, they are apt to go through several books and magazines a month and to pick up pointers on style, organization, point of view and the like from each one.

Sometimes the learning process that takes place when you read is virtually unconscious. For instance, you may barely sense that steeping yourself in Henry James' novels causes you to be more careful about nuances in your own prose; but the effect will have occurred nonetheless and, at a minimum, it will have taught you something about your options in selecting language.

To make learning from reading a more deliberate act, writers often stop to examine each powerful passage they encounter in order to figure out how it achieved its impact (through a succession of startling images, a change of tense, a panoply of facts?). And to further advance their educations, many authors turn to behind-the-scenes books like Virginia Woolf's *A Writer's Diary*, to diaries left by Chekhov, Hawthorne and Thoreau, and to more recent works by accomplished writers like Richard Rhodes, Suzanne Lipsett and Nancy Mairs, which deal with how a writer creates and organizes material, how the raw material of life feeds constantly into present and future writing projects and how to handle writer's block, self-doubt and the other psychological hazards of the trade. Similar subject matter characterizes anthologies like the *Paris Review Interviews*, in which writers not only talk about their craft but also reveal whether they write reclining nude on a sofa or standing up in an A&P parking lot, and *Writing for Your Life*, the *Publishers Weekly* interview series, in which the talk often turns to input from editors and agents.

Because analyzing and explaining how they do what they do appeals strongly to many writers, the commonsense approach to writing has given rise to a body of teachings based on personal experience and handed down over the years in print and through word of mouth. It's from this legacy that the following suggestions derive. For additional guidance, see "Getting the Words Right Resources."

Glimmerings and Gleanings

Writing well for publication demands, first, that you pick a subject that excites you and will attract others and, second, that you flesh it out with examples, images, anecdotes, facts and characters. Many writers meet these requirements with the help of the pack-rat process, which involves hoarding printed materials that interest them along with notes about ideas, snatches of conversation and nuggets of information they find provocative.

In the beginning, these bits and pieces may not mean much, but as they accumulate they'll start to form patterns, and eventually a number of items may cluster around a subject like (for example) building your own house. At that point, the next step is easy: Label a file with that heading and stock it with all the makings for an article or book—notes on background reading, research materials, people to interview, associations to contact, preliminary reflections and angles of approach.

Any subject, as experienced writers know, can be treated in numerous ways, so even before you begin to write you have vital choices to make. Whom shall I write for, and how should I address them? What style will I use? What tone? What do I want to say, and how will I arrange my material for optimum effect?

To get a concrete idea of the range of choice that confronts you, take a subject you're curious about and look it up in the *Readers' Guide to Periodical Literature* and the *Subject Guide to Books in Print* at your local library. Then look up related headings and read around in the materials you discover. You'll confirm that although the topic is unchanging, each treatment of it highlights a different aspect for a different audience, and you'll come away more alert to the decisions you must make at the start of any writing project. (Furthermore, by way of bonus, you'll get a leg up on your research.)

In making these preliminary choices, some writers consult style folders in which they've filed samples of the short, pithy, anecdotal piece; the first-person report; the informal essay in social criticism; the investigative story; and other forms available to authors today. If you start such a folder for yourself you can use its contents as a checklist each time you begin work on a new topic. Perhaps that will prevent you from propping a sprightly personal reminiscence on a scaffolding better suited to *War and Peace.*

Forging Ahead

Writing is scary, as professional writers have bravely testified in memoirs and interviews. And as experienced writers know, the temptation is strong to cope by turning pompous. Beginners are especially prone to say to themselves, "I'm nobody. Who cares what I might have to say? I'd better find a way to sound important." Unfortunately, and for obvious reasons, the attempt to impress is usually counterproductive; just as people at a party groan when someone comes in putting on airs—that old standby defense against social insecurity—readers will be put off by pretentious prose.

As a tool for building confidence in writing ability, many people swear by journals. Ideally, a journal is a free space, inaccessible both to the self-critic and to the critics lurking in the great out-there. In your journal you can experiment by writing whatever comes into your mind without censorship and by following your thoughts wherever they lead, because it's not polished work you're after, but loosening up to feel comfortable with the written expression of your thoughts and observations.

Writers also use their journals to jot down quotes and facts that grab their attention, to try out different writing styles, to test and develop story ideas and to phrase reactions to current events, with the result that the journals serve to complement research, reporting and the more structured writing that goes into a draft of a manuscript.

A writer's journal is "a way of keeping in touch with your inner life in the midst of the rush of daily preoccupations," as Denise Levertov sees it. But, she cautions, "the point of this is not to store up lines and images that may come in handy later. . . . No, the value of the notebook is in the way writing such things down deepens our experience of them in that act itself—enriches our inner life, puts us in more intimate touch with ourselves."

No matter how enlightening your journal is or how extensively you prepare, you may still be struck by panic and confusion every time you sit down to write. The best way to handle the performance jitters—however devastating they seem—is first to remind yourself that fear is normal ("I walk around, straightening pictures on the wall, rugs on the floor—as though not until everything in the world was lined up and perfectly true could anybody reasonably expect me to set a word down on paper"—E. B. White). Then take one simple step. Get something written. It doesn't have to be perfect; it just has to exist so that you will have the beginning of a rough draft to work with, and not merely a pile of notes.

The impetus to get that initial group of words out of your head and onto paper will be strong if selling what you write is the only way you're going to pay the rent. Otherwise, though, writing all too often strikes people as an activity that can fit under the heading "Important But Not Urgent" devised by Edwin C. Bliss in his *Getting Things Done*. To make sure you really do get started, Bliss and other writers suggest that you reserve substantial blocks of time for writing each day, or three times a week, or at whatever intervals are practical in the light of your other commitments and priorities.

You may finish a full morning's stint having completed one sentence; on the other hand, you may become inspired once you're involved in the work of figuring out what you want to say and saying it. But keep trying. "Many times, I just sit for three hours with no ideas coming to me," Flannery O'Connor once said. "But I know one thing: if an idea does come between nine and twelve, I am there ready for it."

Particularly for people working on book-length manuscripts, making the best use of writing time takes practice. "Once I start working, I never go out, ever," Mary Morris told an interviewer. Morris, who writes both novels and nonfiction, has a routine that includes a four o'clock walk every day or something else "to change gears." She always carries a notepad, and she usually uses it to write "a line or two."

Other people work best by getting an early start (novelist Edna O'Brien gets up at 7 A.M., because "it's the closest to the dreaming line, where the stuff comes from") or by interspersing sessions at the keyboard with meetings, lunch dates or anything else that involves contact with other human beings. And still others function most effectively by setting deadlines for themselves. Two professors in this last group, both of whom were carrying full teaching loads and under pressure to publish, found that a deadline buddy system ensured productivity. On target dates, each teacher was required to deliver a chapter to the other; both had finished manuscripts ready for a publisher within a year.

Just as optimum time schedules vary from writer to writer, so the physical situation an author works well within may range from a book-lined cabin on the top of a mountain to a corner of a cramped, urban kitchen. "I prefer small, messy rooms that don't look out on anything interesting," William Maxwell found. "I wrote the last two sections of *They Came Like Swallows* beside a window looking out on a tin roof. It was perfect. The roof was so boring it instantly drove me back to my typewriter." And Susan Brownmiller—among many others—found ideal working conditions inside the Frederick Lewis Allen Room of the New York Public Library's imposing 42nd Street building. In addition to a desk and a shelf for books, Brownmiller got "the companionship of a score of writers who became my own private seminar in how to get the job done. The interrelationship of my Allen Room friends and me is too complex to detail; suffice it to say that each of us struggled together, respectful of one another's progress, in a supportive environment dedicated to hard work and accomplishment, a writer's Utopia or close to it." A setup like that can be created by any group of writers who arrange to share some working space.

Every so often, people who want to write discover that they simply can't manage the task under any available circumstances, and in such cases finding collaborators or ghosts may be a good idea. (A ghost, by the way, should always be given corporeal existence through a shared by-line or, at the least, through an explicit acknowledgment at the front of the book.)

"Getting the Words Right Resources" offers leads to writers and editors who'll work with nonwriters on book and magazine projects (see also "Buying Advice and Assistance"). And editors have even been known to function as unpaid ghosts by reworking manuscripts they've acquired to get important ideas to an audience. But for most people, ghosting isn't necessary as long as they know fully what they want to say and keep readers' needs in mind. "What I ask myself most often," says writer Barry Lopez, "is: How is the reader served by what you are up to? How does what you're doing help?"

Self-Editing

The printed materials you buy at the bookstore or newsstand have generally gone through numerous revisions. "I rewrote the ending of *Farewell to Arms* thirty-nine times before I was satisfied," Ernest Hemingway told an interviewer.

"Was there some problem there?" the interviewer wanted to know. "What was it that had stumped you?"

"Getting the words right," Hemingway said.

Thirty-nine rewrites are several more than most writers will want—or be fully able—to attempt, but you should count on several. "I write every paragraph four times," Margery Allingham reported. "Once to get my meaning down, once to put in anything I have left out, once to take out anything that seems unnecessary and once to make the whole thing sound as if I have only just thought of it."

To make revision easier, be generous with spacing. Read double-spaced drafts on paper silently and then aloud to yourself or a sympathetic listener, and mark trouble spots as you go. Then fix them and repeat the process before you decide you're finished.

Instruction in self-editing is available in several good books (see this section's "Resources"), most of which explain, sensibly enough, that it's wise to begin with the beginning. This is the time to look with a critical eye at those first few paragraphs. Did you breeze through the start just to get some steam? Do they read just as they were written—as a preliminary throat-clearing exercise? If so, dispense with them and find the spot where you really begin to address your subject in a way that will capture a reader's interest.

Devising a good lead is worth all the craft and inspiration at your command. For it's with your first sentence or two that you must convince people to read what you have to say. If you're not sure what constitutes a good lead, look hard at writing you admire. And during all your reading, be on the alert for openings that grab your attention, that attract you and compel you to read on. If you can determine the causes behind the effect—a catalog of precise details, a bold question, an alarming anecdote—you will be better equipped to fashion an exciting lead of your own.

Though the lead is the single most vital section of your manuscript, each word counts, and each should be designed not to dazzle but to communicate. Keep your critical eye sharp as you continue through passages now familiar to you.

Finding the precise word that says what you mean is not, of course, a luxury; it is a crucial necessity. Sometimes the best choice doesn't come to mind right away, but when that happens you can leave signals for yourself as you draft: boldface a word you're not sure about; bracket a choice of two phrases; put a question mark in the margin; write in TK (a printer's abbreviation for To Kum, it's an easy target for a computer search when you're ready to fill in the blanks); then come back later and get the thing right.

As you insert your changes, you may notice that entire sections should be scrapped or reshuffled, or that you shortchanged a point and need to elaborate. Maybe, for example, you left out the illustrative material that would make your message clear on page 6; maybe the paragraph at the end of chapter four clearly belongs with the discussion toward the beginning of chapter two. Because this kind of reworking is the norm, not the exception, for experienced writers, you should move material around with some abandon. And if the first move doesn't work out as well as you thought it would, you can always try another arrangement until you get a smooth, effective draft.

Deleting material is, of course, psychologically harder than moving or adding it, but abridgment is frequently necessary in revision. Although you may have grown fond of a passage, if it duplicates an earlier one, something has got to go. The freedom you allowed yourself in drafting now requires that you be ruthless in pruning the redundant, the irrelevant, the gratuitously showy. And that may mean cutting your first draft by half.

Getting Criticism

To get critical feedback before you send your manuscript to an editor—from whom, by the way, you shouldn't expect a critique—you can approach a variety of early readers. The most obvious source for constructive criticism is another writer, either one who is at your stage of development, or a professional whose work you've read and admired.

"If you really like someone's work, why not write them?" asks Elliot Figman of Poets & Writers, a remarkably helpful group. "The worst thing that could happen is that they won't write back." Most writers are accessible to some degree (see "Resources" for directories that include addresses and phone numbers), and James Harkness found Annie Dillard, Pulitzer Prize–winning author of *Pilgrim at Tinker Creek*, to be very accessible indeed.

I had just finished reading *Points for a Compass Rose* by Evan Connell—about four times, without coming up for air—and I was rushing around to all my friends, clutching them by their coat sleeves and crying, "My God, read this!" Of course no one was paying the slightest attention. I wanted to share my enthusiasm, and I was frustrated. Then Annie Dillard published an essay/review about the book which was rhapsodic and well-written.

I sent her a note via the publisher to tell her I enjoyed the piece and agreed. She replied. We spent several weeks whooping and hollering "Connell! Connell!" and eventually moved on to other topics.

Although Annie knew I was ghost writing for the president of the university where I worked, I kept quiet about the stuff I was grinding out privately. By then I had seen essays from what came to be *Pilgrim at Tinker Creek*, and I had no burning desire to send a bundle of my mawkish scribbling to this obviously brilliant and talented writer who was knocking them out in the aisles.

I don't recall exactly how it came about that I finally did allow Annie to see a manuscript of something or other. She wrote me back an ecstatic paean to the effect that I was "obviously the best writer alive on the planet," a composer of "muscled prose," and on and on. I replied proposing marriage. Too late.

As far as the sort of comments went, they were general and supportive. Mostly she stroked my ego and let the verbs take care of themselves—a strategy, I'll add, that seems to me now not only humane but pragmatically wise. For anyone who has a certain innate potential, the most difficult aspect of learning to write is the long, dreary, often desperate silence that greets early efforts. What is needed there isn't so much criticism, constructive or otherwise, as encouragement. Sooner or later you will begin to get close analysis from editors or critics, if your manuscripts are promising enough, but not many editors or critics will hold your hand and tell you how wonderful you are in the face of much evidence to the contrary. Annie instructed me to try not to be the subject and object of my own prose, an idea I've thought about a lot and attempted to put into practice. But she told me I was the best writer on the planet first, and I suspect the hyperbole was more sustaining, hence more valuable, than the bits and pieces of "objective" commentary.

At various points in their lives, a surprising number of writers knowingly and graciously accept the responsibility of encouraging beginners. "For ten minutes of time and postage costs (they never send return envelopes), I can restore a person's faith in humanity," one established essayist says. "Lots of people write me and send manuscripts. I try to read and comment on them."

Nevertheless, asking for criticism is a hard thing to do, primarily because everyone is afraid of being told their work is rotten. And this fear often makes beginning writers just as skittish about seeking comments from peers as they are about approaching literary luminaries. Friends can be helpful, though, even if they're not writers or editors or professional critics. In fact, when he won the Nobel Prize for Literature, Saul Bellow declared that nonprofessionals may have an edge when it comes to critical comment. Many letters from readers, he told *The New York Times Book Review*, "are very penetrating; not all are completely approving, but then I am not completely approving of myself. In recent years, I would say that I have learned more from these letters than I have from formal criticism of my work."

So consider asking friends whose intelligence you respect to act as critics of your work in progress, not by passing final judgment on it but by pinpointing strengths and trouble spots. As Cynthia Buchanan, playwright and novelist, has explained, "It's a matter of being clear to other people. What I want to find out from friends is, first, can they follow what I'm saying. Then I want to know if it's boring and where it's boring. And third, I ask whether they feel that the language is too baroque and unrealistic in places. In the long run I choose what I want to do, but I need this consensus." Buchanan has given much of the credit for her fine track record in getting published to the informal consulting system she developed for herself.

With an even smaller but equally effective criticism network, Christi Killien and Sheila Bender co-authored a salable book. Killien, who had done six novels for young people, and Bender, a leader of writing workshops, decided to write to each other about writing. Offering ideas, observations, criticism and plenty of encouragement, their letters went back and forth at least once a week for six months and eventually spawned *Writing in a Convertible with the Top Down*, which Warner then published.

To initiate a feedback system that will be productive for you, first formulate specific questions. You might begin, for example, by asking people which passages they had to read twice; which sections they remember best; and which parts they would eliminate if someone were to insist the manuscript be shortened.

If you've written a story for children, the most obvious testing ground is the children's story hour at your local library. And if you're eager to get ongoing criticism of your work, you may want to join or organize a writers' club, whose members will be a ready source of reactions.

It's not hard to do that, as Linda Triegel discovered. In her case, as it happens, the impetus to act came from the first edition of this book, which she read at just about the time she decided she was serious about her writing. Realizing that the author lived nearby, Triegel got together with a couple of other beginning writers she knew and arranged for the library in town to host a Q-and-A session.

"We thought there must be more would-be authors around who would come to hear you speak and, lo and behold, dozens turned up," she recalled. "We had them all sign a guest book with their addresses and a few weeks later invited them to a meeting to organize a writers group. We read our work to one another and critiqued it as best we could. We also, right off, decided to put out a collection of our work just for the sake of seeing it between covers, and this became an annual event."

The writers workshop that Triegel headed for several years functioned in part as a source of moral support for its members. To get "down-to-brass-tacks advice" on markets and contacts and writing techniques, she eventually joined a more advanced writers group in her area.

"Brass-tacks advice" is also available on the Internet through writers news groups and chat groups and lists. Be careful online though, both because it's easy to get hooked (before you know it, hours have gone by and there's no time left for writing) and because you'll be dealing with lots of people you know very little about. Perhaps their goals and standards are compatible with yours. Perhaps their experiences are typical or at least replicable. But then again, perhaps not. Moderated groups and lists are your best bet, provided that you give due weight to the moderator's posts.

Whether they're face to face or in cyberspace, meetings with other people engaged in writing offer several benefits. Frequently, you'll get useful pointers. Sometimes a collaborative project will be sparked. And always your morale will be strengthened by a feeling of support and community—by the knowledge that other people understand and care about what you're doing and what you may be undergoing.

"Writing is a lifelong journey, a slow revealing and minute exploration," Suzanne Lipsett explained in her luminous book *Surviving a Writer's Life*. "Once begun, there will be the stalls and grinding uphill pushes that any ride entails. But there will also be those inevitable glides—through terrains dark and frightening or flooded with sunlight, it doesn't matter—that bring joy to the traveler and stoke the desire that fuels the creative engine."

Buying Advice and Assistance

MAYBE IT'S BECAUSE of the glamour—write and you too may hobnob with the rich and the famous; write and one day they'll all look at you with respect. Maybe it's a simple semantic confusion—writing, after all, is something we learned to do as children, so of course it's easy to bring prose up to publishable level. Or maybe the explanation is that we're just naturally communicative. In any case, millions of people are regularly seized by an urge to write. Naturally—in a culture that believes in advancement through education—lots of would-be writers immediately look for courses and manuals that will start them writing and get what they've written into print. And just as naturally—in a culture of entrepreneurs—there's no lack of individuals and institutions prepared to provide what the public wants.

The goods and services on sale can be summed up under a short list of headings—courses, criticism, software and books. But within these categories, variations in quality are enormous. A few of the writing aids on the market promise a great deal and deliver next to nothing, while others make modest claims for themselves and then yield surprising benefits. Many, it's a pleasure to report, will honestly reveal what they offer, but only to those who carefully interpret their ads and investigate their operations.

Before you spend your first penny on any form of printed, computerized or personal instruction, you should be able to answer these four questions:

1. Is this necessary for the successful development of my written work?
2. What exactly am I buying?
3. What value will it have for me?
4. How much will it cost, both in money and in psychological wear and tear?

The answer to Question 1 is probably No, this is not necessary, and you may therefore wish to go directly from this sentence to the beginning of "A Foot in the Door." But since "not necessary" may still be valuable, and since much of what's on the market is in fact valuable if it's skillfully selected and used, here's a guide to instructional aids.

Classes

Good teachers of writing will tell you that writing cannot be taught; it can only be learned. The teacher's role, they will explain, is to create and capitalize on opportunities for learning so that the students can develop faster and more efficiently than they would on their own. Or, as Lawrence Durrell put it in the catalog description of his course in California's International College Independent Study Program, "While nothing can be taught, the presentation of notions and ideas with precision and enthusiasm can hatch out the talents in people and thus develop them." Word it any way you like, the point is that no writing course can be worthwhile unless you exercise initiative and work hard on follow-up.

First among your required course activities will be writing, arranging words until they form a structured whole. Having written, you will then be asked to submit your work to your teacher and your fellow students for criticism. And after they've commented, you'll have to rewrite, accepting those of their suggestions that your emotions and intelligence can approve and rejecting the rest. Moreover, you will probably be called upon to offer constructive criticism of your classmates' work—which means you will have to figure out where their strengths lie and how their weaknesses can be corrected.

None of this is easy; much of it may be agonizing. And what do you get for your pains?

Motivational energy, for one thing. Whether you call it writer's block or procrastination or just plain fear of failure, the difficulties that many writers experience in getting started can be eased by the presence of an instructor who assigns, expects and encourages the completion of a manuscript.

And despite instructors' protestations, you may actually get some traditional tutelage during class discussions, for good teachers will seize on particular pieces of student writing—good and bad—to illustrate important aspects of literary technique. Teaching creative writing for the first time, Joan Fry found "that students *can* learn to write good fiction by reading bad fiction." Fry is "convinced that's why the workshop method works. People learn to write by identifying what's wrong with other people's work, and by the glacially slow realization that they are making the same mistakes in *their* work."

Particular lessons may focus on dialogue, transitions, point of view, narrative exposition, plot structure or even basic rules of grammar, but whatever the subject, it will serve to sharpen every student's critical perceptions and thus to improve the value of comments on classmates' work and the value of changes in their own.

Most conscientious teachers not only discuss students' writing in class and with each student individually; they also turn manuscripts into teaching tools by jotting comments as they read. As director of the Iowa Writers Workshop, John Leggett edited and copy-edited each piece of student work he read, just as he used to edit books when he worked for large publishing firms. And at Yale, William Zinsser, author of *On Writing Well*, marked up student manuscripts in memorable letters of red. Katie Leishman, one of Zinsser's many appreciative pupils, describes the consequences of his technique for learning.

In the opening lecture Mr. Zinsser asked for a five-page account of "My First Day at College." I still have my notes: Writing is a craft. Good writing is very difficult. One word is better than two. Unnecessary words = CLUTTER. In the margin I've written, "This is all *very* obvious."

All that was obvious a week later was that I had a twenty-two-page draft when Mr. Zinsser wanted five pages. No amount of frenetic snipping and repasting of paragraphs made it any shorter. So I did the only thing I could do. I put the draft and my typewriter in the car and started driving. I suppose I thought that somewhere along the road I would have a vision of the sections I could trim from the article. Then I would stop in a coffee shop and rewrite.

Five hours later I was still driving. At midnight I checked into a motel in the Berkshires and lay in bed wondering, in the middle of winter, in the middle of nowhere, which were the 1,000 critical words of the 6,000 words I had written. I spent the weekend in the bathtub, writing on an upside-down drawer which I laid across the rim of the tub. Saturday, I rewrote ten pages and threw out the rest. By Sunday afternoon I had what I thought were five pages of flawless prose. Satisfied and very clean, I drove back to school.

When I got that paper back it was bleeding—bleeding badly. Mr. Zinsser's red arrows, red question marks and red slashes were everywhere; he had excised entire paragraphs. I slunk out of the classroom, crestfallen, resentful.

That evening, when I could bear to look at it again, I retyped the piece, simply leaving out what Mr. Zinsser had cut and clarifying expressions he'd found vague. As I typed I realized that he hadn't robbed me of my say. Though the edited version ran only one and a half pages, it retained every point of the original twenty-two-page draft.

So "clutter" and "craft" and "the difficulty of good writing" suddenly became real, personal problems to tackle. In later assignments if I used a gratuitous or vague expression, I could almost see a slash or question mark welting over it. Eventually I developed my own sense of what was essential or expendable, of what was my own style and what was imitative. By the end of the course, when Mr. Zinsser joked about students in his "red pen orbit" I knew what he meant. Because, though his principles remained a crucial point of reference, each student was spinning off on his or her own path.

The fact that writing well is a path, not a destination, a process more than a goal, is perhaps the most important truth a writing course can divulge. The ongoing give-and-take with the teacher and the other students makes it clear, as nothing else can, that the effort has no end; it is possible to make progress; it is necessary to accept defeat and go on. Because teachers of writing are themselves writers they can comfort students as fellow sufferers while providing living examples of at least limited success. They are people who have won the right to take themselves seriously as professionals, and they can help you earn that privilege, too.

Carol Lew Simons, having spent three terms in Richard P. Brickner's "Free-Style" Writing Workshop at New York City's New School, summed up the benefits of writing courses this way:

> I am not, strictly speaking, a beginning writer. All my life I have written essays that loyal friends and my mother have dutifully praised; as a literature major at Antioch College I wrote very well-received critical papers; for the past four years I have been writing for a medical magazine. I decided to take a writing course, however, because I felt a gap existed between these slender accomplishments and the claim I sometimes made, more often than not to myself, that underneath it all I was a *real* writer. So far my attitudes have undergone more revolution than my writing, but this fact may suggest the major advantages of workshop courses.
>
> One attitude that has begun to alter rather remarkably is my view of writing as an activity, which has come about largely

through the nature of the workshop discussions. What makes a workshop different from the scores of good literature courses I have taken is that the author is there in the room; the work is being regarded as a thing in process rather than as something that has, as doctors say, passed "into the literature"; and the people considering the work are involved to some extent in trying to do a similar task.

I think, though I would never have admitted to this had I been asked, that before the workshop I regarded writing as an either/or proposition; you wrote something, revised it a little, and it succeeded or not. The workshop has made it clear that writing is something to be practiced very diligently, like the piano. One might never write as well as one wishes, but one can learn to write as well as one *can*—although only with considerable time and concentration. The workshop has given me a much greater respect for writing as a craft and a process, even as it has made me see it as an endeavor more accessible and less mystical than I had once thought it.

To find a course that's as good for you as Brickner's was for Simons, decide first—and honestly—how big a commitment you are willing to make. Depending on your age and station in life, as well as on your financial and emotional wherewithal, you may want to choose anything from a full-scale, two-year creative writing program leading to an MFA degree and a career in writing, to a journalism course or a weekend workshop (though a very short course is likely to be more useful for making contacts than for learning to write). Then, if you're contemplating a sizable investment of time and/or money, consult "Getting the Words Right Resources," read catalog copy and works by your prospective professor, talk with fellow students, and look for these hallmarks:

❖ A commitment from the teacher to comment individually, in detail and in person, on each student's work.
❖ An indication that your classmates will be at approximately your level of writing ability, so you will be able to respect

their comments without developing feelings of inferiority or superiority.

❖ An instructor who has published, who intends to publish again and whose work you admire.

❖ An absence of dogma in the course description. Teachers should be loath to mold you in their image and eager, instead, to point you toward what Brickner calls "that language which is most yours and which is yet to be made available to a readership, to help you impose your specialness in a way that's beneficial to the outside."

The same criteria apply to correspondence courses, which may appeal to those who can't arrange to attend classes. In some cases geography is the problem; there's simply no appropriate course within a reasonable radius. In others, the stumbling block is time; personal or job responsibilities can make it impossible to show up anywhere at the same hour each week. And in still other instances, psychological difficulties arise; taking criticism in front of a group—no matter how similarly situated and how sympathetic the members—may be a terrifying and repellent prospect. In these situations, among others, a correspondence course can be worth considering as a source of motivational energy and critical reaction.

To find likely prospects, see "Resources." Then size up any course you're considering before you enroll. When you read a flyer or an ad ("We're looking for people who want to WRITE," it might say), check on what it tells you about the faculty's qualifications and the students' successes. Is the information specific enough so that you can verify it? Is it recent enough so that you can tell the courses are effective right now? Are there lots of facts, figures and examples or just a few, which might be flukes?

If the school seems promising when you're through with your initial appraisal, go ahead and send for its brochure and its aptitude test, provided, of course, that it's "free (no obligation)."

Then appraise those materials. Look for a brochure that offers bios of all faculty members, who should be accomplished writers, and for a test that calls for you to display and stretch your writing skills, so you learn from your own responses. If, instead, the test seems designed to puff up your sense of yourself as a writer, you might call it quits. But if you're still impressed, keep investigating.

Ask to talk or correspond with students; check consumer and government agencies for complaint histories; write faculty members to inquire about how actively they participate in instruction and how much individual attention you'll receive.

And be sure to get answers to these questions:

❖ What's the refund policy?
❖ How much is the total cost of the course—including any and all finance charges?
❖ What's the school's track record on students' work that's sold?
❖ Are academic credits earned here accepted anywhere else?

Though you won't, of course, need to know who your fellow students are, you should make sure that the other three hallmarks of good writing courses (see above) characterize your correspondence course too. Careful evaluation before you sign up can prevent crippling blows to your psyche and your pocketbook.

Paid Critics

Classroom and correspondence-school teachers generally emphasize writing well at least as much as writing to sell. Paid critics tend to stress marketability above all else. When the paid critic is an experienced freelance editor, this emphasis can be remarkably fruitful. Otherwise, it can hurt.

Freelance editors are numerous now, largely because so many big publishers downsized in recent years. Often called book doctors, they may work closely with former colleagues who are still on staff and with the agents they used to buy books from (yes, even agented authors sometimes need heavy editing to get work ready for submission). As a result of their connections and the interests that led them to publishing in the first place, book doctors tend to be knowledgeable about what at least some editors are buying, and many of them will use their contacts for you when their work on your work is done.

As with everyone else you hire, you should ask about track records, get references and make sure there's a good fit. An editor with dazzling credentials who specializes in science fiction is not a good choice for your public policy book; get someone else.

Often, freelance editors start with an analysis or critique, which can cost $1,000 or more, and then go on to edit or rewrite—provided that's what makes sense and what you want— for fees that run into the thousands.

Criticism services or "agencies" are generally much cheaper. The trouble is, their fees are often money down the drain. When you read their ads (they appear in writers magazines and sometimes in general-interest periodicals too), keep the risks in mind, and remember, too, that while anyone can use the label "agent," most reputable literary agents don't charge for comments they may offer. In fact, the agents' association forbids it.

Perhaps the main thing to worry about with fee-charging critics is that your whole approach to writing will suffer. For what they're selling is not continuing advice on improving a work in progress but, rather, a one-shot assessment of an allegedly finished manuscript couched primarily in terms of its salability. Confronted with this emphasis, you may be tempted to stop concentrating on saying what you have to say as well as you can say it, and to focus instead on giving the public what it supposedly wants. From there it can be a short step to hack writing if you're glib and to writing garbage if you're not.

Of course, hired critics may not know what the public really wants. The chances are, however, that they'll say they do and that, furthermore, they'll have a particular "public" in mind— big-name commercial book and magazine publishers. Now, commercial publishers may very well be the wrong audience for your work, and even if they're right for it their reactions to a given manuscript simply cannot be accurately predicted. Editors themselves are so aware of the variety of tastes in their ranks that they often refuse to comment on a book or article (even if they think it has merit and promise) unless they themselves can buy it; each is afraid to suggest changes that might be anathema to an editor at another firm.

Your money, in other words, may be ill-spent on a criticism service (though the fact that you've actually spent it will provide a powerful and destructive impetus for thinking well of the advice that it bought). And your money may also be stolen. The field is full of charlatans, people who will take what you pay and then vanish where the Better Business Bureau cannot follow.

Consider, as a warning, this portion of a letter from Great Novels, Inc., to writer Wayne B. George: "There is not enough emotion in your book. Instead of the storm in Boston clearing up right away you could have a snowdrift blocking your home in the suburbs. You are slowly starving, and the young lady who is your guest gets sick and needs a doctor. Finally you are both saved from death."

The advice may strike you as insultingly simple-minded on the face of it, but it becomes downright infuriating when you realize that Wayne George's manuscript had no snowstorm scene.

If it's criticism you want, try the approaches mentioned in the preceding chapter; if it's marketing advice, turn to "A Foot in the Door," which comes next. But if you're determined to use a criticism service, take these precautions:

❖ Ask your chosen critic for a current client list, and call or write some of the people on it to discuss the quality of the critic's services.
❖ Ask prospective critics for lists of editors who've bought their clients' work recently, and get in touch with them.
❖ Consult government and consumer agencies about complaints.

❖ Get a written explanation, in advance, of charges and services.
❖ And don't forget that the substantial sums you can pay for advice have no necessary connection with what that advice is worth.

Hardware and Software

Computers' word processing programs are the best thing that's happened to writing since movable type. By now, even technophobes have conceded the point; only a few die-hards stick to their yellow pads, still unaware that these programs let you be remarkably flexible, experimental, demanding and productive as you draft and revise.

Furthermore, expert advice on what software and hardware to buy is abundantly available through books, magazines, the Internet and columns about computers like the ones Stephen Manes does for *The New York Times*. The best tip, according to Manes, is this: "Before you buy hardware or software, make sure that somebody you know—somebody you can call at 3 o'clock in the morning—is already using it." And the second-best may be: Don't rush to buy anything new; with computers, the longer you wait, the faster and cheaper equipment becomes.

Whatever you buy and whenever you buy it, however, some standard features and some add-ons should be used with caution. Take spellcheck, for example. It will catch typos you'd probably miss, but it will also miss typos you'd probably catch, like those in a pithy little poem that ran in the *Bulletin of the Missouri Council of Teachers of Mathematics*:

> *I have a spelling checker,*
> *It came with my PC;*
> *It plainly marks for my revue*
> *Mistakes I cannot see.*
> *I've run this poem threw it,*
> *I'm sure your please too no,*

> *Its letter perfect in it's weigh,*
> *My checker tolled me sew.*

Pitfalls also lurk in "writing software" designed to spruce up vocabulary and style, enliven exposition or create more memorable characters and more dramatic plots. Unfortunately, some of these programs may actually weaken your prose by encouraging you to obey simple-minded rules. In essence, each of them has a finite storehouse of words and patterns it will approve or criticize and/or a finite storehouse of suggestions and questions. Sometimes these are helpful, as, for example, when a program takes you to task for overusing certain words or writing interminable sentences. But sometimes they're harmful, too; given the Gettysburg Address to critique, one program faulted Lincoln for using the passive voice.

The best advice, therefore, is steer clear of software that tells you what to do and make use of software that enhances your ability to do whatever you decide makes sense.

Books

Relax now. Books as instructional aids are easy to access as well as inexpensive and plentiful.

Though they tend to be similarly titled, books about writing divide into three classes: those in which the author becomes your partner in the task of learning to choose and combine words; those in which the author imparts formulas; and those in which the author explains how to find things out.

Partnership books, like good writing courses, see learning to write as an unending process in which the teacher's role is to provide fertile ground for growth. Though the authors here are often men and women of considerable literary distinction, they tend to talk humbly of their work and to speak unblushingly of frustration and failure. As a rule, they concentrate on the development of skills in four primary areas:

❖ *Reading:* "What the writer wants to note, beyond anything that concerns even the critic, is how the story, its language, and all its parts have been joined together" (R. V. Cassill, *Writing Fiction*).

❖ *Creativity:* "To begin with, you must teach the unconscious to flow into the channel of writing. . . . [L]ess elegantly and more exactly, we might say that the first step toward being a writer is to hitch your unconscious mind to your writing arm" (Dorothea Brande, *Becoming a Writer*).

❖ *Diction:* "You will never make your mark as a writer unless you develop a respect for words and a curiosity about their shades of meaning that is almost obsessive" (William Zinsser, *On Writing Well*).

❖ *And construction:* Or learning "how to put words together…so that the reader not simply may but must grasp your meaning" (Jacques Barzun, *Simple and Direct*).

Obviously, this approach involves steady hard labor. You can expect to be stimulated by a partnership book; to be satisfied you must experiment with its teachings (preferably in a playful, almost childlike way), and you must also absorb them, so that they color your perceptions as you work. And rewrite. And rewrite some more.

Few formula publications dwell on the importance of painstaking revision. Instead, they offer to make writing easier. Almost always the authors are professionals setting forth the fruits of their experience as a series of instructions, and they tend to utter commands with great confidence.

Generally, these writers are most trustworthy when they discuss their own activities (by outlining, for example, how they keep records or conduct interviews), and they are least to be believed when they deal with the effects of their systems on editors (beware, for instance, of detailed directions about the physical appearance of a manuscript; if you follow them, you'll signal most publishing people that you're a fledgling writer trying to be slick).

Essentially, formula publications constitute a grab bag for authors in which some of the goodies are much better than others; some may not suit you at all and none is a major gift. For, where writing is concerned, tips on technique and on industry mores, and gimmicks and shortcuts and nuggets of knowledge can be no more than peripheral aids. The central job—developing your individual style, substance and purpose—demands independent, innovative work.

To the extent that gathering data is part of the writing assignment you set yourself, your burdens will be eased by a knowledge of research tools and techniques. As you'll see if you explore your local public library and use the search engines on the Web, the current range of informational materials is astonishing. Whatever you're curious about, you'll find at least one solid starting place.

Research manuals provide starting points too, and most of those that get published offer reliable data and analysis in lively prose (since they can't depend on the glamour of their subject to attract readers, they almost have to be good).

Advice on interviewing procedures is also useful. Since people can be excellent sources of new knowledge, you'll benefit from pointers on how to get human beings to tell you what you want to know.

Wherever you get your information, you may need help in evaluating it because, as this single example from William L. Rivers' admirable *Finding Facts* suggests, the plainest of factual statements can bear a highly complicated relationship to the truth:

[Consider] varying news stories about a simple report on gifts to Stanford University during one fiscal year. The university-published *Campus Report* headed its story:

HIGHEST NUMBER OF DONORS IN STANFORD HISTORY

The *San Francisco Chronicle* headline said:

STANFORD AGAIN RAISES $29 MILLION IN GIFTS

The *Palo Alto Times* story was headed:

DONATIONS TO STANFORD LOWEST IN FOUR YEARS

The student-published *Stanford Daily* announced:

ALUMNI DONATIONS DECLINE; BIG DROP FROM FOUNDATIONS

These headlines accurately reflect the stories they surmounted— which were also accurate.

Clearly, one lesson here is that the way a writer presents a piece of data determines its meaning in the reader's mind. Which brings us around once more to the reason for learning to write. You can teach yourself by following the suggestions in "What the Pros Know" or by devising your own methods or by muddling through. You can take courses, contact critics, plug in to computers and study books. But your fundamental goal must always be the same—full absorption (to such an extent that both your conscious and your subconscious choices are informed as you work) of a crucial principle: What you communicate is a function of how you communicate. Or as Northrop Frye has explained with exemplary clarity, "The words used are the form of which the ideas are the content, and until the words have been found, the idea does not fully exist."

A Foot in
the Door

❖　❖　❖

The Plain Truth About Agents

A MAGIC WAND is basic equipment for literary agents. At least, that's what even experienced authors seem to believe. Agents, it's assumed, can work miracles. They're all-knowing, all-powerful, all-wise. Each one is intimately acquainted with the tastes and needs of hundreds of editors in New York City (and a few elsewhere). At a word from an agent, offers pour in, advances rise, promotion plans expand, ad budgets skyrocket.

Because it's way too much to live up to, many agented authors end up disappointed, even bitter about their experiences.

If you think you want an agent, therefore—as virtually everyone who writes trade books does—it's important to understand how they really operate as well as how to get one, how to work with one and, if need be, how to leave one and find another or function alone. This chapter covers those topics; the next chapters explain how you can place your work without an agent (magazine writers do it all the time, as do authors of textbooks and scientific and technical books and other kinds of specialized work; authors of books for the general reader do it often too, no matter what you may have heard to the contrary).

Submitting

"I go to 10 or 15 houses simultaneously." "I won't take a book on unless I have 3 to 9 houses in mind for it." "I may submit a book to 10 or 15 houses, one at a time." "Usually, I'll submit to 6 or 8 editors." "I start out with 15. As they come back, I do more."

Restated, these reports from agents might read: In the normal course of events, I get half a dozen rejections, a dozen rejections, maybe more than that, for book projects I submit to several editors simultaneously.

Sometimes, it's true, agents will score on the first try, and sometimes they're able to generate competing bids (probably via multiple submissions rather than auctions, which have played out badly often enough to lose much of their appeal).

On the other hand, sometimes agents bomb out completely. "Everyone talks about the books I sell, but they have no idea how many books I don't sell," an agent will tell you in private. In public, the subject of failure rarely arises, but it's a safe bet that 25%, and probably more, of all agented manuscripts simply don't get bought. "Every one of us agents has had something we adored and were not able to sell," Curtis Brown's Ellen Geiger told an interviewer.

What all this proves is that selling literary property is a risky business, even for the experts. And it's doubly risky for agents because they don't just put their reputations on the line every time they offer a book; they also gamble with their finances. Most reputable agents, after all, work on commission. Some still charge 10%; most went to 15% during the '80s; but when a manuscript doesn't sell, any cut yields nothing.

To make their business economically viable, many agents set up shop in their homes, and most agents try to maximize the chances of success in four admirably logical ways: by choosing their clients carefully, by placing books rather than shorter work (periodical pieces take as much time but pay less), by making the projects they handle as appealing as possible and by offering them to editors who are, in essence, their pals.

Maximizing a book's appeal can involve working with the author on a proposal for months and months. (See "Procedures" for an analysis of proposals and their uses.) Agents are not equally gifted as editorial advisers, of course, nor equally willing to put in tremendous amounts of time on spec, but many of the best will critique rewrite after rewrite until a book's strengths are unmistakably apparent.

Even before a proposal is ready, an agent will start the submissions process by talking about it to editors over the phone or over lunch. If the proposal is taking the agent into a new field (it's a gardening book, perhaps, the first one the agent has handled), these editors may be strangers, people ferreted out by research and added to a contact list that numbers between 100 and 200. More often, though, agents bring new book projects to people they already know, like and trust, and who like and trust them right back.

Among the hundreds of editors in New York City and the thousands west of the Hudson, the agent may deal regularly with 40. Or to look at the pattern from another angle, among the scores of agents in New York City and the scores more around the country, any one editor at a large house may hear from no more than 25, while editors at small firms—well-established, professional, profitable small firms—may hear from 6 or fewer.

Provided that your agent is really right for your work, this is all to the good, an efficient chain of interactions between people with similar tastes and interests. If your agent is not quite on your wavelength, though, it may mean that the editors who'd like your book best never even know that it exists.

In any case, the submissions process that good agents follow is lengthy and painstaking. Let lazier authors' reps send material out with a terse covering note—"Perhaps something here will interest you." The good agent not only introduces a book in conversation but also writes a thoughtful, detailed, personal letter to make sure editors have all the information they need to judge a book's marketability, and convince their colleagues of it.

As rejections come in, agents may pass them along to writers in whole or in part, or they may simply dismiss them and move on. When two or three comments make the same negative point about a nonfiction book, it's probably worth rethinking the proposal, most agents believe. Advice about fiction is less useful. In fact, as the agent for several bestselling novels points out, it's generally "worth nothing unless the recommendations resonate or the editor is buying the book."

During the placement process, agents maintain files of all correspondence and records of all submissions and their outcomes. Most agents try to keep their authors abreast of a book's status but no writer should expect a weekly progress report. With dozens of clients, agents find it impossible to pay constant attention to each. In any event, some writers prefer not to know every detail of a flat-out rejection letter and appreciate having a buffer between them and potentially devastating feedback. It's fine to write and ask for news if you haven't heard anything for a while, but don't launch a barrage of phone calls. And rest assured that when something sells, you'll hear about it.

Making Deals

It's when your book is accepted at last that an agent's most valuable skills come into play, for at this point a book publisher will usually offer an advance against royalties, and an agent will usually be able (as a writer probably won't) to get that advance up. Furthermore, as your business representative, an agent can sell your talents and potential to a publisher in a way calculated to get you the best possible terms throughout your contract (see "Getting What's Coming to You" for additional information on negotiations).

For the best agents, negotiating means feeling one's way, not simply following a formula. Or as Georges Borchardt puts it, "There's very little repetition, very little that's standard"; good negotiators are imaginative, they come up with new language, new approaches. Borchardt—whose agency represents Elie Wiesel, Susan Minot, Jack Miles and T. Coraghessan Boyle, among others—sold 100 books last year for publication as originals or reprints. Advances for these books ranged from $1,000 to $1,000,000, a spread by no means unique. Advances reported by other agents run "from two figures to six figures," "from $1,500 to millions," "from $5,000 to the high five figures."

"My secret goal," says one agent, "is to get the advance up at least by the amount of my commission." Trying hard to better other terms too, conscientious agents devote a great deal of time and effort to figuring out what they want for their clients, and then, in effect, they develop their own versions of various publishers' contracts. As a result, when an agent goes to a large firm like Random House or Bantam Doubleday Dell, editors there know from experience what language and provisions will be acceptable to that agent, and they can streamline the negotiating process.

One negative side effect may occur, though. Points that matter to you but not to most other writers may be ignored. Even agented authors should read their contracts carefully and discuss their wish lists with their agents early on to see what's realistic and what isn't.

If, say, you're incensed by the fact that the "satisfactory manuscript" clause gives the publisher power to cancel your deal—and well you might be—you need to know that "publishers can usually get around whatever changes you make in things like that, though it is worth trying for better definition" of their rights.

Limiting publishers' rights is a constant challenge for agents, who must combat attacks on territory that once seemed secure while facing a barrage of new demands. The electronic rights battlefield, recently very active, is a good example. Newly interested in the area, publishers took to asking for all rights now and forever, and agents came up with creative counterproposals. Susan Ginsburg of Writers House, for instance, offered electronic text rights along with the right of first refusal on other electronic applications. As in other areas, the agreements agents reach here will probably become standard, benefiting agented and unagented authors alike.

Usually, it's worth trying to retain as many rights to your book as possible. For if all goes according to plan, the deal your agent makes with a book publisher will be only one of several deals the agent makes for the book. Sales to foreign publishers and movie and TV producers are among those a smart, hardworking agent can generate and shape, and sometimes the money from them far exceeds what the primary publisher paid in advance.

Ongoing Activity

Money due an agented writer will go to the agent first. Agents record payments, deduct what they're owed, and remit the balance to their clients. As a rule, they also attempt to check royalty statements but it's an uphill battle at best and only a few stubborn souls emerge victorious.

Royalty statements are notoriously impenetrable—information is missing, figures won't jibe, streams of income simply don't show up. You can solve some of the mysteries yourself (see "Getting What's Coming to You"), and industry efforts may solve others over time (both the Authors Guild and the BISAC division of the Book Industry Study Group are tackling the problem intelligently).

Meanwhile, agents expect collection hassles and cope as well as they can.

But money isn't all they will keep tabs on. "I'm a partner, not a broker," says Jean Naggar, whose client list includes Jean Auel, Mary McGarry Morris, Elizabeth Arthur and Phillip Margolin. Naggar, like many other agents, sees her mission as developing a writer's career, which means shepherding books through the long and cumbersome publishing process.

At the outset, when editing is going on, the agent's role is generally minor, unless author and editor clash, in which case the agent can step in to restore peace. When the time comes for marketing, agents are more active, although the level of activity varies from person to person and book to book, as does the level of effectiveness.

"We call and nag a lot, but I don't know that it does any good," one agent says, while another reports gratifying success at a meeting with marketing people at a well-known house—which doubled a book's first printing on the spot—and depressing failure in a series of conversations with sub rights people at another—who refused to reject a remarkably low bid from a paperback reprinter. "I want to have an influence on marketing; I really do have things to say that can be helpful," Susan Ginsburg notes, adding that her background as executive editor and editor-in-chief at major publishing houses helps her get publishers to listen.

One relatively easy way for agents to affect marketing is through authors. As "Why and How to Be Your Own Best Sales Force" will demonstrate in detail, lively, savvy writers can boost sales substantially, which is why Berenice Hoffman and others habitually help them use their contacts and energies to advantage.

Does all this sound like a full-time job and then some? It surely is, especially when you consider that most literary agencies are small, maybe one or two people (with an assistant or two or three) serving as advocate, adviser and business manager for 50 to 100 writers. So if you have an agent, make sure to express your confidence and appreciation. And if you don't have one, use the rest of this chapter and the next to decide whether to change that situation and, if so, when and how.

Finding Your Agent

Just any old agent will not do. For one thing, an agent can be a handicap rather than a help. "Everybody knows there are certain agents who send only junk," a veteran editor says, explaining that manuscripts from inept agents arrive with a strike against them. And for another thing, an agent who doesn't quite understand what you're up to probably deals with editors who won't get it either (see "Submitting," above), so that the submissions process will waste time and muddy the waters.

What you want, therefore, is a capable, well-regarded agent who truly understands and admires your work.

You can pinpoint promising agents by using directories and contacting the Association of Authors' Representatives (aka AAR) in New York (see "A Foot in the Door Resources"), but the best way to find out about an individual agent's interests, strengths, and idiosyncrasies is through word of mouth. Long before you're in a position to hire one, you might begin investigating agents by asking published writers you know whom they'd recommend, or by calling a local author you've just read about in the paper for suggestions. Alternatively, you might contact the local writers club, talk to your librarian, scan prefaces for comments on agents' contributions and browse through the book trade's organ of communication, *Publishers Weekly* (see "Resources").

Predictably, good agents are highly selective. "I have to believe strongly" in a book to take it on, says Lydia Wills of Artists Agency. Wills represents "younger writers and edgier writers" but her criterion is virtually universal. For many agents, maintaining the level of personal service they give existing clients means turning away dozens of writers each week. Some won't even take the time to read your work unless you send it exclusively to them (although they may be all in favor of multiple submissions to editors; see "Procedures"). Authors they accept tend to have one of two things going for them: they were referred—by an editor or a current client—or they wrote a wonderful query letter. (Occasionally, agents will take the initiative and go after someone they want to represent, perhaps a chef on local TV who seems to have an interesting new diet or a psychologist whose advice columns embody the theme of a salable book.)

For guidance on crafting good queries, see "Procedures." For more tips on targeting agents (as well as editors), see "Openings." And to get the most from the advice in those chapters remember four things:

1. Boston and Washington, Los Angeles and San Francisco—not to mention all sorts of places in between—are home to agents who are good at their work and possibly right for yours. In the era of jet travel and instant communication by phone, fax

and e-mail, you'd be silly to rule anyone out solely on the basis of geography.

2. People just starting out as agents tend to be less selective than people who've been agenting for a while. *Publishers Weekly* often announces agency openings. As you pursue possibilities, though, you'll want to recall that anyone can use the label "literary agent," and be especially careful to check background and terms.

3. Agents who belong to the AAR have access to a wealth of experience. Through their meetings, their newsletters and their mailings, they share discoveries and breakthroughs and initiate changes that clients can cash in on.

4. The author-agent relationship is intimate and, ideally, long-lived, rather like a marriage. In fact, as you listen to agents talking about writers you'll hear significant-other metaphors time and again. When a client leaves, it's a "divorce." When an agent decides to persevere after 38 rejections, it's because she's "fallen in love" with a book. Trying to decide whether to take a new client on, agents ask themselves, "Can I live with this person?" When the decision is Yes, writer and agent sign a contract that's a "prenuptial agreement."

Agency contracts are sometimes verbal and, when written, often couched in the form of a letter. Some are one page long and entirely intelligible; some run on over several pages larded with legal jargon, and at least one is more draconian than any publisher's contract that agent would let a writer sign.

If the agent you want uses a lengthy form that seems to say "We own you forever," think about hiring a literary property lawyer to negotiate for you (using any other sort of lawyer will be counterproductive because contracts in other industries are so different). Otherwise, you can probably deal direct.

The first thing that strikes most people unfamiliar with literary agents' contracts is that the agents expect payment in perpetuity. A basically reasonable requirement given their investments of time and credibility, it is variously expressed: Commissions are to be paid "for the life of agreements we make on your behalf," "during or after our tenure as representative," on "all sales for which negotiations begin during the term of this agreement and end within six months after it expires, and all changes and extensions in those agreements, regardless of when made and by whom."

But what if the agent goes out of business? What if the individual who is "your" agent leaves the agency and goes somewhere else? What if your agent is acquired by a larger company whose best clients' books compete with yours? As New York literary property lawyer Kenneth P. Norwick points out, it's wise to consider the what-ifs, and Norwick recommends asking that an arbitration clause be inserted in your contract in case of irreconcilable differences.

Just don't get so wrapped up in possible pitfalls that you forget what's really going on here. Two people with complementary skills and congenial personalities who have taken the trouble to investigate each other are joining forces to launch a book and build a career. It may not be any closer to perfect than most marriages but the proper attitude for starters is a blend of confidence, commitment and joy.

Breaking Up

Say it just isn't working out. The agent's not enthusiastic anymore. Worse, your phone calls aren't returned, your letters aren't answered, nothing has sold. Breakups do occur, sometimes to an agent's regret (especially, though not only, when the client who leaves is a moneymaker), but sometimes not. In fact, breakups happen so often that agents form policies about them. "The first step" in leaving an agent "is to find a new one," says Richard Curtis, who's been president of the AAR. "Because some agents have compunctions about taking on clients belonging to agents with whom they're friendly," Curtis adds, "you should make it clear to prospective agents that you have determined to leave your present agent." "I prefer to have clients fire themselves," another prominent agent reports. "I've suggested to several people that they'd be happier elsewhere, because I was getting a twisted stomach every time they called, because I'd lost my enthusiasm or because we'd gotten fed up with each other."

Being dropped by an agent can be terrifying, especially when the agent indulges in negative overgeneralization. "Nobody's buying fiction anymore," one agent told a well-reviewed novelist. "It's hopeless. We've gone to everybody," another one said, summing up seven submissions. In the first case, the novelist got herself another agent—who assured her that the fiction market had not vanished. In the second, the writer decided to proceed on her own and get a publisher interested; Penguin, which apparently fell outside the "everybody" category despite its size and prestige, bought her book. Still, both of these writers had their confidence badly shaken, at least for a while.

But authors anguish during the "divorce" even when they're the ones who walk. "Sure I worried," a nonfiction writer says. Several of his books had been critical successes and one had made a fair amount of money, but now his career seemed stalled and his agent unresponsive. Though he'd decided to sever the relationship, he was nervous. "Will I ever get another agent? Will I get a better agent? What am I doing to myself?"

Yes, he got another agent, and one who was better for him. Although most of his books had been critical rather than commercial successes, this writer had enough pride in his work to "take the position an agent would be lucky to get me." Having "decided to give myself that vote of confidence," he carefully targeted several agents to approach and met with half a dozen. The new agent he chose worked with him for close to a year, first on a proposal that didn't sell and then on one that did—for nearly three times any previous advance he'd ever gotten.

Why the big jump? "Partly because this agent is more on my wavelength than the other one was, which means his contacts are more suited to my work."

The point deserves to be underlined. It's the right agent you want, the one who knows what you're about and likes it. If you can't find that sort of representation, you'll be better off proceeding on your own, at least until you get an offer. With that in hand, getting an agent is easier. Just remember not to agree to any specifics an editor proposes until the agent is on the case.

See the rest of this section for pointers on how to generate offers, and take heart from a statement by Putnam's executive editor, Refna Wilkin: Putnam publishes many authors who come without agents, she said. "Like all publishers, we are anxious to invest in new talent and we hope we will continue to see it."

Who Do You Know?

T HE CHARGE that the publishing game is fixed, that you've got to know an insider if you're ever going to break into print, is part myth, part truth. The myth arises because the easiest response in the face of repeated rejection is to say that everyone but you is pulling strings left and right. It's not a large step from this interpretation of bad fortune to a full-blown conspiracy theory of an entrenched literary establishment. Those who've written superb (and fairly conventional) prose, however, are all but sure to get published by a major company—even if they don't know a soul remotely connected with publishing—for reasons already indicated.

As for the truth: There's no doubt that it helps to have personal contact with people in a position to make acquisition decisions, particularly when your work is good rather than great. The point is not that editors will fight for your work because you're friendly with them (that would not be a good way for them to keep their jobs); the point is that they will be more likely to take a chance on your work if they see you as a known quantity. Editors are as insecure about their own judgments as most other people, and therefore they always find it easier to back a pretested, preapproved author. Anything you can do to provide trustworthy testimony to your skills will help reassure editors that by gambling on you they'll be running a fairly small risk.

The idea of a connections approach to publishing shouldn't

repel you, since in the first place, connections are not necessarily insidious and artificial, and, in the second, most sources of connection to publishing insiders are not only generally accessible but also worth cultivating in their own right.

Think, for example, of writers (including writing teachers), people in publishing (and not only editors) and selected collaborators (including some editorial émigrés).

Other Authors

Any way you can associate with writers is bound to be to your advantage.

Michael Chabon, whose first novel, *The Mysteries of Pittsburgh*, sold for $155,000, placed it with the help of his adviser at the University of California at Irvine, the writer Macdonald Harris. And Amy Tan connected with her first publisher via Molly Giles, award-winning writer and teacher, whom she met at the Squaw Valley Community of Writers. Tan credits Giles with "the sharpest eye, the keenest ear for false steps, insincere voice, inconsistencies." Through Giles, Tan got to Sandra Dijkstra, the California agent who orchestrated the sale of *The Joy Luck Club*.

Some writers make it a point to share their contacts—"I know an editor at the *Atlantic*; I'll write and say you're sending an article in." Others you know may recommend you for assignments they hear about but don't want for themselves.

Taking a writing course (see "Getting the Words Right") will put you in touch with at least one published author, the teacher, who may be willing to link you up with editors. Perhaps others in the class can and will do the same. So ask your instructor and fellow students for the names of people you should send your work to, and ask if you may use their names.

Also explore chat groups hosted by writers, e-mail writers lists that you're qualified to subscribe to, bulletin boards on writing and Web sites that allow interaction with writers. Go to readings by writers scheduled for area bookstores and/or listed in the local

papers' events calendars and steel yourself to approach speakers
after their presentations. Tell them who you are and what you're
working on; they could be valuable links between you and a
sympathetic editorial ear.

Then investigate national, regional and local writers groups.
Joining one or more of those you'll find listed in "Resources"
will connect you immediately with writers by the dozen, many
of whom may become your friends through attendance at the
group's meetings and service on its committees. And if you
can't show up and help out, you can still benefit from the
newsletter and maybe communicate with fellow members regularly online.

No group meets the need you feel? Start one, and prepare
yourself for varied dividends. Four writers in New York founded The Writers Room because they felt a need for long-term
writing space, which the Room now provides for 240 people
(with 50 on the waiting list). But it also provides opportunities
to network, partly through seminars and readings and an old-
fashioned, on-the-wall bulletin board that lets members share
useful information. "It's amazing how supportive the writers are
of each other," according to the executive director, Donna Brodie;
established writers, she reports, constantly introduce newcomers
to agents and editors and offer to read and advise on works in
progress.

Across the country, five Oregon writers had a similar experience. Eager for ways to help each other write and get published,
Jean Auel, Marlene Howard, Lola Janes, Ed Weinstein and
Naomi Stokes established the Oregon Writers Colony. The
Colonyhouse on the beach accommodates not only writers but
also writers workshops and conferences and meetings of church,
business, civic and other groups whose payments help pay for
the facility.

Writers conferences and workshops, of course, provide even
more opportunities for forging useful relationships. Hundreds of
writers gatherings are held each year. On campuses, in hotels
and at vacation spots on-shore and at sea here and abroad, pro-

fessional writers, editors and agents gather to share editorial and marketing know-how, with the result that exciting things sometimes happen.

This is most often the case for writers who come to conferences with manuscripts in hand. Anne Rice, for instance, brought the manuscript of her first novel to a writers conference. An editor from Knopf who was there to lecture read it and was impressed enough to bring it back to New York for consideration. Rice's *Interview with the Vampire*, subsequently published by Knopf, launched Rice's phenomenal career. Also at a writers conference, John Wessel met the bestseller author Sue Grafton. Grafton, who had judged a short-story contest he'd entered, suggested revisions for his novel, and when he sent the new version to her, she sent it on to her agent, Molly Friedrich, who in turn sent it to 22 publishers, stimulating what *Publishers Weekly* called a "bidding fury." In a two-book deal, Wessel's *This Far, No Further* brought $900,000.

To make connections at a conference that will have value for you, you may have to do more than plant yourself on fertile ground, manuscript at the ready, and hope to be discovered. You may have to boldly bring your work to the attention of others. Christina Baldwin's story illustrates the snowball effect that one step of initiative—taken in a mood of nothing ventured, nothing gained—can have.

When I saw an announcement of the Second Annual Women in Writing Conference, on women's personal writings, I wrote the director, Hannelore Hahn, of my work teaching and my intention to write a book, and she invited me to be a panelist at the conference. I headed for it in early August with my third-draft manuscript, and a twenty-minute presentation entitled "The Rituals of Journal Writing." After that everything felt like a hurricane. I gave my presentation and was astounded and delighted with the energy and response it generated. I was asked to do a mini-workshop later in the afternoon and agreed to invite anyone interested. Fifty women crowded into that space, journals in hand, and we shared avidly all we could for the next three hours. Published authors came up to me with advice and referrals for breaking into the New York publishing world. The next day someone introduced me to Meredith Bernstein and told me she was a book agent.

Monday, August 9, Meredith and I had lunch, discovered we liked and trusted each other. I gave her my manuscript copy of *One to One*. She read it that night and called me the next morning saying she loved it, and I agreed to have her handle it."

Bernstein generated an offer quickly and negotiated the contract and the advance within two weeks. At last count, Baldwin's book had been in print for 20 years.

It's possible that all you'll get from a conference is a rudimentary suntan and a dent in your bank balance, but it's also possible that you'll come away having found (1) encouragement from peers and/or professionals; (2) references you can use later in submitting manuscripts or applying for grants or jobs; (3) a demystified view of the publishing business; and (4) proof at first hand that unknown writers do get published. The overwhelming response of many conference-goers is joy, because they discover that the publishing world is not as sealed as they had thought.

Publishing People

If you don't want an agent (or you don't want one now) and if close association with writers doesn't appeal to you, perhaps you'd like to make your connections through people who work in publishing.

First, reach far and wide among your acquaintances to see what leads you can turn up. Maybe your brother-in-law's sister's friend or one of your high-school classmates is a production assistant at a national magazine. Maybe your neighbor heads the new media division of a communications company. Introductions from people like that could be enough to get you a personal response, signed (though not necessarily written) by an editor.

Peter Tauber's entrée to an editor's office for his first book, *The Sunshine Soldiers*, was through an introduction from a mutual friend who'd worked with Tauber on a newspaper. And Ruthie Bolton's key contact was a maintenance man when she was stuck on page 58 of *Gal: A True Life*, which Michael Dorris would eventually declare "succeeds brilliantly as both literature and sociology" in a review in *The Los Angeles Times*. *The New York Times*, which also ran a rave review, did a little feature story as well. The maintenance man, the *Times* reported, worked in a building where the novelist Josephine Humpreys had an office. After he overheard Bolton talking about her work in progress, he asked Humphreys to read it. Reluctant at first, Humphreys was "captivated" by the material. She pitched in to make it publishable and got her own agent involved. The agent, Harriet Wasserman, sold the book to Harcourt Brace.

Even editors who reject a manuscript can turn out to be helpful in placing it. A short, graceful note to anyone who liked your work but returned it anyway might elicit suggestions about colleagues at other companies who'd probably like it too, especially if you suggest that the editor just scrawl names on your letter and stick it in the SASE you've enclosed. "Editor So-and-so suggested I write you about . . ." sends a powerful positive signal.

Sales reps can also send powerful signals to acquiring editors. Reps from book publishing houses travel the country constantly. Always on the alert for salable books, they will be delighted if you turn out to be a "discovery" they can report to the home office. Local bookstore managers can tell you which reps will be in your area when, and then you can arrange to meet some of them. It would do you no harm to learn as much as you can about their work in general, and if you find that one of them likes what you've written, you've gotten yourself an influential sponsor.

In case none of these methods attracts you, there's a still more direct way of building publishing connections: go to work in the field, either informally (by offering editors reliable assistance with clerical chores during your free time) or formally (by getting a job).

Obviously, there's no point undertaking a job hunt in a crowded, poorly paid field just to gain connections. But if you're genuinely interested in becoming an assistant editor, say, or a publicity department trainee, and if you manage to get yourself hired, you'll find making connections among the fringe benefits of your work. Lisa Smith explains why:

> At college I told every teacher and student I knew that I wanted to go into magazines and that I was interested in finding out about an internship program, so I could see what magazines were like without the pressure and commitment of a permanent job. A teacher told me about the American Society of Magazine Editors internship program, and I applied and was accepted. During my internship I made extremely good contacts. In addition to the people I met at the two magazines I worked on during the summer, I got to meet editors from other magazines who came each week to participate in discussions at the ASME offices. A lot of the editors I met face to face were editors I later submitted story ideas to.
>
> After graduation I was offered a job at *Mademoiselle*, where I worked for two years. Because of my work there, I know how to shape ideas and who to direct them to. I know why manuscripts are accepted or rejected because I've been on the other side of the desk. As far as I'm concerned, going into magazine work is one of the best ways to prepare the ground for a writing career.

The same encomiums can be applied to jobs in book publishing, no matter how lowly they may be to begin with. Crossovers from editing to writing are frequent (Toni Morrison, E. L. Doctorow, Michael Korda and Joseph Kanon are examples of the phenomenon), and all knowledge gained on one side of the spectrum is clearly relevant to success on the other.

Collaborators

Connecting yourself to people with good connections is a fine way to win readers and influence editors. You might try quick canvasses of celebrities on assorted subjects (What's the most terrifying event in your past? How do you think we should deal with the federal deficit?). And deeper patterns of collaboration may ease entrée to publishing houses, too.

Consider, for example, the experience of Cherie Mason, an advertising VP and conservation activist who moved to an island off the coast of Maine, encountered a fox who'd been maimed by a trap and wrote a children's book with the fox as a central character. Eight rejections later, Mason read a piece in the *Maine Times* about an award-winning book designer named Lurelle Cheverie. Mason approached Cheverie; Cheverie linked up with illustrator Joellen Stammen, and before long *Wild Fox* was published by Down East.

The expert collaborator category also includes professionals who have newsworthy knowledge but who lack the time, and possibly the skills, to produce publishable prose. Collaboration agreements—with a scholar, a doctor, a designer, an editor or anyone else—should be in writing and signed. Consult a literary property lawyer and/or the legal guides mentioned throughout "Resources" for help in drawing up a contract or responding to the one your colleague proposes.

Endnote on Priorities

Regardless of who its members are, an acquaintanceship chain in publishing (as in any other industry) simply greases the wheels. And any acquaintanceship chain functions best when it ends up not just reaching the right sort of people (editors in this case) but reaching the right individual people (namely, the particular editors who will be most responsive to your work). As you consider making and using contacts, therefore, it's smart to have a wish list of particular editors in hand. "Openings" will tell you how to compile it. Once it exists, you're likely to find fewer than six degrees of separation between you and the people on it.

Remember, though, that the final verdict on your manuscript will be determined by its perceptible merits. For guidance in making those merits show to best advantage, please move on through the next three chapters.

Shaping Subject Matter

T HE MAIN TROUBLE with writing for a market is that editors can't know for sure what they want until they've read it. They know what they wanted in the past, of course (and so will you when you study back issues of magazines at the library or the books on the shelves of your local stores). And they may think they know enough about what they will want in the future to fill out the questionnaires sent by annual marketing guides (though the statement that a magazine is looking for fiction "on contemporary life and its problems" is not likely to help you much, no matter how accurate it is). But what editors want most is something they can't describe because it doesn't exist yet—the untold story, the fresh perspective, the new idea.

Editors spend a great deal of time trying to think up article and book topics. Once they finally agree on a subject, they spend still more time talking about how to narrow it, how to focus it, what facts to go after and what purpose to serve. After that they'll confer about which writers might handle the project effectively. And when they eventually find a writer willing and able to do the article or the nonfiction book they've been discussing, as often as not the project fizzles (obviously, serious fiction isn't likely to result from this process, though formula fiction sometimes does).

Bearing in mind that this is what frequently happens when

professionals try to create prose that will sell, you may be inclined to abandon the effort yourself. If men and women who are not only intimately familiar with the character and needs of their own publications but also knowledgeable about marketing trends and literary talents can't get it right, what's a writer supposed to do?

The best bet is to follow where your enthusiasms lead. When the individual who's excited by an idea is the same individual who develops that idea for publication, the chances of pleasing an audience (including an audience of editors) shoot way up.

Thus, if you're a lawyer who's eager to propose a new legal status for couples who live together but are not married, or a commercial fishing boat captain who longs to write a novel exposing the corruption in the industry, or a corporate vice-president who's desperate to know whether other highly paid executives feel useless too, you don't have to go looking for a strong subject. All you have to do is write up the one you care about and then figure out how and where to get it into print.

Suppose, however, that your trade is not law or fishing or business, but writing, that you continually need new ideas and angles for periodical pieces or books, and that you find yourself fresh out of enthusiasm from time to time. It may look as though you have a serious problem. For enthusiasm clearly can't be created by fiat, no matter how strong your willpower.

Fortunately, however, it can be grown at home. Just provide an environment that lets your natural passions reveal themselves. One good way to do this is by beginning a program of clipping and filing, as outlined in "What the Pros Know." And another is by developing an awareness of readers' motivations and your relationship to them. (What needs could you fill for the reading public that nobody else has filled yet? What needs could you fill that nobody else could fill better?)

Why people read what they read is an endlessly interesting question with plenty of sensible answers. If you keep list of theories in the back of your mind as you examine events occurring around and within you, you should soon find your energies engaged by an idea for a story or a book.

From the multiplicity of readers' motives, here's a selection to get things started.

Readers Want to Learn . . .

Everyone has some knowledge that would be useful to other people. Perhaps, for example, you could write a manual about financial planning or cooking Lithuanian delicacies or even getting published. Eric L. Reiss had always been interested in old phonographs and "thought that maybe it was time someone wrote a book about them," so he tried the idea out on a small publishing house that "specializes in books for oddball collectors." Reiss' *The Compleat Talking Machine* not only got great reviews, he reports; it also sold about 3,000 copies in less than a year, which necessitated a second printing and led the publisher to ask for a sequel. Nina Crews knew what it was like to grow up in a big, big city and decided to do a children's book that would "reflect the energy of the city environment, the textures of it." Greenwillow bought *One Hot Summer Day*, Crews' story with photographic collages about a little girl who beats the heat.

Perhaps what you know—and ought to transmit knowledge of—should serve as the basis of what's called a service piece. Can you explain how to find your way through a complicated morass of information? Could you prepare a *Complete Guide to Home-Swapping Programs* or *A Directory of Occupational Diseases*, for example? Have you discovered a scientist whose studies of genetic engineering excite your interest or a musician who's created a startling new system of notation? By all means, consider making valuable technical data accessible to the general public, and explore collaborating with an expert so that new findings that otherwise would be couched in trade jargon and buried in the voluminous literature of a specialized discipline can reach a wider audience.

To find current research that may be grist for a story, you might sign up for information on recently established Internet lists (see "Resources") and make it a habit to browse through special-interest and academic journals on your library's shelves and in its databases. If a list interests you, subscribe and see if the posts are useful. If an article title intrigues you, get the article. And if it meets your expectations, consider writing the author to ask about other good material on the subject (try the Net and/or biographical directories for an address and, as a last resort, send your letter in care of the magazine). Later perhaps you can interview the author/expert.

Interviews offer a good form for communication between experts and the rest of us because people today value the authentic personal voice, the individual mode of expression, the first-hand, eyewitness testimony. But traditional narrative and expository approaches appeal too.

The most complicated kind of knowledge you can relay to an audience involves not just knowing something but knowing what that something signifies. Many writers succeed because they've developed the perspicacity and skill necessary for asking revealing questions about apparently commonplace events. What's behind the resurgence of affection for the smell and taste of homemade pasta, for instance? Economics? A recommitment to family life and the home? A diabolical plot by a handful of women's magazines and food manufacturers? The answers may provide fresh material that concerned readers will value.

. . . To Amass Experiences

Most of us are avid consumers of experience. What we can't do in fact we're usually eager to do vicariously, so reading matter that can serve either as a trial run or as a substitute for activity has definite attractions.

Thus if you can reveal what it's like to cross the Alps on a bicycle, to experiment with a new method of quality control or to serve on the jury in a murder trial, you have an excellent foundation for the kind of I-was-there-and-this-is-how-it-really-was kind of piece that the media are fond of nowadays.

And if you haven't already had an experience worth sharing, you can set one up. When Marianne Ragins was a senior in high school, she decided to see how much college scholarship money she could collect. She did some research; she sent out more than 200 applications; she got offers totaling over $400,000, and then she wrote *Winning Scholarships for College: An Insider's Guide*. Originally self-published, the book was acquired by Holt and quickly went through three printings. To become an insider of a very different sort, David K. Reynolds, an anthropologist, arranged to be committed to a veterans hospital as a potential suicide. He spent two weeks as a mental patient and then wrote a book with suicidologist Norman Farbow about what happened to him and how his experiences jibed with current research findings.

Whether or not they involve subterfuge and risk, inside stories always appeal to readers' natural curiosity, and there's nothing to stop you from using the form. If you're not an insider by right, you can make yourself one.

. . . To Read About Themselves

It's always exciting to see a movie made in your neighborhood; though you know it's silly, somehow your own life takes on luster after that, and you feel almost as if you'd been featured in that film yourself. A similar pattern of identification probably lies behind the substantial sales of written work with a local focus.

What with diaries and oral histories and natural wonders and the unnatural acts of the couple next door, enough raw materials exist in everybody's town or region to create innumerable poems, novels and works of nonfiction. If you become fascinated by a subject of local interest, you're in luck. The anecdotes and facts that make for a lively manuscript are available nearby, and selling your work will be relatively easy because editors are well aware that Americans love to read about where they live (or where, in this rootless age, they used to live in younger days).

Just as we flock to read about our neighbors because proximity makes us identify with them, we reach eagerly for material about people we recognize as psychological kin. The appeal of feminist literature stems partly from the fact that most women identify to some extent with all women and therefore feel personally drawn to any discussion of the sex in print. So if you can write as a member of any clear-cut group, you can expect other members to form a readership.

. . . To Be Up on the Latest

Check the shelves of your supermarket if you doubt the attraction of the *new* for the American public. Where books are concerned, though, being new means living a year or two in the future because it usually takes a couple of years to get a manuscript from the idea stage to the bookseller. Since even periodicals usually have lead times of several months, bestseller lists and other conventional hit-parade compilations aren't much use as tools for keeping up with the times; though they seem to reflect the present, they actually portray phenomena that will be in the past by the time you get your manuscript out.

A crystal ball of sorts does exist, however, in the bible of the book trade, *Publishers Weekly* (unfortunately, although there are periodicals about periodicals, *PW* has no counterpart as a channel of communication among editors and publishers of newspapers and magazines). *PW*'s circulation may be small but its influence is enormous; almost everyone involved with book publishing reads it and reacts to it, so when the magazine repeatedly spotlights books about money, for example, you can bet (a) that books about money are a big item on current publishers' lists and (b) that they'll continue to be welcomed by editors, who naturally like manuscripts apt to interest an influential journal.

The pleasure of glimpsing such motives behind the dignified façade of publishing is one of the auxiliary benefits of reading *Publishers Weekly*. As you skim through the magazine, you can begin to feel yourself a member of the gossipy publishing community, listening as hard as the next person for the first sound of a new bandwagon getting ready to roll.

Like its treatment of publishing trends—which it covers in reportorial articles as well as through information tidbits—*PW*'s coverage of forthcoming books provides an outstanding resource for keeping current. Its Announcements issues and roundups present annotated lists of upcoming titles at intervals throughout the year, and the magazine often prints items about manuscripts that are still somewhere in the idea or rough-draft stage—books, in other words, that will be published a year or more later. If you can discern a pattern among the new titles, you're on to something that will be hot just when your discussion of it rolls off the presses. Similarly, conclusions you can draw from studying newsletters from small publishers' associations are likely to foretell subjects that will keep readers up-to-date in the near future.

To capitalize on current trends in publications more transient than books, you can begin by noting what's selling on the newsstands. Look at the cover lines on view at a variety of locations over a period of several weeks, and see if you can get newsstand dealers to talk with you about what's selling and why. Then, if one of the subjects now drawing customers captures your interest, you can do a piece about it for a periodical that has a very short lead time—a daily paper, perhaps, or possibly a weekly.

You can also capitalize on trends that may not have made it into print in any form by navigating the World Wide Web. Using a variety of search engines (check "Resources" for specifics), you'll find sites that cover every conceivable topic. Airline safety? Jewish holidays? Poker? Terrorism? Transvestites? Truth machines? All of the above, and countless others.

But if the array of information is dazzling, it's also daunting, or it should be, because the Web can be a trap. Watch out for:

❖ *Mesmerization.* Hundreds, sometimes thousands, of hits will come up for any topic you choose and you may find you've frittered your days away just checking them out. The better way is to define your search as narrowly as you can to begin with and once you find a few useful sites, pursue the leads they offer before you do more exploring.

❖ *Misinformation.* Yes, it's possible to put the latest and truest facts and figures up at a site, but it isn't necessary. Therefore, some of the information you'll acquire may be old (many sites aren't updated constantly); some of it may be wrong (we all make mistakes, after all, and site contents aren't usually checked by copy editors or outside experts); and some of it may be deliberately misleading (lots of Web sites are, in essence, ads or other sorts of special pleading). So be skeptical as you surf.

The most useful information on the Web in terms of trend-spotting may appear in 'zines and in posts about upcoming events—conferences and conventions on topics you're pursuing that you'd probably never hear about otherwise since they're not in your geographic area and you're not yet enmeshed in the subject area. As you study posted program listings, you may decide to call the speakers, to read their published work, and maybe even to go hear what they have to say and meet people who will tell you more. Newsworthy speeches and conversations could be great material for (or great leads to material for) an article or book on the cutting edge.

. . . To Be Prepared for the Future

To see the publishing present, you have to look a couple of years ahead. To discern its future, you'll have to be even more farsighted. Ambitious though this seems, it is worth attempting because the demand for previews of what's coming next is huge. Looking hard for handholds in a maelstrom of accelerating change, people today are greedy—and will be grateful—for whatever helps them predict, and therefore prepare for, tomorrow.

The trick can be done by anyone who realizes that, in fact, cultural, political and intellectual movements of note almost always start small—with one ardent individual or a small group of impassioned people. At first these initiators are unknown to the rest of us. As they begin to focus attention on themselves, we may well regard them as nuts. But gradually the ideas they've championed catch on, often becoming so widely accepted after a time that new small groups form in rebellion against them.

It's through little observations, which anyone can make, that large changes first become visible. If you'd paid careful attention to ages cited in wedding announcement and obituaries, for instance, you might have spotted the trend toward "geriatric marriage" and the rising population of the "old old" before anyone else wrote about them.

And it's through small, specialized publishing companies that seminal thinkers and doers are usually first able to address an audience. You can get a leg up on embryonic movements by reading special-interest periodicals and books as well as 'zines in fields you care about. Check Gale's *Publishers Directory* and *The International Directory of Little Magazines and Small Presses* to see which publishing companies specialize in them. Then skim any titles of theirs that your library carries and/or send for their book catalogs or for sample copies of their magazines.

As you study special-interest material, you may develop an ability to sight coming movements long before the general public has any inkling of them. Then you can be the one who introduces evidence for the rebirth of isolationism or new schemes for redesigning our schools to the wider world as soon as the time is ripe.

Two caveats:

❖ Gauging the moment of ripeness is far from easy, because if the future you're describing is too far off, most audiences will see you less as a forecaster than as a fool. Perhaps, like Margaret Kavanagh-Smith, a Waynesville, North Carolina, writer, you'll decide to do a piece whenever you come upon a portentous subject and then put what you've written away in a drawer until you can see indications of a general readiness to accept its content. (For more on timing, read "Openings.")

❖ While it's true that what's seminal is small, it is not equally true that what's small must be seminal. Again, your own passions are probably your best guide; what you feel strongly about, other people may respond to as well, or at least they may respond to it once you have explained it to them. That way, you'll not only have helped prepare for the future; you'll also have helped create it.

Development

Have faith. Let's assume that one stimulus or another or several in combination have triggered the degree of excitement necessary to launch you on a new writing project. As you begin to flesh your subject out, use the following suggestions to help ensure that your readers will respond with enthusiasm as keen as your own.

❖ If you're writing nonfiction, start by conducting a small, informal survey among members of your intended audience to see who really would like to know what you're planning to tell, and what the general level of ignorance is. Then you can avoid alienating readers either by dishing up background they already have or by beginning your discussion on too advanced a plane.

❖ Unless you think you're the sort who'd make talking a substitute for writing, tell all kinds of people about your project. You may be surprised to see how many of your friends and associates will present you with valuable ideas or data. Moreover, you'll make new discoveries about your own ideas as you listen to yourself talk.

❖ Figure out what special sources might exist for the information you need by following the practice Alden Todd outlined in his masterful *Finding Facts Fast:* On any given matter, ask yourself (a) who would know, (b) who would care and (c) who would care enough to have put it in print.

❖ Keep tugging on the informational chain. You might want a map as background for a short story, or an example to liven up a piece of social criticism, or some word on who could help you understand black holes in space, but whatever you seek you should find if you press each person you talk with for the names of others who could help you end your search.

❖ Refer back to "Getting the Words Right" and review that section's "Resources."

❖ Narrow your focus. The benefits you can offer readers should be carefully delineated and clearly expressed. "Genealogical Research" won't work as a subject but "The Best Way to Get to Know Your Ancestors" probably would. If you can't phrase a working title that tells readers what's in this for them, chances are your subject isn't adequately defined yet.

❖ Widen your perspective. What with the World Wide Web and the multinational publishing empires and the Global Village phenomenon, you may have an international audience. If so, using material that isn't exclusively American will help you reach it.

❖ Be as graphic as you can. Don't just say it if you can show it. Because specifics are much more interesting than generalities, round up generous collections of anecdotes, illustrations, descriptions, dialogue and quotes.

❖ Double-check the draft you think is final against your notes and all your source material.

❖ Put yourself in the picture. Who you are and why you're writing this and what makes you think anyone should listen to you can be important elements of your story.

❖ Bring the wisdom of your lifetime to your task. Writing from experience does not, of course, mean transcribing experience. You have a responsibility to sift and shape your material until it makes sense as a unit and until that unit can be fitted into the context of the reader's life.

❖ Stay flexible, expect changes and setbacks in the normal course of development and abandon all rules—including those propounded here—if ever some combination of gut feeling and dispassionate analysis tells you to try something outlandish. Maybe it's just what the world needs now.

Openings, or Where to Submit Your Manuscript

THE DREAM is a good one. Two book publishers have offered you a contract. You get to choose between Simon & Schuster, which has done a few books like yours, and the Seal Press, which does lots of books that fit in with the one you have to sell, and it always has.

Until very recently, most writers wouldn't have hesitated for a minute. S&S would have been a shoo-in. Even today, you might think the choice is clear, but those who've compared and contrasted large and small houses will tell you that smaller publishers, especially "niche" publishers, are increasingly attractive.

This is true for several reasons. Chief among them:

❖ Smaller publishers pay more attention to authors. "We keep our authors posted on everything," Rich Adin says. Adin—who worked with a couple of the industry giants before he started his own firm, Rache Publishers—goes on to explain that when Rache signs an author on "we send a welcoming gift. When we design our promotional pieces or the cover or anything having to do with their book, we ask for their opinions and suggestions. We tell our authors from the beginning that this is a partnership and for it to work we all have to pitch in."

❖ Smaller publishers give you access to the right readers. The aforementioned Seal Press, for example, sells *Getting Free: You*

Can End Abuse and Take Back Your Life by Ginny NiCarthy not just through bookstores but also to shelters for battered women, YWCAs, clinics and other places where the people who need it most can find it and spread the word about it. As a result, Seal has sold more than 150,000 copies, In the hands of a large publisher that focused exclusively on bookstores, sales figures for *Getting Free* would probably have been much lower. Similarly, if your book focuses on African-American children, or work, or Southern fiction, Just Us Books and Berrett-Koehler and Black Belt (respectively) will probably help you connect with more responsive readers than larger, general-interest publishers could reach.

❖ Smaller publishers keep books selling. Thanks to continual promotion, sales curves for titles from small houses often head upward over time, sometimes rising to impressive heights. Cumulative sales for the Bathroom Reader series are over 650,000, for instance, while sales of *Apple Cider Vinegar Health System* from Health Science have reportedly topped 5 million. At hundreds of small publishing companies, going back to print is the norm. At the largest firms, one printing is all that many books get, and even that one often fails to sell out.

Large publishing operations may still offer advantages, of course, especially for prose that's directed to a very sizable general audience. Since everybody's heard of them, their imprints on your writing tend to confer prestige. Also, they often pay higher advances than small firms (but remember, in many cases a good small firm will net you more over the course of a book's life), and they sometimes have more clout with major booksellers (which they may exercise on behalf of your book, although then again they may not).

On the other hand, big firms may offer you little or nothing in the way of marketing unless you're a celebrity or about to become one. Furthermore, large companies are often—although by no means always—impersonal, and they have an irritating habit of getting tangled up in routines and red tape.

Where periodicals are concerned, big is more likely to be better. The pay's usually higher, for one thing (though you may have to give up a lot in exchange; see "Getting What's Coming to You"), and the exposure is broader (those millions of subscribers will see your piece and some of them will surely read it). But smaller may still be preferable, especially if you're interested in getting to certain sorts of readers. Pieces will work in *Horseplay* or *Aviation Consumer* or *Tactical Knives* or *Homesick Texan* or *Modern Dad* that the mass-market magazines couldn't and wouldn't offer their audiences.

Fledgling writers are frequently advised to start with small companies and work their way up to big ones, on the theory that competition for editorial space is less keen in the so-called minor markets. And sometimes it's true that sales to small publishers will establish a record of achievement that will persuade one of the giants to want you on its list. No press or periodical is designed to be a steppingstone, of course; each has its own independent dignity of purpose. But evidence that one editor thought your work worth printing can serve to embolden another editor to back you, in much the same way that an endorsement from a mutual acquaintance might strengthen an initially shaky editorial judgment.

One good reason not to invest heavily in the steppingstone theory is the fact that some smaller publishers are every bit as choosy about accepting manuscripts as any larger firm. And another is this: At heart, effective marketing of your work has less to do with picking between big and little or top and bottom than with finding the particular publishers who are going to want the particular manuscript you're trying to place right now.

Because the paths to publication are so numerous, you can probably discover a variety of promising markets for every manuscript you create. Book publishers are multiplying fast enough to make your head spin (R. R. Bowker's *Books in Print* database now includes titles from more than 50,000 firms, with thousands of new publishers joining the ranks every year). And magazines keep springing up, too. In 1995, the number of new ones set a record at 838—a short-lived record, it turned out. More than 900 new magazines were launched the very next year. Given the spate of new periodicals and the demise of some older ones, it's hard to keep an accurate count but safe to say that more than 20,000 are out there.

For best results, keep these figures in mind. Then, fully aware of your enormous range of options, use the tools in "Resources" and the pointers in this chapter to narrow it sensibly so that you'll end up sending what you write to the particular publishers and editors who figure to be most receptive to it and most enthusiastic about it.

The Affection Approach

"An editor's enthusiasm is the fuel that makes the project go," says Kate Medina, vice-president and executive editor at Random House. "Unless you have somebody who's nuts about a book you don't get a fire lit under it." It's a view most book and magazine editors would endorse. Despite moanings and groanings in the press about how bottom-line managers are running the publishing show, editors still base acquisition decisions on excitement as well as sales forecasts.

The practice is undeniably attractive. Unlike the outdoor grill manufacturer or the automobile designer or the orthodontist, an editor can—and should and frequently does—allow passion to rule, at least where acquiring manuscripts is concerned. In fact, "love" is a word even the gruffest editors like to use in high praise—"I loved this story," they'll scribble on the back of its envelope without embarrassment.

The chemistry can't be manufactured, of course, but with hard and intelligent effort, it can be encouraged to occur. Fixing yourself up with an editorial partner who's excited about your work—which is the best possible way to ensure a happy publishing future—is largely a matter of learning about individual editors' tastes (and perhaps, at some point—for book authors—

about agents' tastes as well). Try one or more of the following tactics.

❖ Compile a data bank, using your computer or plain old index cards, and enter as much information as you can glean about editors and agents who come to your attention. Perhaps eventually you'll be able to sell a piece about the benefits of smoking because your files led you to a feature editor who'd run two pieces on unpopular positions.

One good way to get information about editors and agents without actually meeting them is by reading about them in a publishing memoir, and once you've made allowances for bias and for that striving after color which afflicts editors as diarists no less than other people, you can use acquaintanceship through print to facilitate acquaintanceship in person.

Publishing memoirs get published a lot (for obvious reasons), but they're by no means the only things that editors write. Poems, novels and nonfiction by editors appear often, and should prove revealing, so skimming reviews and ads and biographical notes to find writing by working editors may be worthwhile.

Other good data for your files can come from comments about particular editors and agents that you collect at writers gatherings or on the Net, from *PW* items about who sold and bought specific new titles; from dedications and prefatory notes that express gratitude to an editor and/or an agent; and from the assorted across-the-editor's-desk jottings you'll find sprinkled through magazines.

❖ Break through editorial anonymity by investigating personal publishing, which is flourishing today on two fronts.

Within the large houses, accomplished editors sometimes get "imprints" of their own that appear on all their titles. The imprint may be the editor's name—Nan A. Talese Books or Lisa Drew Books, the title page will say, telling you just what you want to know. Or it may be a label, like Eagle Brook or Silver Whistle, that translates as Joann Davis or Paula Wiseman, as you'll know if you keep up with industry media.

Outside the large houses, the number of independent, individualistic publishing operations is growing fast. Brief descriptions of such publishing outfits appear in *Literary Market Place*, in the *International Directory of Little Magazines and Small Presses* and in Gale's *Publishers Directory*. The copy won't, of course, say "independent, individualistic," but checking the size of the staff and the nature of the subjects covered should help you zero in on publishers who are kindred spirits. Once you've identified some possibilities, write to ask each publisher for a catalog. Then use the catalog to infer more about the publisher's personality and about the way it might mesh with yours.

❖ Discover an editor through a book you feel passionate about. If you're lucky, you'll open the book to the acknowledgments page and find out who edited it; otherwise you'll have to call the publisher's offices. Try the publicity department first; people there are used to giving out information. Then, when you have the editor's name, you can make sure your query (see "Procedures") explains the bond you sense between the book you loved reading and the book you want to write.

This kind of personal approach can get you off to a great start not only with an editor but also with an agent, you'll recall. "Sure, I'm interested in your material; send it along" is a frequent response, because both editors and agents are impressed by efforts to understand them. And when they learn that you enjoyed a book they helped create, their pleasure may lead them to greet your submission with a small prejudice in its favor.

❖ Use indirect advertising. One method involves sending an item to Authors' Queries in *The New York Times Book Review*. If your project appeals to the editors there, hundreds of editors elsewhere will see it when it runs, and some may well respond with queries of their own about whether you have a publisher yet and, if not, whether you'd be interested in working with them.

To advertise indirectly in another way, use the biographical notes that accompany work you're currently getting published. After you ask the editor who's printing your study of utopian theory to run a line saying "The author is halfway through a novel called *Bravest New World*, about a messianic cult in Washington State," you may hear from publishers and agents who want a chance at the book.

❖ Find a receptive editor by checking the news and "People" sections of *Publishers Weekly*. Editors who have recently changed houses probably had to leave some of "their" authors behind. As they set up shop at new firms, they'll be especially eager to sign new books and develop new relationships with as many good writers as possible.

Matching Exercises

For a straightforward approach to manuscript placement, nothing beats matching the subject matter of your work with the subject matter that appeals to a particular publisher.

Perhaps, without fully realizing it, you've already formed a mental image of what attracts the editors of magazines you read regularly, in which case you'll know almost instinctively whether your work belongs there. Though your sense of a book publisher's range of interests is likely to be hazier, you can start to bring it into focus in a variety of ways. Titles from specialized small houses and from imprints (personal and otherwise) within large houses are easiest to categorize, but even a general-interest publishing giant has a personality of its own, and whatever you can conclude about the likes and dislikes of any size firm will help you with placement.

Information is available not just in *Literary Market Place* (commonly referred to as *LMP*) and other directories you'll find in this section's "Resources" pages, but also in the *PMA* (for Publishers Marketing Association) *Newsletter*, in newsletters from various regional publishers' groups, in the "Call for Manuscripts" notices in *Poets & Writers Magazine* and the "New Mags" section of *Small Press Review*, and through the 'zines and the many other publishing sites on the Web (again, see "Tools" in "Resources").

Furthermore, you can identify openings for your work by using the *Subject Guide to Books in Print*, a mammoth directory listing more than 1.2 million books under a galaxy of subject headings. Start by looking at the titles under several headings that are relevant to your work. You'll probably discover that certain publishers' imprints appear again and again, and you may be tempted to conclude that the editors there are now surfeited with the subject. That's possible. It's at least as likely, however, that they're still hungry for more. They wouldn't have done a second book on exercise for the elderly, after all, if the first hadn't sold well, and the fact that they issued a third or a fourth indicates that they've tapped a responsive market they'll be eager to supply with new reading matter. Specializing in nonfiction about sports, the outdoors and the environment, Sierra Club Books even branched out into publishing fiction when they got an allegorical novel about fishing, David James Duncan's *The River Why* (which, incidentally, Bantam later reprinted).

Matching your subject to a company's demonstrated strength may be the single best placement strategy, but matching it to a company's obvious weakness can make sense too. Is one national magazine you read short on profiles, when the form is clearly fashionable? Are there no multicultural books in the publisher's catalog you've been studying, even though *PW* has just announced that demand for them is rising from parents and teachers? If so—like the high-school student who accused the editor of the local paper of ignoring the kids' point of view and got himself hired to write a column—you've found a gap in need of filling.

Once you've made good matches between your work and publishers' needs, go one step further and try matchmaking with businesses or other kinds of organizations that publish articles and books of interest to the people they serve, as all sorts of groups—including corporations, associations, governmental bodies, schools and fraternal societies—now do. Look for likely candidates to approach in the *Encyclopedia of Associations*, *Thomas Register of American Manufacturers* and other directories you'll find in "The Self-Publishing Option Resources."

Tips on Timing

Consider Judy Delton and her Houghton Mifflin Kitty books for children. When she began to do them in the late '70s, she noted in *Publishing Research Quarterly*, she "wrote about growing up Catholic in the forties. *Roots* had just been published. Ethnic cultures were trendy. I thought, now is the time for me to write about my childhood and get away with it. If I'd waited, I'd be out of luck. The market is saturated with growing-up-Catholic books.

"When my husband lost his job (before it was popular to lose jobs) I wrote *My Daddy Lost His Job Today*. When it didn't sell, I changed the title to *My Mother Lost Her Job Today* and it did. This was 1971. Role reversal books like *William's Doll* were just coming into print.

"Timing is important," Delton concludes, and the point is crucial. Because each moment creates and destroys publishing potential, sensitivity about timing is an enormous aid in placement.

If you are alert to passing events you can sometimes hang an already completed manuscript on a news peg to attract editors. A much-rejected book about Big Foot, for example, might suddenly become salable the instant that new evidence of the creature's existence turned up. Similarly, if an article about the unquenchable desire to do battle has been repeatedly turned down on the grounds of familiarity, a timely new lead might help. Perhaps, for instance, the piece could be sold to a newspaper for the June 6 issue if it began by pointing out that June 6 isn't just the anniversary of D-Day; it's also Korea Memorial Day and the beginning of Superman Celebration in Metropolis, IL (this celebration, along with hordes of others that delight and inform, is listed in *Chase's Annual Events*; see "Tools" in "Resources").

People unprepared with manuscripts can also take advantage of propitious moments for getting published. Was it your town the tornado hit? Your aunt who gave the governor a ticket for jaywalking before the speech at the travel agents' convention? Your college that voted overwhelmingly to reinstate single-sex housing? When you're involved in any way in a newsworthy event, it makes sense to offer an eyewitness report to interested publications that have no representative on the scene. If you can plan ahead for the story, query selected editors about it beforehand (see "Procedures"); otherwise make a few phone calls to see if you can get an expression of interest.

Either way, you might consider parlaying the temporary position of on-the-spot reporter into an ongoing job as a stringer for one of the national newsmagazines or large metropolitan papers that like to keep up with news breaking locally around the country; get in touch with the nearest bureau chiefs if the prospect appeals to you (you'll find their names on mastheads). Stringers' assignments are sporadic; their copy is generally rewritten beyond recognition; both their by-lines and their pay may be virtually invisible. But think of it this way: Magazines such as *Time* and *Newsweek* make nice additions to anyone's list of credits, and being even partly responsible for what millions of people get to read has its charms.

Not every story needs, or should have, explicit links with current events, but no manuscript can be sensibly submitted unless targets are selected with timing very much in mind, because every publishing enterprise has a definite position on a temporal spectrum. As noted in "Shaping Subject Matter," special-interest publishers tend to congregate near the leading edge, getting to the future way ahead of most mass-market, general-interest publications. Thus a piece that *The Fish Sniffer* might like this month probably won't be suitable for *Field & Stream* until sometime next year and might not be welcomed at the *Reader's Digest* until long after that (for tips on making several sales with the same story, see "Spin-offs").

Art Harris, a prep-school teacher turned freelance writer, learned his lesson about timing the hard way: "Having three sons and a wife who was reading all these articles on 'How Safe Are Birth Control Pills?' I had a sterilization operation—the vasectomy. What a great idea for an article, I thought. It even tied in with another subject—zero population growth. 'You're a nice fellow,' the editors said, 'but frankly nobody wants to hear about your operation. Forget it. It's too personal a subject.' So I put the idea aside only to see a whole crop of articles on the subject a year or two later. If I were to approach an editor today with 'My Male Sterilization,' I would get laughed out of the office; the subject has been well covered, thank you."

However painful Harris' education, he learned enough in the end to write a piece called "Timing the Submission" that he sold to *The Writer*. The advantages you'll derive from developing timing skills may not be quite as direct, but they're sure to aid your progress nonetheless.

Easy Access

"We regret that we are unable to consider unsolicited manuscripts" is a sentence that causes a lot of needless anguish. It's true, as enraged would-be authors are quick to point out, that many publishers make it a rule to return unsolicited material unread. But that policy can't debar anybody's work as long as editors respond to queries and proposals with invitations to submit the manuscripts those documents describe (see "Proce-dures"). And besides, no matter what rejection slips may say, the periodical press is open to new contributors. Consider:

Reader-Participation Departments.

Magazines and newspapers of all sizes and sorts are now actively soliciting material from the general public. Like modern physicists and politicians, publishers have discerned that our deepest sense of reality demands some confluence of subject and object, of actor and acted upon. The results of this realization—which is especially powerful because it's not entirely conscious—vary among disciplines, but in publishing it has led editors to try making writers of readers. "The magazine game has tended to look on readers as spectators," editor Tony Jones explained when he sparked the trend with *Harper's Weekly.* "We think they should be players, and we're looking for ingenious ways around the limitations on how many can play."

Not long ago, the only place open to readers as players was the "Letters to the Editor" column but today ordinary folk are cordially urged to contribute to "Viewpoint" in *Glamour,* the "My Turn" column in *Newsweek,* the "Metropolitan Diary" section of *The New York Times,* the "Celebrations" section of *The San Jose Mercury News* and the Op Ed pages of innumerable newspapers, to name a few reader-participation departments.

In all these columns, and in the letters column too (which remains a good launching pad for an idea and maybe even a writing assignment), short pieces that emphasize specific, signifi-cant experience and observation rather than abstract theory are most likely to succeed. But so are pieces that offer small wisdoms of everyday life, personal stories that will resonate in readers' minds and lives.

Book Review Columns.

In addition to sections that solicit contributions from readers, a good many periodical departments are entirely open to the public, though they seldom proclaim that fact. One of these, as Robert Cassidy discovered, is the book review section. Cassidy, who got his start with a review, is the author of *What Every Man Should Know About Divorce*, among other books. You can follow his example by checking publishers' catalogs and *PW* for forthcoming titles you'd be able and eager to write about, and then querying editors to see if they'll either sign you up to review a book (mention title, author, publisher and publication date of the one that appeals to you) or try you out on a title that's up for grabs. Many book review editors' names are listed in *Literary Market Place*, and their preferences as to style and substance can be inferred from the reviews they ordinarily run; check the Net and your library for copies. The pay is generally poor (in fact, the book itself may be your only payment), but the rewards in terms of exposure and contacts and credits and pride of performance can be considerable.

Other editors who are especially receptive to newcomers include those who work on:

Community Newspapers.

Even beginners can apply to a neighborhood weekly about covering a particular beat. Once you've regularly reported on leisure-time activities, say, or profiled local businesses for a small periodical, you've got credentials to present to a big one. And if you've written anything with a local focus, you should find a ready market among community weeklies.

In-house Magazines and Newsletters.

Both profit and not-for-profit organizations need people to discern and relay ideas relevant to their concerns. Here again, the pay for a piece may be low or nonexistent, but the audience can number in the thousands, so you can expect dividends in the form of exposure.

E-zines and other new publications.

The supply of good material is relatively low, as a rule, when a periodical is just getting started. At that point, therefore, the editors may be more than receptive if you offer them an appropriate article. They may be ecstatic. Of course, they also may be undercapitalized, as many publishing start-ups are, with the result that you have to choose between withdrawing your work and trying to sell it elsewhere or letting them publish it for free and enjoying the excitement of a new venture along with them.

Campus Publications (Including Alumni Magazines).

The connection between you—or your subject—and the school will give you an edge here, and though the pay scale varies widely, most editors in this field, like their counterparts on other small publications, are generous with assistance. "We have to scratch harder for good stuff," said Elise Hancock, editor of *Johns Hopkins Magazine.* "So if something has possibilities we'll work on it rather than turn it down because the possibilities weren't quite realized. I once published a piece called 'Bald Is Beautiful,' a magnificent parody on radical manifestoes that maintained (quite rightly) that bald people *are* discriminated against. The author was urging the *Ten Commandments* be refilmed starring Woody Allen. It was a great piece, but *Esquire* had turned it down. I think they just weren't willing to spend the hour required to cut it by two-thirds, which was all it needed. So that's a plus of working with alumni magazines."

It would be misguided to treat the easy-access openings with less respect than any others; what you've written must be right for the specific publisher you send it to in terms of subject matter, style, tone and timing. But if you submit to the most hospitable editors with the same care you'd use for the most forbidding, you can anticipate better results.

Danger: Dead Ends

Almost any publication opportunity you can seize may be worth seizing; ever-widening ripples move out from even the smallest splash. But something more like a self-contained plop is all you're likely to get if you resort to a vanity press or an exploitative poetry "contest."

You can recognize the contest scams by the pricey anthologies and plaques you're supposed to buy if you're a "finalist," and you can recognize the vanity presses by their come-hither ads. "An invitation to authors of books," they'll say (or words to that effect), going on to offer a free (no obligation) manuscript evaluation and a free (no obligation) brochure about the publishing operation. Usually vanity houses wait until you've begun corresponding with them to mention their fee. Be advised, though, that a vanity press is likely to charge you far more for producing your work than you'd spend if you hired your own production people or handled production tasks yourself. (Please don't decide you lack the necessary skills before you've read "The Self-Publishing Option" chapters. And don't be dismayed if you recognize vanity as one of your own motives for getting published, as long as it's not the only one you see; virtually every writer is seeking glory to some extent.)

Most vanity houses issue impressive-looking pamphlets that explain their operations with varying degrees of candor and detail. These booklets generally fail, however, to stress two crucial points:

❖ The press has no stake in the success of your book; it takes its money up front by having you pay all the costs of getting a manuscript into print—plus a handsome sum that's pure profit for them. Then, if the edition actually earns anything they'll take a cut of the revenues from sales too, and have the nerve to charge you for any copies you buy over and above the allotment mentioned in your contract.

❖ Distribution efforts by vanity presses can be worse than useless because libraries, bookstores and book reviewers have learned to distrust the imprints. Though some authors do manage to rack up sales, it's virtually certain that self-publishing would have produced far better returns on investments of time and money.

Testimonials from happy authors are a regular feature of vanity press catalogs, which don't, of course, print any litanies of complaint. The complaints are a part of the picture, though ("I never realized that binding all the copies in the first printing wasn't included in the deal" commonly heads the list). If you're considering vanity publishing, become familiar with "The Self-Publishing Option" and consider that instead. Those who remain determined to throw money away in producing a book might give some thought to having their manuscripts bronzed. That way, at least they'd get what they paid for.

Procedures, or How to Submit Your Manuscript

A LOT THAT'S WRITTEN about the fine points of submitting a manuscript not only can be disregarded; it should be. Editorial etiquette is mainly a matter of common sense; for obvious reasons, your copy should be neatly typed, free of misspellings and coffee stains, consecutively numbered page by page and clearly labeled with your name, address, telephone and fax numbers and e-mail address. Those rules that have no commonsense basis will only divert your attention to minutiae when it ought to be focused on your primary purpose: getting editors to publish what you write.

Any pieces of paper you send editors—from three-paragraph queries to thirty-page proposals—will persuade them either to move your manuscript one stage closer to publication or to reject it right then, depending on whether they've been led to answer yes or no to the two all-important questions that echo in editors' heads:

❖ Will this article (story, book), if it's skillfully handled, add to my company's prestige and/or profits (and therefore to mine as well)?
❖ Can this writer handle it skillfully?

If your idea comes across in the beginning as notes jotted down in a hurry, no editor is likely to take it more seriously than you apparently have. It's best, therefore, not to think of any approach to an editor as a preliminary move designed merely to feel out the situation before you submit your "real" work. Even the shortest introductory note, though it should look effortless, probably ought to be the end result of several drafts.

Essentially, what you're doing when you first make contact with an editor is applying for publication, much as you might apply to college or for a job. And just like a director of admissions or human resources, the editor you apply to will be only the tip of a decision-making iceberg. Almost always, the power to accept or reject rests with a group (or groups) rather than with an individual, and if your proposal succeeds in winning one editor's vote, that editor in turn will have to convince colleagues that your project is worth backing.

Queries and proposals generally circulate among editors, with more and more people becoming involved when the risks of commissioning a project are high; some book publishers insist that every manuscript under consideration be reviewed by two or more sizable committees before an editor gets clearance to buy it. In certain cases, decisions are influenced by the author's appeal on video tapes and/or in face-to-face meetings with marketing bigwigs. But no matter how many people participate in the process and how many media are involved in the presentation, what you've set down on paper had better be good.

To give yourself every advantage in approaching editors, you'll need to use the forms of communication they favor, as they've developed over the years. Here's a roundup.

Queries, or Don't Get Stuck in the Slush Pile

On the surface, a query is simply a letter that asks editors whether they'd be interested in work you're planning or have already produced. It's an introductory move, used to pave the way for submitting articles to periodicals and proposals or finished manuscripts to book publishing houses (and to agents too). With magazines, queries may also function as proposals, in the sense that they can earn you an assignment—complete with guaranteed minimum payment (although they're not likely to do that if you're unknown). And in all cases they obviously make for efficiency; evaluating a letter takes a lot less time than reviewing the entire manuscript it describes, so the winnowing process is speeded up. But the query's most important function is often—and oddly—ignored: A query is a tool for steering your manuscript clear of the slush pile.

Judging from the number of unsolicited submissions that reach editorial offices daily, most writers either don't know this or don't believe it. The fact is, though, that queries get manuscripts solicited status, with benefits all around. Even the most elitist editors respond to them. "For the record, we are generally unable to review unagented material" a letter from a New York editor recently noted. "However," he went on to say, "I am intrigued enough" to ask for more.

Queries about nonfiction offer editors the opportunity to become involved in shaping your material at the outset. When the subject you've suggested is one they're interested in pursuing, they'll welcome the chance to share thoughts on how the story should be approached, what length it merits and what information should be included. Their suggestions will improve your manuscript, at least for their purposes. And to come closer to what an editor has in mind—as long as doing that doesn't violate the essence of what you want to say—is obviously desirable.

With fiction, phrasing a query is more difficult, but if you write an intelligent letter in which you show that you understand the publisher's goals, that you have the approval of people the editor respects and that your subject is important and timely, you should succeed in building editorial interest in you and your work that will help it over the final decision-making hurdles. Acquainting editors with *Rhonda the Rubber Woman*, Norma Peterson described it as "a novel about women who derive their strength from their jobs at a time when 'women's work' is all that is open to them" and herself as a writer "published in periodicals ranging from *The New York Times* to *McCall's*, *USA Today* and *Green Mountain Review*." Editors from several houses asked to see her material, and Permanent Press bought the book.

When an editor responds positively to your query, your submission will land in that editor's personal in-basket rather than in the unsolicited-manuscripts bin when it arrives. Expressing interest obligates editors to read, or at least to skim, what you send. That's all it obligates them to do, however, unless they've agreed to commission your forthcoming work; when editors say they'd be delighted to see your manuscript "on spec," they mean they think it has promise but they're guaranteeing nothing. Many magazines do offer "kill fees," especially to writers they've published before, which may be somewhere between 25% and 40% of the fee for the piece if accepted. But even without the guarantee, it's usually smart to go ahead when an editor expresses strong interest. "Send it on spec and give it everything you've got," one experienced editor has advised, partly because editors don't encourage writers lightly and partly because if the piece doesn't succeed after all that time and effort, at least you'll have impressed the editor by the work you put in, which means that you'll have a sympathetic, receptive audience next time around.

To get a positive initial response to your query you need to do more, of course, than ask to be invited to submit your manuscript. The question "Would you like to see my story about snow-mobiling being hazardous to health?" can call forth only one reply: "Well, it depends." It depends on what, exactly, your point is and how you're going to express it.

As Mary McLaughlin, executive editor of *Working Mother*, explains, queries must present a very specific idea. For McLaughlin, the best queries are the ones that "at least promise to illuminate a part of a problem in a new way." A piece designed to help Mom cope with separation anxiety, for instance, might appeal to women's magazines that usually cover the topic by talking about helping the child.

Whatever the topic, every query must work fast. One page is the best length; one-and-a-fraction should be your limit. Within those confines, the query has two important tasks to accomplish. First, it must sell your idea to the editor it's addressed to, who—it's good to remember—is always looking for new talent. "Talent is the magazine. Writers are the magazine," according to *The New York Times Magazine*'s editorial director, Adam Moss. And second, it must help that editor sell it to colleagues, who—it's necessary to remember—will be asked and can say No.

The checklist that follows outlines the elements of a good query letter about a nonfiction manuscript; if you adapt them creatively, they'll serve for fiction as well.

❖ *Explain why you believe each editor you're addressing will be interested in the work you're offering* (because they've edited material on similar subjects or material displaying similar sensibilities; because they come from areas where your story is set; because you've discovered they share your interest in or indignation about or passion for whatever your topic may be). This portion of the query, which is usually the first sentence, must obviously be different for every editor you approach.

❖ *State your specific idea* (as opposed to your general subject). In addition to a catchy title and a subtitle that conveys the substance of your article or book, a "tagline" that expresses its appeal will be useful here. To create an effective tagline, look to book cover copy and magazine cover lines for inspiration and then focus firmly on the benefits your work offers readers. More than any other element of the query, the tagline can help interested editors convince marketing colleagues of the project's merits (eventually, it will also help the marketers sell it to wholesalers, retailers, media people and the public).

❖ *Describe the main point your manuscript makes, the ground it covers and its style,* with specifics by way of illustration.

❖ *Mention your relevant credentials and connections:* professional expertise and achievements, publishing credits, mutual friends, mentors and acquaintances—whatever makes you more of a known quantity and more credible in terms of promotion will be helpful. Even beginners should be able to cite some relevant achievements. A young writer who has worked during the summers on a newspaper or won honorable mention in a high-school short-story contest has credentials worth mentioning; in fact, some editors ask their first readers to direct manuscripts from anyone who lists such credits to their personal attention.

❖ *Say where and how you got (or are getting) your raw material* (from interviews? primary sources? personal experience? laboratory experiments? exhaustive research?).

❖ *Show how what you have to say is fresh and different from specific articles and/or books already in print* (hit the highlights here—you have information such-and-such a piece didn't reveal; you hook your findings to a narrative instead of presenting them in the scholarly format of such-and-such a book).

❖ *Estimate length.* A figure that's appropriate to your topic and to the publishing concern you're writing for gives an editor a clue that you do your homework.

❖ *Provide a tentative delivery date for your manuscript.*

❖ *Convey your enthusiasm for the project.* Enthusiasm is infectious, which is lucky because (as noted above) it's also essential. "I wouldn't buy a book I was lukewarm about," Bob Bender reports at Simon & Schuster, where he's VP and Senior Editor. "More than ever, enthusiasm is a necessary prerequisite for acquisition," Bender says. If the editor isn't passionate about a book, the sales force isn't likely to get behind it.

It should be needless to say (but experience indicates it's not) that every query should be directed to a specific editor by name, not to The Articles Editor or The Editorial Director; that the editor's name should be spelled correctly; and that the editor-in-chief isn't the only one on the staff. Associate editors, assistant editors, department editors and others still lower in the ranks may give your manuscript more personal attention than the higher-ups who get most of the mail.

To target editors, refer back to "Openings" and consult the

directories listed in "Resources" or the most recent issue of the magazine you're aiming at. Then, because editors are notorious job-hoppers, call and find out whether the one you've chosen is still with the company before you write.

Some writers shy away from queries for fear that editors will steal their ideas. Well, in the first place, they probably won't. In the second place, they may well get similar stories from other writers, so if it looks as if they stole something of yours they probably didn't. And in the third place, what alternative does an author have? You can't sell your work without describing it. So conquer your paranoid tendencies. The grain of truth that may lurk behind them in this instance is a rotten reason to give up one of the best door-opening tools you have.

Person-to-Person: Calling Up and Calling On

Occasionally, telephone calls or personal visits to editors will provide the best way to acquaint them with your idea for a piece. Early in her career, for instance, Delia Ephron dropped in unannounced on the editor of the magazine supplement of the Providence *Journal* to propose writing about sports from a woman's point of view. He said sure, on spec, and bought the first piece she did. Ephron, now a much-published author, then used that clip to get an assignment from a national magazine.

Once you've got an editor listening, you're in a make-it-or-break-it situation, so be 100 percent sure that you've formulated what you have to say in the best way possible. Boiling your story down to three or four sentences or coming up with a descriptive title beforehand will help you arouse an editor's interest during the few minutes of time you've requested.

Perhaps, following the lead of successful freelancers, you'll want to equip yourself with three or four well-developed story ideas before you enter conversations with editors. Then if all those fail, two other tactics will remain to be tried. You can turn the tables and ask editors whether there are any weak spots on their upcoming lists that they'd like you to work on; maybe after they tell you their editorial problems you can mull them over and return in a week or so with ways you might help solve them. Or you can see whether editors will suggest other markets or other topics that might work for you.

Like the written query, a well-planned phone call or visit gives receptive editors the chance to help shape your idea and ensures personal attention to your manuscript once they've encouraged you to send it in. Established writers approach editors in person all the time; and for beginners who are effective in one-to-one situations, it offers an exceptionally good means of entrée.

Book Proposals, or Sell It Now, Write It Later

In essence, what you're asking when you send a query to a magazine editor is, Will you buy my manuscript or at least tell me you think it sounds promising and ask to read it? When you send a query to a book editor, though, what you want to know is, Will you look at my book proposal? (See below for a checklist of what a proposal should contain.)

It then becomes the book proposal's job to give editors the information they need to answer the harder question, Will you buy this book or at least ask to read it?

Editors routinely bid for nonfiction books on the strength of a proposal alone (the payments can be made half on signing, half on delivery of a satisfactory manuscript or in thirds or even quarters), and although it may be hard to convince them to buy a first novel if they haven't seen the whole thing, it's by no means impossible. With second and subsequent novels, the proposal can become a more powerful selling tool. If publishers are to advance money for books, however, they must generally be convinced that the book they're buying will be a book they can sell.

Book proposals can be submitted to agents (who will take you on—or not—having read them) as well as directly to editors, and the basic principles that contribute to the success of a query apply to proposals too: Because it's much shorter than a full man-uscript, a proposal can be considered more quickly and easily, and because it represents raw possibilities, it has the power to ignite editors' imaginations and get them involved in what you're trying to do.

Editors commonly define a book proposal as "an outline and a sample chapter," but what they really want is anything on paper that will give them some sense of how you write (which excerpts from several sections may demonstrate better than a chapter in a book's early stages) and some reason to believe that your subject, as you plan to develop it, will interest readers they can reach (which no rigid I, II, III, A, B, C outline of contents is likely to convey).

The following checklist for organizing a complete and effec-tive proposal will keep you from omitting elements of impor-tance to editors, but it won't serve as a guide to phrasing or arranging your presentation. Only you can figure out how to mesh your proposal and your earlier query so that together they do justice to the book you hope to write.

❖ *Remind the editor that this is a solicited submission.* Or as one publisher puts it, "Use the magic words 'you have asked to see,'" so whoever opens the editor's mail doesn't misdirect it. And refer back to the links between you that you mentioned in your query. Having targeted editors with care, you want to make sure they remember what aspects of their professional or personal lives connect them to you. The stronger the con-nection, the more receptive they'll be.

❖ *Describe your book well enough so that editors can easily con-vey its appeal to colleagues.* This usually involves restating the tagline and perhaps expanding on it.

❖ *Give at least one anecdote or example that illustrates your theme and its significance.* Take whatever space you need for this—a paragraph, a page or more.

Ralph Keyes, for instance, used a string of specifics in the proposal that won him a contract for a book called *Timelock:*

How Life Got So Hectic and What You Can Do About It, including: "We all notice life's quickening pace in different ways. During two decades of writing for magazines, I've watched the preferred length of articles halve, even quarter. A Florida court reporter says today's witnesses speak 20 to 40 words a minute faster on the average than they did in the 1950s."

❖ *Identify the audience to whom the book is addressed* (lawyer-bashers, singles, people who've found psychotherapy unsatisfying, everyone who loved John D. MacDonald). Sometimes you can direct editors' attention to several possible markets and thus inspire them to think of still others.

Since salability is a vital consideration, it's a good idea not only to identify your markets but also to suggest ways of reaching them. If you're planning to write about St. Louis architecture, for instance, you might mention that you're game to approach architects about your book at their upcoming convention and that you'll be writing articles for publication in their professional journals and shelter magazines around the time the book comes out.

❖ *Talk realistically about the competition and how your book is different,* so both editors and sales reps will understand why it needs to be written, why it will be read and how to distinguish it quickly when booksellers say, "But we're already well supplied on that very subject." Although a summary statement can be useful, explaining the overall differences between your book and its competition isn't enough. You'll need to pinpoint roughly half a dozen comparable titles and highlight specific aspects of each one that you handle differently or better.

❖ *Show how you plan to develop your book.* Indicate the breakdown by chapters, and sketch your primary sources of information (where will you go, whom will you talk with; what facts and figures will you gather?). Many nonfiction writers offer a Table of Contents with meaty, chatty annotations. For fiction, meeting this requirement means providing a synopsis that reads as well as the book, exemplifies its style and echoes its tone.

❖ *Explain your credentials.* Cite publishing credits as evidence of your ability to write, and any experience or training that qualifies you especially well for this project. And don't forget that publishers large and small rely on authors to help with promotion. If you're an experienced public speaker, an authority reporters call for quotes, an amateur actor who's great at readings, make sure prospective publishers know that.

❖ *Enclose a sample of your text.* There is no normal length for text samples. Many run between twenty and forty pages, but it's best to send whatever chapter(s) or excerpts reflect your book's content and style most accurately and most favorably. Make sure the sections you choose won't confuse readers out of context, and if you're a novelist, end with a suspenseful scene. What you want is for editors to want more.

❖ *Express any passion and excitement you may feel about the project.*

"I decided that, no matter what it took, my students would write simple, honest, readable prose that showed they were in some way connected to the words they wrote," Elaine Hughes said with some gusto on the first page of her proposal for *Writing from the Source*.

Hughes wanted to put the exercises she'd developed as a teacher into a book for writers outside the classroom. Having queried Carol Cohen at HarperCollins and been invited to submit her proposal, she used the proposal checklist in this chapter to create a 40-page package divided into many short sections ("The Basic Premise and Theme of the Book," "The Audience," "The Competition," "My Credentials," "Book Plan," "Student Comments") and included a handful of very brief excerpts and exercises.

"I consider both the title and the current draft of the manuscript only a work in progress at this point," Hughes explained, taking note of a phenomenon editors know well: Books always change in the writing. "The breakdown of chapters will go something like this," she continued in the same vein. "I expect that each category will have 6 to 8 different exercises"; "I think this chapter will include suggestions for clustering the exercises."

Writing another book, Hughes would probably have structured her proposal differently and used a different tone. Indeed, every book demands its own distinctive document. It's a pleasure to report, though, that this approach worked for this project. Hughes' "writing and meditation exercises that free your creativity, inspire your imagination and help you overcome writer's block," retitled *Writing from the Inner Self*, has now been helping writers for many years.

Poetry

Certain guidelines will serve you well no matter what kind of manuscript you're trying to place. It's always a good idea, for example, to address an editor by name and to triple check for typos. Often, sending a stamped, self-addressed envelope is a good idea too, since that makes it easy for editors to get in touch.

What makes sense for poetry submissions does, however, differ in some respects from what makes sense for prose. In the first place, poets don't need to use query letters since the material they submit won't run to dozens or hundreds of pages. Instead, it's best to start by sending roughly half a dozen poems ("five has always felt comfortable to me as an editor," said Diane Kruchkow, editor of *Small Press News*), along with a brief covering letter that shows you're familiar with each publisher you approach and tells publishers about your credits if you have them.

Poets often aim their work at magazines first because, as Alice Quinn has noted, "In general, poets enjoy and require the reinforcement magazine publication provides." Quinn, a poetry editor for Knopf and a fiction editor for *The New Yorker*, has observed that some poets use a lazy-Susan system. Instead of agonizing when something is returned, they send it right out again: "The three poems *Grand Street* turned down go straight to the *Atlantic*; the two that *Poetry* didn't want go straight to *Southwest Review*."

A lazy-Susan system can, of course, also cover magazines that aren't devoted to poetry. The poet Judson Jerome found that "specialized publications are a wonderland for those of us swamped in the miasmic plains of literary magazines." Jerome was particularly taken with the notion of submitting some poems about horses to *Arabian Horse* in Waseca, Minnesota, at $10 to $75 apiece, and to *Toys "R" Us Magazine* for pay that could be called handsome—$200 to $700.

Going to the other extreme, certain literary magazines have lately begun to demand payment from poets by charging what they call "reading fees" for considering submissions. The practice is common, and conceivably defensible. But the consensus among poetry editors is that self-respecting magazines don't charge to screen manuscripts for publication, so credits from those that do aren't likely to count for much.

Having poems appear in reputable magazines gives you credibility with book publishers, as Jonathan Galassi points out. Galassi, editor-in-chief at Farrar, Straus & Giroux, thinks magazine credits are a poet's most important credential when the time comes to try for a book.

Should that time come for you, consult the preceding section on book proposals, and bear in mind that it's often better for poets to publish with a smaller house, partly because the smaller house will keep their work in print longer and partly because a small house is more likely than a large one to think poetry books are important enough to merit marketing energy.

Children's Book Channels

The main difference between children's books and adults' books in terms of procedures is that you can sometimes make your first move with an entire manuscript. If you're working on a lengthy book for older kids, you should still approach editors first with a query letter, but if what you've done is a picture book, you should know that "at Greenwillow, any unsolicited children's book manuscript will be looked at," according to the editor-in-chief, Susan Hirschman, and editors elsewhere are equally welcoming.

To target editors and publishing houses that will want your work for kids, browse through the children's books sections in nearby bookstores (they're increasingly popular nowadays). Consider going to writers conferences (Scholastic's editors often connect with authors there, the publisher, Jean Feiwel, reports). Study the children's books on your library's shelves (although they don't dominate the market the way they used to, libraries are still big buyers). And visit Web sites that feature books for kids. Then use any applicable "Foot in the Door" tactics to make your approach.

Unless you want to illustrate your book yourself and you're as good an artist as you are a writer, do not send illustrations along with your manuscript. "We do not require or encourage authors to seek out illustrators for materials they plan to submit," children's book publishers say in submissions guidelines. The editors, who regularly review artists' portfolios, would rather pair authors with artists themselves.

Covering Letters

Several marketing manuals suggest dispensing with a covering letter when you mail your manuscript, on the theory that if the thing's going to sell, it will sell on its own merits and that a letter saying simply "Here is my manuscript" only wastes an editor's time. But there's much more than that to say.

You can use your covering letter to reestablish personal contact with editors by reminding them of previous exchanges between you. You can use it to convey thoughts or information of the sort that might have appeared in your original query or proposal but didn't. And you can use it to indicate that you're eager to improve your work even now, after you've tried hard to do your best.

Listen to an editor vacillating about a submission: "A very interesting idea, I think—'romanticizing the Holocaust.' It's good. But he is heavy-footed, repetitive and clumsy in places. Excessively wordy. It could be helped by a few passages of quotations, to refresh our memories if not to make the point. Is it worth sending back for fixing?"

In a case like this, the fact that your covering letter proclaims an openness to criticism and a willingness to make changes might be enough to keep rejection at bay. Although major revision is a headache and a gamble for both editor and writer, it is also a much-traveled route to publication.

Authors of magazine pieces are regularly asked to revise on speculation, but book editors are cautious about requesting substantial changes without committing to buy the improved version of the work. Because their judgments are highly idiosyncratic, one book editor's idea of an improvement may be another's idea of a change for the worse. You'll have to assess your own position carefully before you decide whether the risk/reward ratio is reasonable enough for you to proceed. As a general rule, it's unwise to make changes that don't feel right after careful consideration, and it's smart to follow an editor's suggestions when your inner voice says, "Of course! Why didn't I think of that?"

The Question of Multiple Submissions

Only a few years ago, writers who sent out queries, proposals or full manuscripts could anticipate one of two fates. Either they'd wait several weeks—or months—and then be rejected, in which case they'd have to start all over again. Or they'd wait several weeks—or months—and be accepted, in which case they could take whatever terms they'd been offered (perhaps with minor modifications) or start all over again. Now, however, thanks in large part to innovative agents, all that has changed, and the vehicle of change has been the so-called multiple submission.

In book publishing, where long periods usually go by between the time you present your work and the time you get a response to it, multiple submissions are now standard operating procedure, and anyone who receives positive responses from more than one publisher may be able to play them off against each other a bit before picking the one that's best. (See "Getting What's Coming to You" for a further discussion of choosing among offers.) For periodicals, one submission at a time is still common, but by no means the rule. The fact that magazine editors respond more quickly than book editors makes multiple submissions less necessary and less usual where they're concerned.

Follow-up

Queries normally elicit a response within a few weeks; book proposals can have you checking the mail for months. It's a good idea, therefore, to keep records of everything you've sent out and to follow up on magazine pieces after about a month and on books after roughly six weeks. Editors do get bogged down, go on vacations and sometimes even lose manuscripts (this is as good a place as any to remind you always, *always* to keep a copy). Furthermore, delays may result when a project hovers on the borderline between acceptance and rejection. A polite letter of inquiry is a reasonable and perfectly proper way to find out what's holding things up.

If and when you do get a positive response from an editor, acknowledge it with thanks and with some word on when you expect to deliver your finished manuscript. Be as realistic as you can about the due date; then if you find it impossible to stay on schedule, let your editor know.

Any rapport that you establish with particular editors obviously works to your advantage, and can be strengthened by simple gestures of courtesy—saying thank you for comments, for example, or expressing gratitude for encouragement offered along with rejection.

And speaking of rejections—well, everyone gets them, even the best of writers. And everyone feels the same way: rotten and hurt. But bear in mind that it's probably true if editors say that they really liked your piece even though colleagues didn't, or that everybody liked it except the editor-in-chief (whose no means no). And remember, too, that the roots of rejection are infinite: An editor who had a marital spat last night bristles at your piece about how to achieve a blissful relationship through yoga; a story like yours just came in from a house author and, while it isn't any better than the one you wrote, it isn't any worse either; your book just doesn't strike the sales manager as a good bet; or your article sounds too much like one that just appeared in *Business Week*.

Rejection after rejection may mean it's time to cut your losses. If you've followed the advice in these chapters without garnering a single encouraging word, you'll want to take stock. Perhaps your logic is not as sound as you first thought, or your point is not so fresh and crisp after all. Sigh one sigh, file the manuscript away, and get on with something new. And if, heaven forbid, you've received nothing but printed rejection slips without so much as a personal note scribbled at the bottom, go back to the beginning of this section and start rereading.

On the other hand, it's well worth reiterating that one editor's rejection may be another's acceptance. "I keep a hair-shirt file," a respected editor once confessed; the file held correspondence about books he'd spurned that went on to become bestsellers. So bear in mind that you're still free to try other imprints at large houses with several independent divisions, and that you may find a rejection a steppingstone to acceptance (the editor at Philomel who turned down Linda Wikler's first picture book, *Alfonse, Where Are You?*, suggested trying it on Tracy Gates at Crown, which then published it), and you can always explore "The Self-Publishing Option."

A Note on Improving
Your Vision

The next two sections present complementary perspectives on the same set of processes. "The Sale and Its Sequels"—which approaches publishing from the point of view of authors who want someone else to take charge of producing and selling their work while they assist—should provide self-publishers with valuable information on the standard operating procedures that have helped conventional firms succeed over the years. And "The Self-Publishing Option"—which approaches publishing from the point of view of authors who want other people to assist in producing and selling their work while they take charge—will prove a good source of innovative ideas for conventionally published writers.

Therefore, whatever role you want to play, please read both.

The Sale and
Its Sequels

❖   ❖   ❖

Getting What's Coming to You

RECEIVING WORD that a publisher is interested in buying your work is just cause for celebration. What follows, however—the business of talking money and rights—can be (and usually is) an ordeal, especially where books are concerned, because although you and your publisher share many goals, your aims diverge on the division of profits and risks.

With magazine pieces, areas of contention are relatively minor. You can ask to be paid on acceptance rather than on publication; you can ask for a kill fee; you can ask to be reimbursed for expenses; you can ask to retain everything but first serial rights. Your publisher can then refuse any or all of these requests. If your wishes are largely ignored, though, it may not matter much, and in any case, writer/publisher relations are likely to be amiable.

The situation is quite different with books, as a quick glance at the average contract will convince you. Book publishers, who must sink substantial sums of money into each title they issue, have developed complex, formal mechanisms for minimizing their losses and maximizing their gains, which tend to put burdens on—and take rewards away from—authors.

Authors, understandably, resent this, and many of them are tempted to vent their anger on their editors, whose earlier support may now seem suspect. You'll be better off, though, if you can manage to treat yours with kindness. After all, the editor has just assumed the unenviable role of mediator between you and all the publishing people who will be handling aspects of your book; and besides, you'll probably never have a better friend at a large house. With everyone else there, you might as well gird yourself for an adversary relationship; expect the worst and be prepared to fight for the best.

Comparing Offers

If, having made multiple submissions, you've attracted two or more interested buyers with your book proposal, your first task is to consult with your agent or a literary property lawyer and decide which one to accept. The house that offers the most money? Maybe not. Although the size of an advance does provide a tangible index to the publisher's level of commitment, as well as an all-but-guaranteed income, you should investigate each publisher's abilities to prepare and sell your book in addition to each one's proposed down payment on it before you make a decision. These are areas to explore:

❖ *Distribution (i.e., sales to booksellers)*. Does the house have its own sales force? How large is it? What territories does it cover, how often does a sales rep visit each one and have the reps been successful with books like yours?

  Houses that can't afford to maintain their own sales departments depend either on sales reps from larger firms (who handle books from a number of houses besides their own), on commissioned sales representatives (who sell books for lots of different publishers), on independent distributors (who also sell books for lots of publishers but otherwise function in much the same way as a salaried, in-house sales force) or occasionally, on wholesalers (who are in business to fulfill orders rather than generate them).

❖ *Backlist policy*. Many houses actively market brand-new books only, paying no attention to older titles—aka backlist—

which means that books they issue usually die fast. As a number of small publishers regularly prove, however, there is an alternative. Continual promotion, updating and/or repackaging can give a book not just a long life but an increasingly profitable one. So ask about predictions for—and commitment to—your book over time.

❖ *Subsidiary (aka Sub) Rights.* As publishing (like other industries) becomes increasingly international and book format distinctions become increasingly blurred, many houses push harder for more rights. Instead of buying the right to issue a book in hardcover *or* in paperback, they'll try to buy "hard-soft." Instead of buying English-language rights, they'll say they want world rights ("foreign rights have become increasingly lucrative and sometimes mean the difference to a U.S. publisher between the financial success and failure of a book," according to foreign rights consultant Mildred Hird). Moreover, apparently persuaded that new technology means new revenue streams, they'll specify that "electronic rights" belong to them. Such demands can occasion some horse-trading.

Maybe you and your representative will decide to swap some rights for a bigger advance, a better royalty schedule or a higher discount on copies you buy for resale. Maybe, if the public would like audio tapes of your book, video tapes or multimedia products derived from the book, toys or clothing inspired by characters in the book or other related products, you'll bargain to keep control of them (provided, of course, that you're as well equipped or better equipped to attract buyers). And maybe, if your book figures to sell outside the U.S. and the publisher wants world rights, you'll grant them conditionally. ("I'll be happy whoever sells to publishers overseas," a first-book author told his editor, "but any foreign rights you haven't sold after six months should revert to me." "We can work with that," the editor said.)

In any event, though, it's important that authors and their representatives arrange to get clear, complete and timely information about sub rights deals the publisher makes and sub rights income it collects. Realizing that millions of dollars regularly get lost in sub rights transactions, BISAC (the Book Industry Systems Advisory Committee) devised a contract clause and a Subsidiary Rights Payment Advice Form to help money flow through to publishers, agents and authors (see "Resources" for information on how to get it and use it).

❖ *Library sales.* Since libraries account for big chunks of book sales in many categories—including children's books, mysteries and other adult trade titles—attention to library promotion is important.

❖ *Sales to schools.* Trade books are increasingly popular in classrooms at every level, and always popular at school book fairs and college bookstores. So find out how the house deals with academia even if you're not the author of a textbook.

❖ *Mail-order sales.* Authors who have concluded that their books can be sold easily through the mail should find out which editors agree, which houses have mail-order departments and what freedom they'll have to sell through the mail themselves.

❖ *Cyberspace sales.* Houses large and small are present on the Web, but because they highlight different books in different ways, you'll want to find out what exposure your work will get, and for how long. Questions to explore include: Does the site ballyhoo bigbooks only? Would the publisher link to your site if you set one up, and do its current links work well? Is it easy to order on-site, even when readers want backlist?

❖ *Special sales.* If you've written a book about cross-country skiing, perhaps sporting goods stores would move lots of copies. If yours is a kids' activity book or an illustrated history of cigars, catalogs might do well with it. Because "special" or "non-traditional" sales channels can be extremely profitable, you'll want to know whether the house takes advantage of them and, if so, which ones it uses and with what results.

❖ *Pecking order.* The importance of your book in relation to others on a publisher's list is significant because you will be competing with every other current title for the time and money budgeted to all departments in the house. Perhaps your book would not be considered a "big book" by any publisher, but even second-rank titles get appreciably better treatment than those on the bottom of the heap, so try to feel editors out about their expectations for yours; most will be quite frank about the prospects.

❖ *Personal compatibility.* Don't be ashamed to ask a lot of questions; naïveté, coupled with an eagerness to learn may prompt an editor to talk with you at length, and the longer you converse, the stronger will be your sense of how well the two of you would work together.

Contracts, or the Agent's Hour

Because a book publishing contract is a complicated legal agreement in which the commitments of both author and publisher are defined (by the publisher) and the financial terms of the partnership are set forth (by the publisher), an agent or a literary property lawyer should be on board to represent your interests when you get an offer for your manuscript, if not before (once more, a warning: Don't agree to any dollar figures until your representative is in there fighting for you).

If you hope your first book will be only the beginning of a long writing career, an agent will probably serve you best (remember, once you have an offer from a publisher, you're a desirable client, one who guarantees the agent a commission). If the first agent you approach dumps on the offer and advises submitting elsewhere, however, keep looking. And if writing isn't on your agenda for the future, then consider a lawyer with expertise in publishing who will advise you, bill you and be gone (though the lawyer can stick around and actually negotiate for you if that's what you prefer and can afford).

There's only one case in which you'd be wise to proceed without the help of either an agent or a lawyer who's familiar with publishing, and that's when you're signing up with a small house that uses a simple, straightforward contract to buy rights that are strictly—and appropriately—limited. If all they have to deal with is a short memorandum of agreement and a one-person publishing operation, assertive authors can probably handle negotiations themselves by using one or more of the relevant guides in "Resources."

Authors who are represented are obviously not relieved of all responsibility for shaping a contract that's acceptable to both sides; at the least, you should be familiar enough with your publisher's contract form to know what changes you'd like to make. You'll have to read the thing, therefore, and probably more than once.

Much of it, you'll find, is intelligible, and what you don't understand you can ask about (consult your editor and/or your lawyer and/or the Authors Guild and see other entries in this section's "Resources").

But comprehension of a contract's basic provisions is about all writers can hope to achieve on their own. For common sense (which this book has touted before and will encourage again by and by) has a relatively minor role in the highly stylized negotiations of the usual contract quadrille. And that's where the agent's or the lawyer's expertise comes into play. Almost as if there were annotations throughout the contract that were visible to authors' representatives but invisible to authors themselves, your champion will X out and add in and modify clauses, acting a part that's as predetermined as the patterned figures of a dance.

Each house has a different contract—page after page of fine and pompous print—so standard changes vary a bit, but both sides know which moves will be made; in fact, even your editor will know (and might tell you in advance if you ask) roughly what terms the whole maneuver will produce in the end.

Why, you may well wonder, go through the motions? If every expert is aware that an author with clout can get the paperback split changed from 50/50 to 60/40 (author's favor) this year, and that clauses D, H and Z are always deleted by authors' representatives, who regularly add identical riders to paragraphs 3, 7 and

12, wouldn't it make sense to amend the forms before issuing them and skip the back-and-forth that comes afterward?

Well, arguably, no. For one thing, although the initial round of demands and counterdemands about changes in a publisher's standard contract is pretty well determined by custom, its outcome and the outcome of all subsequent rounds can be influenced to some extent by an astute and aggressive bargainer. For another thing, no matter how generous the form contracts were, authors would always want more. And for a third, publishers still scent the possibility that unrepresented writers may swallow the package as printed.

Don't do it. If you're forced to conduct contract negotiations yourself, consult relevant guides listed in "Resources" and see if you qualify for membership in the Authors Guild ("Resources" gives the group's address and phone number), so you can get a copy of its recommended trade-book contract. Designed with full knowledge of the contract quadrille's choreography, it can help every author understand the best possible terms.

Payments

Controlling payments from periodicals is fairly simple, the idea being to collect once, for a single use of your material by a magazine or newspaper, and then, if your article, story or poem is reused, to get paid again by the subsequent user or users. Thus, you have only two things to watch out for:

❖ *Get the going rate.* To learn what a magazine or paper normally pays its contributors, read its guidelines sheet (if it has one) and check to see whether it's listed in *Writer's Market;* then multiply any figures you find by roughly 150 or 200 percent (because they're directed to neophytes, published prices almost always fall at the low end of a periodical's payment scale).

❖ *Don't sell more than you must.* Ask the editor who offers to buy your piece what rights you'll be selling and when you get your check, be sure to examine it front and back for fine print before you endorse it. Otherwise, you may sign away rights you'd arranged to keep, with the result that the periodical will get the fee if your piece is reprinted in an anthology, say, or sold for use on TV, and you won't.

Like their counterparts in book publishing, many periodical publishers were quick to envision, and loath to share, cash flow from the Internet. Out on the Internet themselves, the American Society of Journalists and Authors took to reporting changes in periodicals' policies and individuals' agreements on the "ASJA Contracts Watch" List. To subscribe, see "Resources," and to improve your own cash flow if some magazine insists on purchasing all rights to your work, insist right back that they agree to return some of those rights to you later on. You may well need them if you plan to recycle your material, but do this even if you have no such plans at the moment.

Payments for book manuscripts are, predictably, far more complicated, and consequently far more likely to provoke and prolong aggravation.

The first money you get for a book will probably be your advance; as much as a half or as little as a fifth of that may be paid when you sign your contract, with the remaining payments coming due per contract specifications, usually on delivery of satisfactory sections of your manuscript. Occasionally, a publisher can be persuaded to pay the entire sum up front (this is worth angling for if you need the money to catch up with bills or to keep a roof over your head while you write). Occasionally, too, perhaps in the case of a very small publisher, no advance at all will be forthcoming. And sometimes, with university presses, authors may even be asked to supply money, in the form of a "subvention" to defray publication costs. As Beth Luey points out in her *Handbook for Academic Authors,* there are differences between this and vanity publishing, chief among them the fact that university presses requesting author subventions "separate the decision to publish from the author's willingness to pay," though "the differences can become blurred."

When money is due—as per most book contracts—collecting is likely to be a challenge, mostly because of sloppy bookkeeping on your publisher's part. Payments that go astray or are slow in arriving are no rarity in modern publishing circles. Payments that must in the end be returned are a somewhat less frequent phenomenon, but if you fail to deliver a manuscript that's satisfactory to your publisher (or if you fail to deliver any manuscript at all), you may be obliged to repay any advance you've received.

Nowadays, partly because advances have escalated into five, six, and even seven figures and partly because some publishing houses' new corporate parents have new financial standards, it's increasingly common to find a publisher demanding its money back when a book project doesn't pan out. If your advance was relatively small and if you tried your best to write a good book and if you're poor and starving anyway, your publisher probably won't pull out all the stops to try to get money back from you. But don't count on it.

Assuming that you turn your manuscript in on time, or nearly so (editors grant extensions on due dates much as professors do, although here too they are getting stricter), and assuming further that it's found acceptable and subsequently published, the next money due you will be paid after your advance has been earned out, and it will come in the form of royalties.

If you have an agent, your contract probably takes some subsidiary rights out of the publisher's hands and puts them in yours; among them, you'll usually see first serial rights (for excerpts in magazines and newspapers before book publication) and motion picture rights, but you'll almost never see reprint or book club rights, which are too lucrative for publishers to part with.

All monies from subsidiary sales effected by agents go directly to them; they subtract their commission and forward the rest to their clients. When writers are not represented by agents, their publishers can sell all subsidiary rights and will keep the monies received until they've been reimbursed for whatever advance they paid. Thus, if *Sports Illustrated* bought an excerpt from your book for $3,000, $450 would go to your agent (assuming the agent takes 15 percent), and $2,550 would go to you; if you had no agent and were represented by your publisher, 10–15 percent might go to your publisher no matter what and the remaining 85–90 percent would also go to the publisher until such time as your advance had been earned out, unless your contract specified otherwise.

The sooner your advance has been earned out through one sort of sale or another, the sooner you begin earning royalties. For a typical hardcover from a large house, you'll get 10 percent of the retail price on the first 5,000 copies sold, 12½ percent on the next 5,000 and 15 percent on all copies sold thereafter (*n.b.*: A percentage of list price is still standard for trade book contracts, although some smaller and specialized houses tie the author's percentage to wholesale price or publisher's net receipts, using numbers that yield substantially lower dollar figures). Royalty rates on paperbacks are lower and royalties in general may differ a good deal, depending on such factors as the book's format, the publisher's financial situation and the author's clout.

Essentially, royalty figures represent your cut of the money a customer pays for your book. But if you get $2 per copy on the first 5,000 sales of a $20 book, where does the other $18 go? One big chunk is for bookstores and wholesalers, who will buy your book at roughly half off, which gives them their margin of profit and means that all they actually remit to the publisher is something in the neighborhood of $10. After your $2 has been subtracted, the balance of $8 or so must stretch to cover the costs of editing, manufacturing, advertising, selling, shipping, warehousing and, of course, the publisher's overhead (rent, utilities, payroll).

Taking all this into consideration, it's easy to see why large publishing houses maintain that they must sell thousands of copies of a book just to break even, and why they may sometimes engage in a variety of shenanigans to hang on to whatever money finally comes in. One author who suspected that his publisher was keeping cash it owed him was lucky enough to discover an interview in which his editor bragged about sales of his book. Since sales figures quoted in the interview far exceeded those indicated on his royalty statements, the author called at once to discuss the matter; it was then settled in his favor.

The point of this story is not that all publishers will try to cheat you or that if you read widely enough you will catch the ones who do; instead, it's that you may need to take the offensive not only to get the money you're entitled to but also to find out how much it is. Royalty statements don't divulge a great deal (few note, for example, how many copies have been printed and how many are still on hand), and the way in which they're issued makes the data that do appear hard to grasp.

At periodic intervals, the income generated over a specified time span is supposed to be reported in a royalty statement. Usually, there's a lapse of three to four months between the closing date of the royalty period and your receipt of that period's statement, which means that money for a sub rights sale consummated in February will show up not on the statement you get in April but on the one you get the following October, some eight months from the date of sale, unless your contract provides otherwise. To make matters worse, money earned just before a given closing date is sometimes not included in the statement where it belongs; instead, it's held for the next statement because a publisher "forgot" to list it (and thus gave itself an interest-free loan at your expense).

How do you figure out whether what you're being paid is what you should be being paid? For starters, "You have to understand the structure of your royalty statement and keep track of your royalties yourself," Stephanie Winston believes. Because she had been in book publishing, Winston, the author of *Getting Organized*, knew that the financial information she'd be receiving as a writer wouldn't be the financial information she needed.

Since she also knew that agents can be flummoxed by royalty

figures, she developed her own personal auditing system. She identifies someone on her publisher's staff who can explain the company's royalty policies and practices—the chief financial officer's assistant, perhaps; she gets a copy of the publisher's basic royalty statement, and she calls her editor's assistant every so often to find out about new printings (though it would make an author's day, editors rarely share the news that a book is going back to press).

With the information she gathers, Winston can see right away whether a royalty statement's figures are reasonable. Then, if gross discrepancies appear, she calls her contact in the publisher's financial department to say that something's wrong.

Catching errors and oddities is more than half the battle (publishers can usually find the problem and fix it) and well worth the effort. By flagging mistakes on a short succession of royalty statements, one astute author brought in an extra $50,000.

But if you still suspect you're missing money, you'll want to consider an audit. Book publishing audits—which every contract should allow over the life of the title—are too complicated for authors to handle on their own, and too dependent on industry idiosyncrasies for auditors experienced elsewhere. Consult the Authors Guild and the National Writers Union and consider hiring a specialist who will assess your situation and work for a contingent fee (see "Resources"). One recent audit recovered roughly $7,000; another recovered more than ten times that amount. Using your recent statements, an experienced auditor who knows the book business can often estimate the minimum you'll get before the audit even starts.

Fringe Benefits

Authors who know the ropes routinely ask their publishers for a host of extras that no contract will ever stipulate. As long as you're not greedy in your requests and not churlish if they're refused, you may well follow suit. What you have to gain, among other things, are the following benefits.

Office Space.

Occasionally, you can arrange to use an empty editorial office, and sometimes you can manage to get access to a computer, a telephone and a variety of office supplies as well.

If you regularly spend time in your publisher's quarters, perhaps you'll meet and make friends with employees who'll get interested enough in your project to give it special attention.

And even if you show up only occasionally, you may gain the privilege of using the company's copying machine.

Expenses.

Particularly in the case of a magazine piece that involves extensive research, it's worth asking for an expense allowance that will cover the costs of travel, interviews, postage, copying and research materials. Expense allowances are sometimes forthcoming for nonfiction books, too, and unlike advances they don't have to be earned out before you can collect royalties.

Free Books.

The most obvious fringe benefit for writers under contract to publishing firms comes in the form of reading matter. Don't expect to stock your library from your publisher's warehouse, but if you see a book you'd love to have, go ahead and ask for a copy of it.

Power Plays

The self-fulfilling prophecy has doomed many a book. Here's what happens: Your editor views your manuscript as nice but minor; if it breaks even on sales, everyone figures to be satisfied.

Because it seems minor, the editor won't lean on anyone in marketing or publicity to create an energetic sales and promotion campaign that would attract the buying public. And because no special efforts will be made to publicize and distribute your book, it will end up nice but minor; if it breaks even on sales, everyone will be satisfied. Except, of course, you.

This scenario—a common after-the-fact explanation of "why my book was remaindered after three months and I never got a penny more than my advance"—can seem inflexible enough to convince writers that their books' failures were preordained. Feeling helpless and anguished at this realization, they'll turn on their publishers, who will respond to shrieks of outrage and demands for bigger advertising budgets with veiled (or possibly not so veiled) anger, and nothing else.

But there's no need for writers to place their books at the mercy of editors and marketing directors until it's too late to do anything about plans for them but scream. With determination, tact and knowledge, you ought to be able to steer clear of the minor-category catch. (The analogous exercise for magazine pieces would consist of working to make yours the cover story, the lead or one of the articles in the "well," or center, rather than one of those in the front or back of the book. As with contracts and payments, however, positioning is relatively unimportant for periodicals and relatively simple to fight for if you're inclined to argue.)

The first step in positioning a book with a publisher is to grasp the fact that it will be categorized very early, in some formal way, on paper, and/or informally, in the minds of editorial and marketing people. One popular system involves an *A, B, C* scale designed to help publishers allocate their limited supplies of staff and money. All publishers obviously want the maximum return on their efforts, so when half a dozen books on a forthcoming list seem likely to bring the house a profit if they're heavily promoted, those titles will be designated *A* books and slated to get the bulk of the promotion budget. The *B*s and the *C*s will have to compete for what's left over (which may not be much), and it's more than likely that the *C*s will end up with no budget whatsoever. Authors today are more and more apt to ask for promotion provisions in their contracts, but since publishers aren't eager to grant such requests, most writers still have to rely on plumping for position. And the optimal time to begin doing that is immediately after you sign your contract.

Normally this is the very moment when writers are most anxious to get out of business hassles and back to the business of writing. But the hours you put in now planting seeds for the full campaign to come (see "Why and How to Be Your Own Best Sales Force") can mean the difference between a book that is ignored or mishandled and one that is granted the most favorable treatment possible.

Your primary goal between the day your manuscript is accepted and the day it's published should be to get everyone—from your editor to the publicity director to the people handling all sorts of sales—involved with (and, if you can manage it, excited about) the future of your book. To make them envision that future the way you want it to happen, you'll have to reinforce and supplement the marketing suggestions you made in your original proposal through occasional short, informal notes to your editor.

Since most editors have numerous authors to deal with, an outpouring of "me first" epistles is not recommended. Just write in an enthusiastic, contributory spirit ("I've been invited to do a series of workshops in Oregon in June and a bookseller out there suggested that I do bookstore programs at the same time") and use suggestive tones (*coulds* rather than *shoulds*; *we might* rather than *you'd better* will make it clear that you're willing not only to fire off suggestions but also to do the work entailed in executing them). Each of your letters, if it's well worded, will encourage your editor to think about a new dimension of your book and provide at least one viable idea the editor can pass along to sales and publicity people. Keep copies; as publication date nears and promotion plans are firmed up, you'll want to refer back to these early memos.

Among your efforts to gain momentum for your book in its early stages, you might include the following:

❖ If there's anything in the news that's relevant to your book's contents, write a short piece for newspaper Op Ed pages or letters columns or for a magazine's opinion department; include a biographical note mentioning that your material comes from a book you're working on; and use clips of published pieces as evidence to convince your publisher that you're dealing with a timely and important subject.

❖ Keep your eyes open for gatherings relevant to your subject; volunteer to be on a panel or to participate in a series of readings. Ask for, or collect, a list of names and addresses of attendees to whom you can send notices and order forms when your book is published, and after a successful speaking engagement drop a note to your editor about the event and the enthusiastic response.

❖ Once you develop the habit of thinking in terms of positioning, you'll be visited by enticing ideas at all sorts of odd moments. To keep them where you'll be able to find them, start a file that will include:

- *Names (and addresses if possible) of writers, critics, broadcasters and anyone else who's famous* and who, because of their interest in your subject or their ideological bent, might give your book favorable advance comments for use in cover blurbs and press releases.
- *Names of magazines, newspapers and Web sites* that would have good reason to run excerpts from your book or to review it or plug it or sell it.
- *Potential sales pitches.* "This book is for people who . . . and we can reach them by . . . "
- *Titles.* Improvements in your working title are likely to occur to you as you write, and if you keep a record of them all—even those that don't quite make it in your mind—

you may eventually come up with one that works beautifully.

All of these steps, along with others to be discussed in the chapters that follow and still others that you'll think of on your own, will help give your book its best chance. But that's not all the good they'll do: When you're so stymied in the actual writing that you've begun to think nothing will ever be published at all, they'll give you a psychological boost. Even (and sometimes especially) when you're disgruntled, it's just plain fun to work on ways of making your book the biggest deal it can legitimately be.

Editing, Copy-editing, Design, Production and Part-and-Parcel Advertising

T HE IDEAL AUTHOR, from the point of view of practically everyone in a large publishing operation, is the one who's happy to revise, quick to provide documentation and intimidated enough to keep quiet about design and production processes. The message from editors, copy editors, art directors and production managers may be unstated but it's often loud and clear anyway: You're dealing with experts now. Listen up.

It's true, of course, that these people have knowledge you lack and that an amateur's mistakes can cost dearly in money and time. But it's also true that these people have varying degrees of expertise, and that many (if not all) of them can devote only a fraction of their time and their smarts to you.

Partly because they are less compartmentalized and partly because their general approach assumes a partnership, people in smaller firms are far more likely to welcome an author's participation. In fact, many of them insist upon it. The message they send, often explicitly and more than once, is: There's work to be done and you get to do a lot of it.

But if the tone of the proceedings differs between larger and smaller publishers, the steps are the same, and it's important for every author to play a constructive role.

Groundwork

The best preparation for smooth passage through editing and production shoals for a book is a thorough dry run through your manuscript. After it has been accepted and before editing begins, go over what you've written, marking every textual and stylistic point you care deeply about. Is it important to you that a particular example not be cut; that footnotes appear at the back of the book instead of on the bottom of each page; that section headings seem twice as powerful as chapter headings; that dialogue be punctuated exactly as you've indicated? Expressing preferences of this sort may not get you everything you want (and perhaps you'll eventually be glad if it doesn't), but it will help you avoid some conflicts, and it will maximize your influence on the outcome of others.

It's intelligent also to state clearly and in writing—before work starts—whether you want the right of approval for any or all of the following (and to insist on reviewing at least the first three for periodical pieces as well as books):

The edited manuscript.
The copy-edited manuscript.
The title, and the subtitle if there is one.
The index.
The typeface(s) and layout.
The illustrations (if there are any) and their captions.
The book cover design and copy, or the magazine cover line.
The catalog copy.

You needn't—in fact, you shouldn't—be strident or combative when you make your request. A friendly, informal note to your editor explaining that you want to be involved (and that you don't intend to be obstructive) should serve you well. Backstop the note, though, by becoming familiar with your manuscript's timetable. The anti-snafu checklist that follows will let you identify key opportunities for input.

Here's what you need to find out:

❖ When will editing and copy-editing be done? The edited, copy-edited manuscript should go to you before it goes anywhere else. After you've gone over it, consider making copies to send out with requests for early blurbs that you can use on your cover.

❖ What's the designer's deadline for sample pages and layout? If you want to have some effect on layout and illustrations, get involved while rough sketches are in the works and be prepared, even that early, to meet resistance; editors and designers are apt to have sharp preferences of their own about how your manuscript should look in print.

❖ When will copy go to the printer? Any changes you want to make should be on record well before that date.

❖ What's the schedule for preparing the index?

❖ When will you be getting the author's questionnaire the publicity department sends out and how much time will you have to complete it? (Remember: Your editor may use material from the questionnaire in writing promotional copy.)

❖ Which catalog(s) will your book be in and when is copy due? Overworked editors may be glad if you offer to draft catalog copy, and you'll want to check it before it goes into print anyway to make sure that your name is spelled right, that your new, improved subtitle is included, and that your bio credits you with the degrees you really earned.

❖ Which sales conference will cover your book? Once you have the dates, prepare materials that display your work's strengths and give them to your editor at least three weeks before the sales conference begins (see "Why and How to Be Your Own Best Sales Force").

❖ When will the cover design be ready? Again, you'll need to see it to check for accuracy.

❖ When is cover copy due? It's wise to ask to OK final front and back cover copy and flap copy, if any, and it's important to get blurbs in early enough to be included, of course.

❖ What day does the cover go to press?

❖ When will you be getting proofs and how fast will you have to read them?

❖ What's the timing of the press release? As with the catalog copy, consider drafting or ask for a chance to check the publicity department's draft.

❖ When are bound galleys due and how many sets will be available for people who might provide blurbs? Galleys should also go to reviewers like *Publishers Weekly* and *Kirkus Reviews* that need materials well before publication and to periodicals that publish once a month or less often and that may review your book or buy serial rights. This is SOP, but watch for glitches; they do occur.

❖ When will finished books be ready? That's the time to check on copies for radio and TV programs and for reviewers and rights buyers at weeklies and dailies.

❖ What's the official publication date? After that, you can start collecting reviews and comments to add to cover copy if your book goes back to press.

Editing

Editors come in two varieties at some giant firms: acquiring and line. Acquiring editors scout for material, take authors and potential authors out for lunch or drinks to discuss projects, and herd manuscripts through the acceptance stages. Line editors edit. Most companies, big and little, are set up so that every editor is an idea person and a blue-pencil person, but if your publisher divides the functions—or if your editor turns editing jobs over to junior colleagues—try to arrange to deal face to face with the editor who's actually working on your manuscript as well as with the one who was in charge of it to start with.

How much editing that person will do depends on how much your work needs, on individual style, on time pressures and, obviously, on ability.

Ideally, an editor will clarify what you have to say, suggest cuts and additions to strengthen the impact of your work and change nothing unless change means improvement. In fact, some may habitually overedit and some may hardly ever edit at all but most vary their activities markedly with each manuscript they handle, deleting large chunks of the flabby ones, moving sections around in the disorganized ones or making detailed suggestions about revisions to authors who seem capable of fixing their own text, given guidance.

It generally takes an editor a week or so to edit an average book and roughly a day to do a normal magazine piece, but with heavy rewrites these figures can easily triple. If you have a complicated book and a first-rate editor, you may find yourself poring over suggestions about revisions, which editors commonly offer in memos and marginal notes, that are themselves thousands of words long.

All this editorial attention may feel oppressive short-term, but the converse—as growing numbers of writers can unfortunately testify—is far worse. For most books, no editorial attention means a far weaker finished product. So if any book manuscript of yours seems headed straight for copy-editing and production or, worst of all, straight for production (because your editor is too busy, your editor left, your manuscript came in too late or for any other reason), do your best to stop the process and fill the gap. Hiring an outside editor is one option; see "Getting the Words Right" and its "Resources," and ask in-house editors for recommendations.

Despite individual differences of style and speed, editors everywhere generally agree that any manuscript can be improved (the opening should build up momentum more quickly; the mother's speech in the confrontation scene should be foreshadowed; readers ought to be told the basis for the findings in paragraph 4). And they tend to agree, too, about what not to do. Editors remind themselves and their assistants—often and with conviction—to refrain from superimposing ideas on or changing characters in an author's work. Editors are supposed to realize your story's potential; if they have tales they themselves want to tell, they should tell them on their own time.

"I think the difference between an editor and a writer is that nugget of creativity," Fredrica Friedman said at a symposium. "It was the author's idea . . . it wasn't my idea. Where I can help is in the execution of it." For Friedman, as editorial director at Little, Brown, helping in the execution meant analyzing "what the purpose of the book is, who it's trying to reach and how we're going to do it," or in other words, enabling authors to do whatever they "set out to do."

Good editors take pains to treat their authors with care. In fact, some editors are so solicitous of writers' egos that they've developed a special diction for suggesting revisions. "Your careful probe into all aspects of the topic is invigorating but I'm afraid that there may be too much material here for one book," an editor might say in a letter, translating from the sterner language of the in-house memo: "The author really needs to go back and rethink the structure and contents."

Almost always, the subtext of an editorial critique is "I genuinely admire what you've written; I know how hard it was to write; and I don't want you to feel hurt because the final product is less than perfect. What you don't know and I do, however, is that every manuscript has notable weaknesses; for your own good, I want to correct the flaws in yours." Maybe the midsection is verbose and confusing and needs to be cut by a third. Maybe the startling observation that could grab readers and reviewers alike isn't at the beginning, where it belongs. Maybe you have confused cause and effect in Chapter 8.

To forestall the defensive reaction that's likely to arise when editors come along and tell you, tactfully or not, that they can make your manuscript better than you've made it, think about these contrasts:

❖ Editors don't have to cope with a blank piece of paper or a blank screen. You've originated a story or a line of argument that's worth transmitting to readers; all they have to do is fine-tune the signals.

❖ Editors are intimately familiar with a wide range of literary techniques because they've worked with dozens of writers, while you've got only your own experience and learning to draw upon.

❖ Editors know their audiences. Sometimes, by using their hard-won knowledge of readers' predilections, they can reshape a manuscript so that it will draw a bigger and more receptive crowd.

❖ Your editor isn't sick of the whole damn thing. After endless rewriting, both your words and your concepts may blur and grow stale in your mind, but the material is new to the editor, who can therefore come to it clear-eyed and energetic.

In spite of everything writers can do to persuade themselves to adopt a professional attitude toward being edited, some find it impossible not to bristle. If you're in this group, go through your editor's suggestions once, fast, and take a breather. Walk three miles or play a couple of sets of tennis before you look at them again. Then pretend that you're considering the work of a total stranger and try to imagine what your publisher's problems with it may have been. (Does the magazine have a particular tone of voice to maintain? Are cuts of 23 pages necessary to keep your book's cost down to the point where bookstores will stock it? Did that lovely descriptive section you struggled with for weeks destroy the story's pace?)

Whatever complaints survive a dispassionate reading should be taken up—calmly—with your editor. Especially with books, you can probably have the final say, which should help you keep the tension level down. It's best to avoid squabbling if you can, because you and the editor are jointly responsible for creating and nurturing a piece of writing, and creative, nurturing tasks are best performed by teammates who focus on the good of the offspring rather than on failings in each other.

Copy-editing

A mutually satisfactory working relationship with your editor is at least as important after editing is finished as it was before and during the editing phase, since from now on you'll have to rely on the editor to help settle disputes with everybody else. The odds-on favorite for most-likely-to-be-disputed-with is the individual who gets your manuscript next: the copy editor. (On many newspapers the editor who's called the copy editor will have general, high-level responsibilities, but you're not likely to have much direct contact with people of this stripe.)

Copy editors have a lot to put up with. Their status is low, as is their pay, and their job—which tends to be literally thankless—demands a peculiar, contradictory blend of character traits: Copy editors must be highly intelligent, dazzlingly knowledgeable, keenly alert nitpickers.

To copy-edit is to be responsible for making a manuscript correct in all its details. Authors are generally uninterested when a copy editor conforms their work to house style ("theater," not "theatre"; *The New York Times*, not the *New York Times* or the New York *Times*), and they're grateful, on the whole, when copy editors catch and correct their mistakes, by supplying appropriate double consonants in "accommodate" or "desiccate," for instance, by taking Mesa Verde National Park out of New Mexico and putting it back in Colorado where it belongs, or even by pointing out that the action in a particular story couldn't happen. (Take the tender scene in a leading novelist's work in which a father tiptoes in to place a goodnight kiss on the cheek of his child as she lies asleep in her crib. "Listen," said the copy editor, "you can't kiss a kid in a crib unless you balance on your stomach over the railing." "God, how embarrassing," said the novelist; "thanks very much.")

It's when the copy editor presses for documentation or defines as a correction something the author sees as a distortion that trouble starts.

More and more, documentation is the author's job because fewer and fewer publishing concerns can afford to have a fact checker on the staff nowadays. To protect against lawsuits and to ensure accuracy, the copy editor must often call upon writers to cite (and perhaps to produce) their sources. Writers who have kept careful records will naturally find the task less onerous than writers who haven't, but even the most rigorous recordkeepers may have to exert themselves considerably, because copy editors know—from long and sad experience—that what sources tell you is not necessarily so.

Satisfying their rule of thumb—when two out of three authorities agree, that's good enough—generally calls for additional research, which few authors undertake without grumbling.

The grumbling turns to groans, or even screeches, when writers come up against copy editors who have a context to contend with (is yours the second piece in a magazine's May issue to use the Mad Hatter's tea party as a metaphor? If so, you'll probably find the allusion has been cut) or whose ideas of correctness don't jibe with their own. Robert H. Pilpel, who repeatedly referred to Churchill as Winston throughout his "affectionate portrait," *Churchill in America*, was furious to discover that a copy editor had laboriously changed all his "Winstons" to "Mr. Churchill," "Churchill," or "the PM" on the grounds that "Winston" sounded disrespectful. Pilpel thought it conveyed just the tone he wanted. He won the point.

You can win similar arguments with copy editors if you treat them with kindness and respect. In fact, as with editors, you can probably have your way most of the time; after all, it's your story. It's important that you not make an issue out of everything, however, and it's vitally important that if you're going to take a stand, you take it early. After the copy-editing stage, it's costly to fuss with the text. (For more about copy-editing, see "Creation Processes" in "The Self-Publishing Option.")

Indexing

All too often, an author assumes that providing an index is part of the publisher's job, while the publisher assumes that an author who doesn't ask for an index doesn't want one. Since a nonfiction book with an index will sell many more copies than the same book without it, you should check your contract on this subject and take appropriate steps in good time.

Conceivably, you'll decide to do an index yourself if you can't get the publisher to pay for it. Indexing software is not hard to come by. But don't make that decision until you've checked out some professional indexers (see "Resources") because the job is not as easy as some people think. Besides, your time may be tied up on other things you need to do for your book just when indexing has to happen.

Design and Production

Designers provide full sets of specifications for typefaces, column widths, spacing and the like. Production managers arrange for and supervise their implementation. The smaller the firm, the more likely it is that the designer and the production manager will be one and the same; in every firm, their functions are intimately related.

To get a firm grasp on design and production, you can turn to books listed in "Resources"; to learn enough about these operations so that you'll know what their effects are, read on.

At its simplest level, design has to do with how a manuscript should look in print. Given the available space, a range of type options and possibly a budget for artwork, a designer will select one or more sizes and styles of type for text and several others for headings; the designer will also devise a format and perhaps commission or secure drawings or photographs—all this with specific goals in mind: making your work readable and visually reinforcing its message without overspending. Once the basic choices are made, the designer combines text and titles and pictures to create an effective array of pages.

Since most writers know little or nothing about layout and type, and since many book and periodical designers have a strictly limited range of options, there's usually not much an author can contribute at this stage; in fact, you should feel free to turn your attention elsewhere all through the production phase—which consists of purchasing materials and services, scheduling and routing the manuscript, coordinating printing and binding with distribution and keeping everything straight and moving along with the help of detailed written records. A production cycle lasts several weeks at most magazines and six months to a year or more for books, and unless you're responsible for coding and correcting your manuscript on your computer, you can safely leave it to the specialists. Do read your galleys and/or page proofs, though, to catch any mistakes you and the copy editor missed and any that may have crept in, and return them on time because deadlines matter more now.

As publication date approaches, your manuscript's schedule gets increasingly inflexible and changes get more and more complicated and costly. There's a little bit of give at every point of every production timetable (despite what you'll hear to the contrary from people who don't trust you to meet a real deadline), but by the time page proofs are pulled, things are generally moving so fast that only minor and absolutely essential corrections can be made.

Part-and-Parcel Advertising

As a book or article goes through the publication process, its author should devise and develop a variety of ways to let people know it exists and to make them want to read it. ("Why and How to Be Your Own Best Sales Force" and "Managing Sales" will elaborate.) One marketing tool, which is conceived and executed well before publication, is an all-important part of this work. For a book, this crucial marketing tool is the cover; for an article or a story, it's the cover line (only a few items from a magazine's table of contents get listed on its cover; if you can come up with a phrase that will attract buyers to yours, perhaps it will be one of those that's featured).

Like coming-next-issue squibs and headnotes, magazine cover lines are presented as the publisher's work rather than the writer's. That being the case, editors frequently feel no obligation to check them with authors, and authors usually don't mind.

Almost always, however, writers want to preview their book covers and unfortunately, almost always, they don't know how to evaluate what they see. Controversy in this area erupts when publishers define covers as point-of-purchase ads, while authors assume they should be works of art. Since the first point of view is demonstrably healthier for sales, you'd be wise to adopt it and, having adopted it, to decide then what ideas and/or sketches and/or leads to picture sources you might usefully contribute.

Out of politeness, publishing people may pay lip service to your suggestions, no matter how off-base they think you are. But if you want them to act as well as to listen once you get into the conflict-ridden area of publicity, advertising and sales, you will have to convince them that you don't fit the conventional writer's mold. For a writer, as pictured in publishing's collective unconscious, is a babe in the business woods, an impractical type who's understandably eager to succeed and infuriatingly misinformed about how success is achieved. Because this mental image has a substantial foundation in fact, overcoming it means absorbing knowledge and terminology. You can start by realizing that your book's cover may be the only ad it ever gets, and by the time you've read the next chapter you'll have learned enough to position yourself verbally and intellectually on your publisher's wavelength. Then you can really start to fiddle with the controls.

Why and How to Be
Your Own Best Sales Force

Call it the curse of abundance; with roughly 120,000 books published each year, and periodicals starting up all the time, only a small percentage of what's out there catches the attention of the public. This reality comes as a shock to most writers, and as an especially severe shock to authors of first books, whose expectations about sales and reviews always escalate as publication day approaches.

To help cushion the inevitable blow, many editors deliver a standard prepublication speech. At small houses, the gist of it is, We hope to rack up sales over the years, but making a big splash now just isn't in the cards. And at large houses, an editor may say, in effect, Don't expect much (or for most fiction writers and poets, don't expect anything); your book is not going to sell 100,000 copies—we'll be lucky if it sells 5,000; we won't be running any ads for it in *The New York Times*, and no, you won't get on *Oprah*. "The house is allocating promotion funds for only three of the books on its current list," an editor recently told a writer, "and yours isn't one of them." The sad fact is that unless a major rights sale improves its image or your advance was well up in six-figure territory, your book will vanish without a trace very shortly after publication.

Fortunately, as the ghost said to Scrooge, these are the shadows of things that will be only if you don't get busy.

To promote a magazine or newspaper piece, about all you

need to do is draw up a list of influential individuals who figure to comment on it and ought to get copies, draft a covering letter to them and tell your publisher about any contacts you have with media people who might focus on your story. (If you want extra copies of your piece for your friends or your files, order them before the issue they'll appear in is printed; they're cheaper that way.) To promote a book, however, you can do a great deal more, and you'd better.

Profit and Loss and the Bigbook Bind

It's part of publishing's proverbial wisdom that each book is unique and that it therefore requires individual attention—"This isn't toothpaste we're selling" is the standard comparison. In fact, though, publishers generally produce and distribute their wares assembly-line fashion. For this apparent contradiction, they have a ready, and thoroughly plausible, excuse: With dozens or hundreds of titles to sell and strict limits on time, money and staff, routinization is essential.

Why do publishers continue to produce so many books if they lack the resources to sell them? Why, to put it another way, does a $20-billion business accept it as a fact of life that book after book after book will fail to bring in a penny of profit? A full examination of the reasons would make a book by itself, but four of them deserve mention here.

❖ The largest, most commercial houses sometimes publish books that don't seem likely to make any money because editors there think those books are important to contemporary thought or literature. (Does the preconception inhibit sales, you wonder. Probably. But that's another discussion.)

❖ There's some truth in the this-isn't-toothpaste argument, not because each book is unique (most current titles have obvious counterparts in the publishing past), but because the public will greet it as if it were until they've been educated to believe otherwise. The educational process is expensive—conventional book publishing houses, after all, have few brand-name loyalties to draw upon and no subscription systems to guarantee that money they spend initially to round up an audience will be paid off over time—so large firms quite naturally concentrate on telling the world about those titles that have a huge potential readership and leave the rest to luck.

Since each book is a one-shot deal, publishing people must base initial commitments to a particular title on the rough guidelines their experience offers and on apparently unquenchable sparks of hope. Usually, though, the hope proves forlorn because, in the end, the routine measures that publishers have time to put into effect almost never suffice to locate and arouse a particular book's best audience; and authors, who might inject some nonroutine verve into the proceedings, don't know how to help.

❖ Some books succeed anyway. Smaller houses strive for profitability over the long haul but the revenue stream from "backlist" is impressive at larger firms too. Thanks perhaps to an industrious author, an adulatory reviewer or a providential newsbreak, a non-blockbuster title sometimes, somehow keeps selling. "Ah ha!" its publishers say to themselves. "No need to change the system; neglect works after all."

❖ The bigbook has the industry in a bind. On the one hand, bestsellers (not unlike toothpaste) appeal to a relatively large general market, and that enables publishers to benefit from market research (of an admittedly informal sort) and from economies of scale. On the other hand, however, they draw funds and attention away from the majority of the books on a publisher's list, and they demand a strenuous commitment to hype.

Increasing Your Influence

Bigbooks get much of their power from implicit comparisons. This is the cream of a very large crop, goes the unstated bigbook message; thus, it can damage your chances by defining your book as inferior (it's something other than cream, quite clearly, and perhaps no more than watery milk). And, of course, the big-books can also hurt you (along with any publisher's overall track record) by preempting the major portion of all sales resources (that initial advertising blitz is expensive, and so is the tour, and after sales reps push a bigbook as hard as they're often instructed to do, they won't have much time left for selling the rest of the list).

To counter the forces that will work to keep your book just one more title on "the rest of the list," you'll have to attract an audience for it, and the most efficient way to do that is by identifying the connections that already exist between you and your work, on the one hand, and classes of readers, on the other.

Focus on people who know you and people who share membership with you in a formal or informal group of any sort. But focus most of all on people who will feel a sense of kinship with the subjects, settings and people your book features. Is your protagonist a liberated house-husband? Tell women's organizations and men's clubs. Does your message apply to college students? Reach the campuses. Is there a scene in Chicago, a narrative account of abortion, a proposal to abolish free public education? Across the country, people who identify in some way with these areas of interest (and with almost any others you can think of) regularly convene, and communicate through newsletters, meetings and the Net. If you use their particular concerns to provide points of entry to selected aspects of your work, the whole of what you've done will get its fair chance to capture their attention and earn their admiration.

Once you succeed in stirring up interest, you can use evidence of your success to convince the staff at your publishing house to back you. When they see signs (even small ones) that you're a winner, they may be more likely to include your book among the titles they urge on booksellers, librarians, reviewers and all the other intermediaries who stand between conventionally published writers and their readers.

Persuading your publisher to get out there and sell your book is a never-ending job that demands a good deal of gall (though they don't want to be quoted, publishing people admit that books by demanding authors get more attention) and some skillful maneuvering. For best results, you'll want to devise sensible promotional plans, figure out how to fit them in with your publisher's standard operating procedures and then get up the gumption to see that they're put into effect.

The following descriptions and suggestions should tell you what you need to know to manage all three steps.

Major Departmental Development

Publicity, Promotion and Advertising

At large houses, separate departments may exist to handle each of these areas; at small firms one person is often responsible for them all, and for other things besides. In any case, though, all three are closely related, and the first two are extremely important.

Probably the only request these departments will ever make of you is that you fill out a questionnaire providing them with an autobiographical sketch, a description of your book, an account of how it was conceived and written, a list of its newsworthy aspects and a roster of names and addresses of people who might provide blurb copy or otherwise help focus attention on what you've written.

In a rational world, all writers would complete these forms immediately and with care. What actually happens, however, is that publicity people have to plead for information—"Please answer the questions here as thoroughly as you can" is the way one house introduces its questionnaire; "we know it's a time-consuming exercise but your responses are very important"— and when they finally get writers to hand the forms in, they discover half the time that the data supplied are either too sketchy or too voluminous to be usable.

This, of course, bolsters the view that authors are clueless, a view often supported still further when writers express unbounded (and ungrounded) faith in ads, or seem to believe that bookstore clerks who say they've never heard of a book are saying something true and significant. Having been badgered so often by inappropriate demands, most publicity people don't count on help from writers. In fact, their response to the idea of author participation tends to be horror.

Before you can make a contribution, therefore, you'll have to demonstrate that you're different, that while others may try to nag and second-guess marketing people, what you intend to do is provide extra information and elbow grease.

For starters, see what you can do about blurbs. These prepublication comments from relevant celebrities and authorities can be the spark that ignites a publicity campaign. So make a list of important people who might say good things about your book, and scrounge up addresses for them (remember that lots of famous folk reveal their whereabouts in directories; see "Resources"). Then draft letters explaining what you need and why you think they might be happy to give it to you.

"I read what I could about each author on my list so I could personalize my approaches. For example, I learned that one author had worked in advertising so I made sure to mention that in my book the tourists on safari are advertising people," Karin McQuillan reports. A therapist as well as a novelist, McQuillan actually enjoyed the process of asking for blurbs for her novel *Deadly Safari*, once she psyched herself up for it. "It was fun to make contact with the authors I love, tell them so, talk a bit about their books and my book. I'm always telling my clients that their needs are legitimate and that it feels good to ask for what you want even if you're told No; at least you stood up for yourself. Besides, it felt as much like sharing my enthusiasm, and joining the club as asking for something."

Tony Hillerman, Robert B. Parker, Aaron Elkins and other giants of mystery fiction were among those who said Yes, so McQuillan's sheet of "Advance Praise" quotes became a powerful marketing tool.

To add to your marketing tool chest, look hard at your book, remembering that many of the people at your publishing house may never have read it. In fact, you'd do well to assume that the publicity personnel and others in charge of selling a book will know nothing more about it than its central subject. Thus, if your title is *A History of Fitness Fads*, they'll realize it would be smart to alert health and fitness groups and periodicals to forthcoming publication, but because they won't have read the chapter on next year's Be Fit Fair in Cleveland, they won't be able to develop potential there.

You could, though; you know every chapter, every scene, every sentence, and if you assess them as candidates for fairly standard promotional efforts, they can give you quite a lot of mileage.

Consider, for example, review copies. Most publicity departments have a list of review media that runs just a page or two and includes trade journals like *Publishers Weekly, Library Journal*, American Library Association magazines and *Kirkus Reviews* along with major newspapers and magazines. As each new title gets to them, they earmark it for some of the periodicals on that list and off it goes. Some houses will also send review copies to selected columnists and to some special-interest magazines and Web sites.

But unless you're working with a small, highly specialized house—and sometimes even then—there's no way the publicity department can identify all the people who figure to cover your book. It becomes your job, therefore, to create a supplementary list. Include small-town papers and neighborhood throwaways published in places you've mentioned in your book, along with pertinent special-interest periodicals and relevant sites on the Web; supply contact names whenever possible, and mention any relevant relationships you have.

As a general rule, between 100 and 500 copies of a new title go out for review. Though the number of press releases regularly issued by publishers varies at least as widely, they too constitute powerful selling tools for any sort of book. You should be able to think of good places to send them by creating appropriate conclusions for the sentence that starts "This book will be of special interest to you because . . . "

What people or groups would be especially interested in the people or groups your book mentions? What local papers serve the places you've described? What associations care about your subject? What directories exist in the field? And how can you get your work listed? (The Bowker and Gale catalogs, which are described in "Resources," will be helpful here.)

If you know about meetings of people active in your book's area, write a memo about them. If you think the book would be valuable for supplementary reading in schools, draft a letter to teachers explaining how they might use it, and pass the draft along to your editor. And if you've spotted the newsworthy side of what you've written, by all means develop your thoughts and share them as soon as you can.

Remember, too, that publicity departments frequently send announcements to notify friends, family and interested others that a particular author's book has just been published. This is a relatively inexpensive practice (much cheaper, for example, than mailing out review copies or scheduling ads), so you're not likely to meet much resistance if you press for its use.

Mailings also go out from publicity departments to radio talk shows, of which there are hundreds. Because the telephone lets authors appear on radio anywhere in the country without incurring travel expenses, you may well find that your publisher is happy to do a "phoner" mailing for you. And if they're not interested, you can do it yourself; see "Resources" for directories to use in targeting appropriate shows and their producers.

Kenneth C. Davis, whose hardcover publisher had "low to modest expectations" for *Don't Know Much About History*, appeared on scores of talk shows—21 of them in the course of one "exhausting but exhilarating" July 4th weekend—to promote the paperback edition that became a bestseller. Crediting the successful launch of his bestselling Don't Know Much About . . . series mainly to radio, Davis notes that it's a medium he's comfortable with (many writers find it far less stressful than TV) and that you get generous amounts of time to cover your subject (sometimes an hour or more, compared to TV time measured in minutes).

The best way of all to sell a book is face to face with a prospective buyer, which is why many publishers arrange interviews and speaking engagements for nonfiction authors at bookstores and elsewhere (and why they now often ask for videos of author appearances and face-to-face meetings before taking a book on). But if no one else schedules you, you can schedule yourself.

Molly Peacock, whose books of poems include *Raw Heaven* and *Take Heart*, repeatedly generated invitations from people in charge of readings with a package including a copy of one of her book jackets, copies of reviews, a précis of her professional accomplishments, several poems that show the quality and flavor of her work and a letter beginning "I hope you will consider me for a place in the [Such-and-Such] poetry reading series," which went on to talk about the magazines that had published her poetry and the readings she'd already given. Assessing the new readings that resulted, Peacock said, "The psychic rewards are terrific."

The financial rewards can be pretty good too. A poet who's "completely unabashed" about selling her books when she reads, Molly Peacock found that giving readings plus judging poetry contests plus getting grants could propel her annual income from poetry into five figures. Readings also work well for novelists. And writers of all sorts can do practical, factual presentations to groups.

Where speaking to groups is concerned, your knowledge of your book is again your best asset, and you should use it to select upcoming conferences and conventions that will be worth attending. Since many authors have been successful in selling their own books at conventions and fairs, your publisher may be willing to cover your expenses at such gatherings. (If you do go, don't count on your publisher to have copies on hand, and do try hard to get a list of names and addresses of the attendees; it could supply productive leads for mail-order sales.)

Whether or not the publisher will reimburse you for expenses, you can tie talks in with your own travel plans. Whenever Lois Tschetter Hjelmstad plans a trip, she consults her AAA map to find hospitals in the areas she'll be visiting and calls ahead to tell them about her book *Fine Black Lines: Reflections on Facing Cancer, Fear and Loneliness* and to offer to speak. Then she sends a packet of information and makes a follow-up phone call. This approach has created a speaking career. "People are thrilled to hear from me," she reports, and she regularly sells books to her listeners, sometimes to every single one.

The publicity department should be pleased if there's enough evidence of interest in your book to warrant keeping it alive. And when and if a book starts to take off, they may try to help it along by issuing periodic announcements to the trade journals about favorable new reviews or large new printings. The more developments there are, the better; so keep working to interest the local bank, the library, the schools or the stores in displaying your book; keep sending material about it to suitable Web sites and to periodicals and talk shows whenever a news story can serve as a news peg; keep looking for groups that might welcome you as a speaker; keep monitoring coverage (try Nexus, through your library, your publisher or your friends), and above all, keep telling the publisher what's happening. Each new sign of interest and enthusiasm you can report may stimulate still more attention.

As for ads, the important thing is not to plump for space in the standard book review media. Ads there are exceedingly expensive—a full page in *The New York Times Book Review* costs approximately $20,000—and what they get you may be only a fraction of what you'd get from two tiny coupon ads in publications that focus on your area of interest. (See "A Foot in the Door Resources" for ways to track them down.)

Subsidiary Rights Sales

Once upon a time, there were publishers who produced books bound in cloth covers to sell in bookstores and publishers who produced books bound in paper covers to sell elsewhere. Hardcovers appeared on books coming out for the first time; softcovers were for "cheap editions," and sub rights departments in hardcover houses became profit centers by selling rights to paperback reprinters.

The picture is not so simple anymore. Having realized that their profits may be greater if they're the only house issuing a book (however many formats that book may have), publishers that used to do hardcovers only and publishers that used to do nothing but paperbacks now publish hardcover and softcover books; any house may decide to issue reprints of material they originated, and any house may produce or co-produce or license editions in other formats, other media and other countries.

You can see which rights areas are active by looking at boiler-plate contract provisions. But whatever rights your publisher wants and whether or not you have an agent who refuses to part with some of them, your biggest contribution will probably relate to "serial sales"—i.e., sales of rights to excerpts that magazines and newspapers run before and/or after publication.

Here again, your intimate knowledge of your book can lead to getting offers instead of getting ignored. If you suggest that the analysis of sitcoms on pages 85 to 90 might appeal to *TV Guide*, that chapters two and three, with some connective tissue and a new lead, would work for *Rolling Stone*, or that your section on old country inns should interest *Southern Living*, you'll please—and help—your rights director (or your agent, if serial rights are among the ones the agent reserved).

Left to their own devices on serial submissions, overworked people are likely to send a complete set of galleys of your book out to a magazine that shares its general area of interest. When the galleys arrive, magazine editors will be faced with a choice: (a) plow through three hundred pages of material in hopes of finding fifteen that might, with some work, make a piece; or (b) eyeball the book and risk missing a decent article. Quite often— and quite rightly, given time pressures and priorities—an editor will opt for the latter. If you want portions of your work to appear in the periodical press, therefore (and you will if you con- sider either the money or the publicity you can gain that way), you'll have to carve them out yourself and help direct them to the most appropriate openings you can find. Confer with your editor on timing, and consult "A Foot in the Door" and "Spin- offs" for targets.

Sales to Bookstores

The job of getting books into stores is performed by a sales force, perhaps as many as a hundred people for a very large pub- lishing house or a sizable distributor. Salespeople generally con- vene at least twice a year for a full-dress presentation of their firm's new books. Sometimes an in-house sales force will meet in the publisher's own locale and editors will introduce their own titles; sometimes a conference will take place at a spiffy resort where the editor-in-chief, along with other members of upper management, announces the entire line, describing each book and suggesting how to sell it.

It's important to get your book presented favorably at the sales conference because if the reps sense that it's a loser they'll classify it mentally as a "skip book" (one they can use to build confi- dence with booksellers by saying, "Between you and me, you can skip this"); and then, of course, a loser is what it will be. To avoid this fate, you should prepare a package of selling docu- ments and pass it along to your editor in the hope that the editor, in turn, will relay copies to all the marketing people. Consider including a list of promising markets together with notes on how to reach them, an analysis of the distinctions between your book and its competition, a particularly engaging excerpt and/or a table of contents, and your strongest pre-pub comments.

In addition, you might offer to provide a short audio tape

and/or a short video and to talk with the assembled sales reps if they're in your area, either by addressing them at a meeting or by attending one of the parties the house may be giving for them during a sales conference.

Since more than a hundred titles may be presented at each sales meeting and since each sales rep will have about 20 seconds to sell a book in the stores, it's a good idea to create a "handle" for yours. "Handle" is the first heading on one publisher's Editorial Fact Sheet because it's what the reps need most. The term, as one rep explained, means "key words or phrases that will be sure to catch the attention of the retailer." What the retailer wants to know, of course, is whether the book will attract readers, so the best handles are those that emphasize benefits. Think in terms of what your book will contribute to readers' lives rather than what material it contains. Good models include a line Random House used in ads for *Dr. Susan Love's Hormone Book* ("The menopause book that asks all the right questions—for the generation that questions everything") and a line for Ballantine's *Hunger Pains: The Modern Woman's Tragic Quest for Thinness* ("Mary Pipher...helps all women to see themselves—and to like what they see").

When sales conferences end, after close to a week, each sales rep goes forth—armed with catalogs, book covers, bios and photos of authors and a quota to meet for every title—to call on accounts (a single rep may be responsible for contacting 50 or a hundred booksellers). Because most books sold to stores are fully returnable and because the sales reps' bonuses are usually based on sales minus returns, it does them no good to load retailers up with copies of a title the stores won't be able to move. Still, once the books are on the shelves the manager will try to find customers for them (or so the theory goes), and besides, quotas help publishers provide an objective correlative for impressionistic first-printing orders.

Unfortunately, despite quotas and clever sales pitches, many new books have a hard time getting into bookstores, and those that do make it onto the shelves aren't likely to stay there long.

Because they know they can return most titles they stock, bookstore managers take little risk in ordering, have little incentive to sell most books aggressively or imaginatively and tend to go with our cultural flow toward the new, new, new and the big, big, big. Ninety days after a book's publication, booksellers who want room for other titles may simply return it to the publisher for credit, and unless they're convinced that would be a mistake, it's just what they'll do.

Everyone agrees that present systems of distribution are unsatisfactory all around and perhaps at their worst in those moments—known to authors, publishers and booksellers alike—when it's impossible to cash in on a surge of interest in a particular book because the damn thing isn't in fact "available at your bookstore," as the ads and media coverage promised, but is, instead, stuck in the warehouse, lost in the mail or held up in its second printing by a strike at the bindery.

On the whole, the transience and unpredictability of a book's life in the stores make everybody miserable. You can take a small step toward sanity, however, by reminding yourself that—just like the publicity people and the subsidiary rights people—sales reps can't be relied upon to have read your book and that they need you to tell them what's between the covers.

If you've written about alternative medicine, for example, and you know that Boston, New York and San Francisco are among the cities in the vanguard of medical change, write a memo suggesting high quotas for stores there. Try to isolate as many promising geographical markets as you can, whatever your subject, and prepare a list, complete with explanations (I grew up in Newtown, Connecticut; my parents live in Boise, Idaho; chapter six is set in Helena, Montana). Selecting three cities for special attention, Joanne Leedom-Ackerman helped propel her first novel, *The Dark Path to the River*, into a second printing shortly after its publication date. With good reviews and a schedule of public appearances in hand, she arranged to autograph books and deliver posters at chain and independent bookstores in Los Angeles (where she lived), New York (where the novel takes place) and Dallas (where she comes from, where her supportive publisher was based and where her book soon made the bestseller list, which it stayed on for weeks). "Targeting a few areas and making personal contacts with the booksellers there was one of the most successful things we did," Leedom-Ackerman reports.

Special Sales

For a variety of reasons, many people never set foot in a bookstore. They do, however, watch television (including QVC), surf the Web (with stops at Amazon and other bookselling sites) and go to stores that cater to their special interests (which sell books along with sporting goods, yarn, toys, health food and a host of other products). Moreover, all sorts of people regularly hear about and buy books through periodicals, associations, catalogs and conferences. Reaching readers through these and other special-interest, "nontraditional" channels is a primary goal for smaller publishers and increasingly important for larger firms. Often, the responsibility falls to special sales departments, which can bring in sizable amounts of money—more, for some books, than bookstores ever will. Suggestions from authors are usually welcome in this area, so find out who handles it for your publisher, get up a memo pinpointing channels the publisher could use to get your book directly to its natural readership and explore opportunities until they're ripe for action on the publisher's part.

Did the local paper report that a big company will be setting up headquarters in your area? Maybe the human relations VP would buy cartons of your regional guidebook to help employees get adjusted. Is repainting high on the list of your book's decorating tips? Sound out local paint-store managers about adding it to their stock mix. Would you enjoy hosting an AOL chat group about your book's subject or interacting with visitors to your own Web site? Investigate ways to tie in with existing sites (including your publisher's) and service providers (including the one you use). And see "Managing Sales" for more ideas and examples.

Sales to Libraries

In addition to selling directly to retailers, some salespeople deal with book wholesalers, who get a large discount because they buy in bulk and who sell their inventory to retailers and libraries. These wholesalers (or jobbers, as they're sometimes called) handle titles from the biggest houses and from thousands of smaller firms, offering all the advantages typical of one-stop suppliers in any industry, such as simplified ordering, billing and shipment procedures.

It's their greater efficiency and their discount policies that recommend jobbers to librarians, who order from them after studying publishers' catalogs and reviews in professional journals. Since libraries are obviously a crucial market and since books lead comparatively long lives on library shelves, you'll want to establish contact with librarians in your area, and perhaps you'll decide to include an index in your book (a "no index" note at the end of a review in a library journal can mean "no reference value" to a librarian and thus no sale to you).

Bear in mind that libraries often host author appearances, that library associations have meetings and newsletters, which might focus on your work, and that the librarian who greets you at the checkout desk can help you reach the right people.

Fighting the Fear of Hustling

Authors rarely lobby for their books within the houses that publish them (which means less competition for you if you follow this chapter's advice), and they're even less likely to go out by themselves in search of sales. Somehow, they seem to think, it's not dignified to hustle for anything you yourself created. Well, dignified writers do it, and for a dignified reason: Believing that what they have to say is worth saying, they accept the responsibility of finding those people who will benefit from hearing it.

Even famous, well-established authors get out and give their latest book a nudge or two. A buyer for the Radius Book Store on the West Side of New York City, Susan Bergholz, reported that Joseph Heller, who was a neighbor of hers as well as the author of *Catch–22* and other memorable novels, periodically came into the store to autograph a few copies, to check the stock and positioning of his book and to see how many copies had been bought.

And other writers also roll up their sleeves to reach readers. Cases in point include Joshua Meyrowitz, whose *No Sense of Place* has won three awards and gone into multiple printings; Ann L. McLaughlin, whose first novel, *Lightning in July*, went back to press and earned her a contract for a second and a third; and Terry McMillan, whose *Waiting to Exhale* became a cultural phenomenon as well as a bestselling book and a hit movie. "When I was at some writers' conference, I read this book, *How to Get Happily Published*," McMillan told *Publishers Weekly*, going on to explain what she did to market her first book, *Mama*. "Even without strong reviews," the editor for the paperback edition recalls, *Mama* had sold out its first hardcover printing of 5,000 copies, "a mystery until McMillan explained what she had done...she'd sent out thousands of letters to bookstores, college organizations and news media—with a strong emphasis on black groups—urging them to stock and promote her book and invite her to read from it."

To set up readings or other personal appearances and profit most with the least psychological strain, start by talking before audiences that will think of you as a neighbor or a friend. Arrange to speak to the Chamber of Commerce or the PTA. Check with groups in your area that might sponsor meet-the-author get-togethers. See if a bookstore downtown will display your book and invite people to your related workshop. And whether they'll do that or not, arrange to autograph the store's copies of your book (since autographed copies are more likely to sell, it's smart also to sign copies in bookstores outside your area whenever you travel).

While you're stalking the home front, query the local papers about feature stories; call talk shows about appearances; see whether local periodicals might like to serialize your book. And by all means drop a note to the book reviewers of all local publications to tell them that a local resident has been published. In her hometown (Portland, Oregon), Rose Naftalin sold 6,000 copies of her cookbook. As that figure indicates, it's hard to overestimate the value of promotion on your own turf.

Wherever you speak and whether you bring your own supply of copies or ask your publisher to get books into the area, be sure also to give out flyers that include ordering information (preferably e-mail and toll-free phone numbers). Maybe your editor can get the sales department to prepare some for you; if not, you can produce them yourself. Be sure, too, to let the publicity department know at least six weeks in advance about any speaking engagements you've lined up so that they'll have time to alert the local media and bookstores and so that you'll have time to take advantage of any public-speaking services your publisher has to offer.

Some houses provide coaching for their authors before scheduled TV and personal appearances, but whether or not lessons are available, you should make up a list of provocative questions that an interviewer might ask, and then practice answering them fast and fully. Since the average interview lasts eight minutes, there's plenty of time to establish eye contact with your audience and to mention the title of your book with fair frequency; all you need by way of preparation is a few rehearsals.

Those of you who still feel shy may be emboldened by the story of Diana Brown, told here in her own words.

As a librarian, I was well aware of the number of titles published each year, so when my first novel—*The Emerald Necklace*—appeared, my family and I put our heads together to explore what we might do to save an entertaining book from possible oblivion. We sought out all our contacts: personal, professional, educational, ethnic, and told them of the novel's release.

Attending a political convention, my husband had "campaign" buttons made up for each of us announcing "My wife [or mommy] [or I] wrote *The Emerald Necklace* by Diana Brown." These we wore to an ever increasing number of talks I presented to local groups—friends of the library, schools, service and women's clubs.

May's birthstone being the emerald, we approached a local jeweler with a chain of stores in busy shopping centers who agreed to display my book along with his emeralds, and with a sign noting it was by a local author. We also purchased a small advertisement in a local shopping guide suggesting *The Emerald Necklace* as a May birthday gift.

I wrote a press release on the novel, its progress, and my own background for distribution to local papers. When *The Emerald Necklace* was featured in *Good Housekeeping* and later by *Buenhogar* (the Spanish-language version of that magazine) we had this release translated for Spanish-language papers and radio stations in our area.

Our summer vacation was turned into a promotion trip. Armed with the press release and copies of reviews, we called on newspapers, radio and television stations along our route. Since *The Emerald Necklace* had been chosen by the Sunday supplement *Family Weekly* as suggested summer reading, we made sure to approach each newspaper that carried that magazine. The trip resulted in numerous reviews and feature stories.

Using photocopies of the book jacket, we designed our own notepaper and envelopes. We also reprinted the publisher's catalog copy, and no bill payment or letter left our home without one of these promos being inserted in the envelope. Our Christmas card was also designed from the book jacket—which happened to have been adapted from a handsome portrait by Sir Henry Raeburn.

All of these personal and family efforts resulted in *The Emerald Necklace* going into three hardcover printings. It has since been reprinted in paperback and published in England, Argentina, and Greece. Undoubtedly its success added to the publisher's enthusiasm for my later novels—including *Come Be My Love*, *The Hand of a Woman*, and *The Blue Dragon*.

The Editor Exits and Other Evils

Authors are prey to strange malevolent forces. When the reviewer assigned by a prestigious magazine to cover your book does a lousy job and the piece gets chucked, you get no coverage there. When delays of one sort and another mean your tap-dancing guide comes out after the craze is over, you'll have lost your audience. When two books with subjects like yours suddenly fail, you'll forgo the support of the sales force. And when your editor is feuding with the publicity director, you will suffer.

But no matter how events conspire against you, if you believe in your book you can change your luck. Here's a sampling of suggestions.

❖ When your editor leaves the house, don't panic. As soon as you hear the news, find out who might adopt your book once it's orphaned (its original editor should be able to supply some names), and then meet with candidates to assess their enthusiasm for your work and their ability to do well by it. Finally, after you've been assigned a new editor, make a date to explain your book's strengths in detail. (Resell your book also when a new sales manager, special sales director or other key player enters the picture.)

If, as sometimes happens, no editor on the premises seems likely to handle your book well, then explore ways you might get the project away from its present publisher and resell it to another house. (Your original editor may be helpful here, too, and writers with agents should seek their counsel.)

❖ Consider hiring a publicist or marketing consultant (see the *Literary Market Place* listings). Some publicists won't work for a book that's already out, and no publicist or marketing consultant can promise results. Still, marketing energy and expertise have breathed new life into many a title.

❖ If you have plenty of convictions but very little money, try hiring an energetic student you can train to be your own personal publicity agent. With a week's study of the standard publicity guides (see "The Self-Publishing Option Resources"), even an amateur should be able to put ten good ideas into practice.

❖ Alleviate the no-books-in-the-stores problem by calling bookstores in areas where you'll be getting publicity to explain when and why they'll profit by having your book in stock. One writer who went this route was initially afraid that bookstore managers would hang up on her, but in fact they were grateful for her calls and—more important—they did arrange to have copies of her book on sale when she was in town.

❖ Start fresh, by arranging for your book to be reissued, preferably by a publisher equipped to attract its special-interest audiences.

  • Books get second lives all the time. Look, for instance, at remainder dealers, who buy publishers' leftovers in bulk at below-cost prices, offer readers a bargain and sometimes sell so many copies of a particular title that they wind up reprinting it over and over again. Or consider the experiences of Gloria Bley Miller with *The Thousand Recipe Chinese Cookbook*. Remaindered a year after pub date—despite good reviews, a major award and outstanding media coverage—the book was resold two years later to another house, which then cheerfully racked up sales year after year after year.

Instead of finding a new publisher, as writers and agents often do, you may decide to become your book's new publisher. Consult a literary property lawyer and/or your agent, if you have one, about severing your current publishing ties and see the next section for guidance on how to proceed after that.

The Self-Publishing
Option

❖ ❖ ❖

The Case for Doing It Yourself
or
Don't Skip This Chapter Unless You're Willing to Let Prejudice Stand Between You and What May Be Your Best Destiny

A DEMONSTRABLY FALSE series of assumptions keeps a great many writers from seriously considering self-publishing, which is a shame because a lot of people could earn more money and have more fun if they brought out their own work. Constructed with one part ignorance, one part laziness and one part unadulterated snobbery, the chain of thought might be summarized as follows: I am a writer; a writer's job is to express ideas, images and information in words; after a writer has done that job, noncreative types should pronounce it good and take it over, leaving the writer free to write some more.

At first glance, the argument seems logical enough, but closer examination reveals a fatal flaw. If expression is a writer's goal, why is a publisher necessary? Why, indeed, is anything necessary besides a desk drawer big enough to hold manuscripts?

The answer, of course, is that expression is really only a preliminary goal, a necessary first step toward the ultimate end of writing, which is communication.

Once you accept the fact that when you write you want to communicate, you'll realize three things: (1) You need people to communicate with; (2) You're most likely to communicate effectively with people who'll be receptive to your writing's particular style and substance; and (3) Finding those people is the only way to fulfill your role as a writer.

In theory, you can get a publishing company to track your audience down for you. In practice, though, busy professionals handling masses of titles are not likely to concentrate on drawing receptive readers to yours. Thus, if you want to reach as many people as possible you'll have to plan selling campaigns on your own (and maybe execute them on your own as well) whether you're self-published or conventionally published. Those who self-publish, however, will be spared one burden: They won't have to start by putting their ideas across to a publisher with an impulse to ignore them.

Looked at in this light, do-it-yourself publishing may seem a more attractive alternative than it used to. Writers who are beginning to like the idea but who are not yet convinced that they'll be able to implement it should read the next two chapters to resolve their doubts one way or the other. And writers who are troubled by the always sticky matter of money may ease their minds with the following string of comparisons.

Self-publishers pay to have their work issued. People who use vanity presses pay to have their work issued (though they pay much more and get much less; see "Openings"). But the group that pays the highest price of all is composed of writers of best-selling books. True, they don't pay to begin with. But advances can sometimes be matched by self-publishers (see "Finding Funding"). And besides, by the time successful books go out of print at a major house, their authors will have repaid the publisher many times over, not only for their advances but also for all expenses, through the portion of their profits that the firm keeps for itself.

Therefore? Therefore, who pays what and when and to whom is not, by itself, a useful gauge of publishing worth.

Instead of allowing yourself to be diverted by quibbles about front money or picturesque notions of the cloistered literary life, why not assess the attractions of self-publishing in terms of the particular kinds of writing you do and the particular kind of person you are.

Natural Candidates

If a major publishing house that has produced many related best-sellers wants to give your book its bigbook treatment, then you will probably do better under its auspices than you would on your own. In other circumstances, it's not so easy to decide whether conventional publishing or self-publishing will be the better bet.

Often, both options are available, with the result that many writers move back and forth between the two alternatives, sometimes with the same book (after the writer's edition appears, a bigger publisher shows up and asks to take it over; after an established house gives up, the writer becomes the publisher and generates sales through the years).

Historically, the roster of self-publishers has included many names that now appear under publishing's most prestigious imprints. (William Blake, Washington Irving, James Fenimore Cooper, Walt Whitman and Mark Twain are among those cited by Bill Henderson in his classic *Publish-It-Yourself Handbook*.) And crossovers continue in present times.

Maggy Simony, for instance, began by self-publishing three volumes of *Traveler's Reading Guides*, which list and describe fiction and nonfiction about anywhere anyone might be going. Then, after getting excellent reviews in library media and write-ups in travel and consumer publications (including *The New York Times*), she sold rights to Facts on File, which brought out an 800-page, one-volume edition that also became available through the Book-of-the-Month Club and the Quality Paperback Book Club.

It's by no means unusual for a major house to pick up a proven self-published work; in fact, self-publishers who are tired of business aggravations and eager to devote themselves full time to new writing projects frequently go after bids from conventional houses once their books are launched—and get them. Any self-publisher who makes a deal with a big firm, though, ought to be represented by a lawyer who's thoroughly familiar with the publishing industry and who's a bit of a scrapper besides.

Nor is it unusual for authors to pick up—and succeed with—books major houses have dropped. When her publisher gave up on *American Harvest: Regional Recipes for the Vegetarian Kitchen*, for example, Nava Atlas bought leftover copies of it so that they "wouldn't end up on the remainder tables," and after that she sold the book through channels like mail order companies, gift shops, health-food stores and wholesalers that reach her market, some of which the original publisher had failed to approach. Similarly, Vicki Lansky, the author of many books from major houses, gave second lives to some that went out of print by publishing them herself and going after "special" as well as trade markets. Her edition of *KoKo Bear's Big Earache* sells about 5,000 copies a year (pediatric ear, nose and throat specialists are good customers), and her edition of *Vicki Lansky's Divorce Book for Parents: Helping Children Cope with Divorce and Its Aftermath* had 30,000 in print 18 months after pub date (partly because of mailings to divorce lawyers, mediators, therapists and other professionals in the divorce world).

But if it's true that almost anything a commercial company can publish (and some things it can't) can be self-published instead, it's also true that two classes of writing are particularly well suited to the self-publishing process:

❖ Works that are clearly of interest to at least one well-defined, relatively large, easy-to-reach audience, because a single individual can market them as well as an established firm, and if you do it yourself you get to keep all the profits.
❖ Works that figure to interest a very small group of readers, at least to begin with, because established firms aren't likely to take them on, and if they do, they'll probably let them die in short order without ever giving them a decent chance to live.

Whether self-publishers sell hundreds of copies or hundreds of thousands of copies will depend on their level of skill with words and with business arrangements, as well as on what it is that they've written. Diverse kinds of material offer good self-publishing potential across a wide sales spectrum, though. For instance:

Valuable Data

The thirst for information persists. Even on vacation, we like to improve our minds, which is why there are hundreds of educational travel programs, and why Evelyn Kaye saw a reason to create a book about them. She can make money on *Travel & Learn: The New Guide to Educational Travel* with annual sales of about 3,000. Now in its third printing, it launched a publishing company, Blue Panda (formerly Blue Penguin), whose informative travel titles include the *Active Woman Vacation Guide*.

To satisfy a hunger for information about freebies by mail, Robert and Linda Kalian decided to publish *A Few Thousand of the Best Free Things in America*, which quickly sold more than 700,000 copies. Later titles from their Roblin Press include *Great Stuff for Aquarium Lovers* and *Great Stuff for Seniors*.

Other writers have produced substantial profits with such items as a newsletter describing job openings in the federal government, a brochure explaining how to get rid of groundhogs and a book analyzing the management of paperwork.

Community Coverage

When the locality in question is a region and the self-published work is a full-size book or periodical, sales may easily mount into the high thousands (regional books pay the rent for a good many commercial publishers). But even if both the area and the self-publishing project are defined by more modest limits, success is still possible.

Jan Zobel and some colleagues created and published *The San Francisco Bay Area People's Yellow Pages* back when the idea was new. They sold 40,000 copies and went through five editions.

Across the country about a quarter of a century later, Nuria Clarke and Hernando Reyes created *Vea*, a Spanish-language guide to New York City. Realizing that tourism from Spain and Latin America was growing fast, they thought they could attract advertisers as well as readers. They were right. And serving the non-geographic academic community, Jeffrey Kittay attracted awards along with subscribers to *Lingua Franca*, a magazine built around "nourishing, sexy, witty, sometimes off-the-wall" shoptalk, with shoptalk defined as "the information that circulates in faculty lounges, off-campus cafes, cafeterias and conference hallways," which is *critical* to our understanding of what's going on in our profession and where each of us stands in relation to it."

Scholarly Papers and Classroom Texts

Circulating ideas and information is essential in the classroom too, of course, but teachers who write or compile materials for academic use can't rely on publishing houses to produce a book that only a few hundred people figure to read. Fortunately, though teachers' markets may be small, they are solid. Thus, by computing sales accurately in advance, self-publishing scholars can arrange to keep costs down to the point where they'll surely be matched by revenues.

One caveat: Now that it's easy to create the customized books known as course packs by duplicating written material, it's also easy to overstep copyright boundaries. If you do decide to publish a collection of other people's work, be sure you have the permissions you need and be prepared to pay for them. (See The Authors Registry in "Resources.")

Special-Interest Literature

Thousands of self-publishers have tapped into specialized markets with gratifying consequences. Consider Patricia Johnston, for instance. Johnston started Perspectives Press to publish

Perspectives on a Grafted Tree, her collection of poems about adoption, and much to her surprise "found a new career" publishing for its market. With 21 titles in print by authors involved with adoption personally or professionally, her press has won awards; one of its books has sold more than 30,000 copies; annual sales per title average in the thousands; and the giant bookstore chain Barnes & Noble took the initiative on carrying her books. Or look at *Women Who Kept the Lights: An Illustrated History of Female Lighthouse Keepers*, by Mary Louise Clifford and J. Candace Clifford. Fascinated by lighthouses, Candace Clifford published the book and sold more than 12,000 copies in its first three years, mainly through gift shops at lighthouses and maritime museums and parks and through catalogs that feature lighthouse-related products. "Each year has shown a steady increase in sales," she reports.

The special interest focus works for periodicals too. Glen C. Ellenbogen, author/publisher of the satirical *Journal of Polymorphous Perversity*, made a 3,300-copy bulk sale to Smith, Kline & French Laboratories, which wanted to distribute an issue featuring its pharmaceutical products (eventually, by the way, he also made a paperback sale to Ballantine, which brought out a collection of "Readings from the *Journal of Polymorphous Perversity*" called *Oral Sadism and the Vegetarian Personality*).

As every newsstand habitué knows, special-interest magazines that focus in on crafts, computers, cars or some other well-defined area far outnumber magazines that cover a wide range of topics. Dealing with still more specific subjects, today's 'zines—with titles such as *Murder Can Be Fun* and *Bust*—are numerous enough to have spawned still another sort of special-interest periodical: the 'zine review. M. Teresa Lawrence founded *Curio* to publish pieces about them along with excerpts from them, and reviews of 1,500 'zines appear in issues of R. Seth Friedman's *Factsheet Five*.

If what you've written will serve a special-interest audience, you may find it relatively easy to get financial help when you put on your publisher's hat. But even if you bear all initial expenses yourself, you shouldn't be out of pocket for long, and you should reap major rewards in the form of response quite quickly.

Novels, Short Fiction and Poems

No matter who the publisher is, fiction is usually harder to sell than nonfiction and poetry is harder still.

Nonfinancial rewards may be plentiful. Take camaraderie, for example, one of the nicest side effects for many self-publishers. "When I decided to self-publish *Blinkies: Funny Poems to Read in a Blink*, everyone I know got into the act," reports Alma Denny, talking about her collection of light verses, most of which ran first in *The Wall Street Journal, Gourmet, English Today* and various other periodicals. "An artist offered to design a cover and do 51 cartoons for my short poems. A printer in Washington, DC (her father), set the poems up in type. (He also owns a bookstore!) She is arranging with a book packager in Ohio to do the production. A friend in Washington State wants to handle distribution and mailing. A professional PR person has asked to do the promoting. A beautiful actress wants to do readings at meetings to sell the book. And my sisters have asked for 100 copies each to sell to their Sisterhoods. What I'm saying is the idea snowballs."

Denny's experience highlights the fact that people working together toward a common goal often forge or strengthen close personal ties, and self-publishing writers can convene as big a group of collaborators as they like. Conventional houses react badly to having more than two people on the other side of a publishing contract (both profits and decision-making powers will, they fear, be spread too wide and thin). But works produced in concert do succeed when self-publishers are in charge.

The people who labor along with a self-publisher on a particular project aren't the only ones who offer aid, comfort and affection, however. Members of the country's vast small-publisher network may also be ready to help. Many small publishers are generous with advice and assistance, and coming to know them by joining their associations frequently means coming to like them as well.

Are financial rewards available with fiction and poetry, too? Often they are and occasionally they're huge. E. Lynn Harris sold 5,000 copies of his first novel, *Invisible Life*, mainly through beauty salons and black-owned bookstores. Then, after *Essence* magazine named the book one of the year's ten best, he made a deal with a big publisher. James Redfield and Richard Paul Evans also eventually made deals with big houses, but after *The Celestine Prophecy* and *The Christmas Box* had each sold hundreds of thousands of copies in their self-published editions.

The big-publisher buyout isn't par for the course, and in many cases it isn't necessary for profitability. But rights sales can be enormously lucrative. Take *A Solitary Dance*, for example. Robert Lane's story about a schizophrenic child was originally published by Serrell & Simons (i.e., Bob and his wife, Mary). They sold rights to Reader's Digest Condensed Books, New American Library's Signet paperback line, several foreign publishers and a couple of book clubs. At last count, more than two million copies of *A Solitary Dance* were in print in 16 countries and nine languages.

Activist Arguments

In nonmilitary battles, the call to arms is often sounded by words. Self-publishers today use books, magazines, newsletters and Web pages to rally supporters to a multiplicity of causes—from saving the Earth or reforming the electoral process to reinvigorating religion or embracing alternative medicine. Published by somebody else, they might have had to water down their views, wait for their turn in a leisurely publication schedule and forgo the chance to be directly in touch with the readers they need to arouse.

The Aptitude Test

So far so good? If your current project fits one or more of the "Natural Candidates" categories, you'll want to know whether your personality fits the profile of the successful self-publisher.

When the self-publishing boom began in the '60s, self-publishers were often a bit quirky—people, perhaps, who wanted a physically beautiful product above all else or who insisted on writing about a subject most readers found repulsive or ridiculous; people, in other words, who probably had no choice because established publishers weren't interested in what interested them.

Today, with established publishers and self-publishers producing the same sorts of products, the typical self-publisher is far harder to describe but three attributes are crucial.

❖ *Successful self-publishers love to be in control.* It's the first reason they're likely to mention if you ask why they decided to go it alone. You're in charge, and you can even adjust the degree of your commitment. Suppose, for example, that you've written *The Complete Small-Engine Repair Manual.* With a modest cash outlay, you can get 1,000 copies printed up to offer local hardware stores, department stores and bookstores on consignment, and to sell personally at programs you give for nearby vocational schools and continuing-education centers. Then, if those markets work well, you can go back to press, begin to experiment with mail orders and wholesale distribution over a wide geographical area and perhaps wind up selling hundreds of times as many copies as there were in your original print order.

Or suppose (to frame another example drawn from actual experience) that you've just moved to the Ozarks and that you want to share observations on your new homeland with friends you've left behind. If you begin by duplicating reports to them, and if they pass your pieces on to friends and acquaintances of theirs, and if the chain continues to lengthen, you will have founded a newsletter or a magazine before long and developed a mailing list that more scientific periodical publishers will envy.

In the self-publishing arena as in others, however, control is far from absolute and it can't mean bossing other people around. Getting anything done will involve motivating them.

Though you may not have a staff, you undertake to run a small business when you become a self-publisher. You'll have to supervise an editor, a designer, a printer, wholesalers, retailers, reviewers and more. Recognizing that your concerns will be low priority for them and that their operations are not 100% efficient, will you get steamed or sympathetic? Or, to put it another way, can your definition of control include understanding their problems so that you can help solve them?

❖ *Successful self-publishers like fast starts but have staying power.* Impatience is high on just about everybody's list of Reasons I Self-Published. Why wait 10 months or a year or two years for some conventional publisher to get your work into print when you can get it out so much faster? This argument, which is most obviously appealing with timely topics, has force even for material that doesn't date.

Launching a print product takes time, however (see the next two chapters for explanations). In fact, as business school teaches and businesses know, launching a new product of any sort usually takes years. Yes, you can get your book or periodical out there quickly, but getting it to pay off is another matter, and more often than not where self-publishers are concerned this comes as a big—sometimes panic-inducing—surprise.

"Stick with it," "don't get discouraged," "build on whatever happens"—keep on keeping on is the message veterans send first-timers. Large, established, book-publishing firms, which must make room in their catalogs for hundreds of new titles at least twice a year, can't afford to keep a book in circulation for more than a few months unless its initial rate of sale is impressive. The life span of articles in established magazines is even more severely limited; one month after the March issue comes out, it's off the stands, no matter how many copies remain unsold or how many people are just now beginning to show an interest in the piece you wrote for it. But a self-published work can be—and must be—granted the gift of time.

With time, it may well attract a following. Many books that make no splash when they're released become profitable over the years as appreciative readers begin to wield the single most powerful selling tool any publishing company ever has: word of mouth. And once word of mouth begins to operate, it's relatively simple for self-publishers to capitalize on it (see "Managing Sales").

❖ *Successful self-publishers are either idealistic realists or realistic idealists.* Unlike a writer whose book circulates in the hands of a publishing company's sales force, self-publishing authors must often navigate serpentine, swampy marketing terrain themselves, dealing face to face with distracted people enmeshed in complicated systems.

Much of this real-world activity is no fun in and of itself. But most writers who self-publish take it in stride because it gets them what they want—a shot at enriching the world with their words. Although economic sustenance or ease is often *a* goal, it tends to be relatively unimportant (most self-publishers don't even think to mention it when they explain what got them into this). *The* goal is more likely to be affecting readers.

So ask yourself one last question: Is what I have to offer important enough to be worth the effort (which will be considerable), the time (remember, that's long) and the money (count on investing several thousand dollars at least)?

If the answer is Yes, if you believe that the analyses and aesthetic experiences and entertainment and insights and information and ideas captured through your work will make substantial contributions to personal lives and/or to the culture we live in, you're a likely prospect for self-publishing, an option more writers choose with every passing day.

Creation Processes:
From Editing to Entity

Is $14.95 the best price? How do I find a good printer? Why do I have to have an ISBN (whatever that is)? What's camera-ready copy? What's CIP? What's dpi? What's RFQ? First-time self-publishers may find themselves bedeviled by questions like these and tempted to conclude that the real questions are, What did I get myself into and how do I get out?

If this happens to you, don't worry. It's true that you'll need to learn new terminology and understand unfamiliar processes. But the technical terms will soon be familiar and you don't have to handle any or all of the work by yourself. Free guidance is available (read on); help is not hard to buy (see this section's "Resources"); and as you progress, you can effect any number of trade-offs between expenditures of your time and energy, on one side of the equation, and of money to procure professionals' services, on the other.

So rest assured that with judicious use of manuals and specialists, with modest amounts of information and with easily available equipment, any amateur can produce a bound book, a pamphlet, a periodical or—please note—an effective piece of promotional material for whatever's being published, no matter who's publishing it. Moreover, special pleasures accompany these literally creative acts. In our push-button era, self-publishers are privileged to share the I-made-it-myself elation usually reserved for children and for those few adults who build things they love with their hands.

Here are the stops along the road to that reward.

Editing

Although you may have grown heartily sick of reworking your words, two more editing efforts will be worthwhile.

The first involves reviewing the manuscript in terms of marketability. This is your chance to add material that will strengthen the appeal for readers (such as a foreword or preface by some relevant Somebody) and to delete or change material that may turn certain audiences off. Bookstores and libraries in one region of the country may reject work with cusswords in it, for instance, so if profanity is not essential you might want to eliminate it. Buyers overseas may be turned off if all the examples are American. And a company whose product you recommend may decide against buying copies for their customers if you praise the competition too, so when one brand will surely serve your readers best, you may want to leave the others out.

While you're thinking of your market, think again about your title (is it as resonant as it can be? does it clearly convey what benefits readers will derive from your work, not just what the work is about?), and come up with a name for your publishing operation (something general and neutral is fine and so is something that signals your subject; don't use your own name, though, because some people are still prejudiced against self-published work; and check *Books in Print,* at a minimum, to see if the name you want is already in use).

If you plan to hire a marketing consultant, this may be the time to do it. In any case, after the marketing edit, you'll want an overall edit, preferably from a professional who comes to the project fresh. Self-publishing writers are often tempted to skip this editing stage, sometimes (1) because they believe it's of little value, sometimes (2) because they're afraid of having their work distorted, and sometimes (3) because they don't know how to find a good editor.

Well, every piece of writing can benefit from sensible editing (many will be significantly improved) and good editors don't distort (on the contrary, they clarify and strengthen).

To locate an editor who'd be right for your work, you might start by finding out who edited some similar published work that you admire and asking them if they'd work for you (call or write the publisher's publicity departments to get names if you can't deduce them from internal evidence). In the event that the editors can't afford the time or you can't afford their fee, perhaps they'll suggest colleagues you might contact.

Alternatively, you can choose a freelance editor from those who are listed in *Literary Market Place* , enrolled as members of the Editorial Freelancers Association (see this section's "Resources") or recommended by writers you know. It's important, of course, to get references and samples before you make a commitment, and it's helpful to have an editor whose computer is compatible with yours (once you know that, you'll want to find out whether the editor will work on hard copy or on a diskette you supply).

In any case, you should arrange to proceed in well-defined stages. You might begin, for example, by asking the editor to look over the whole manuscript and give you a rough critique along with a ballpark estimate. Many editors work by the hour (rates vary widely, from about $20 to about $150); many will quote a project fee. Second, you might propose paying the editor to do a comprehensive memo about revisions and to actually edit the first chapter or two. If that goes smoothly, you can then make a deal for the rest of the work. And if serious disagreements arise, you and the editor can either devise ways to avoid such snags later or you can call it quits.

Copy-editing

The same approaches should suffice to find a good copy editor. Copy-editing is generally freelance work, even when giant publishers are involved, and generally billed by the hour at rates between $15 and $30. Because it requires a special set of skills, you may want to use a pro (see "The Sale and Its Sequels" for tips on interaction), or it may turn out that you yourself can read critically in this different way.

Copy-editing means making sure that a work is correct and consistent, fact by fact, word by word and even letter by letter. The best way to do that is by following a copy-editing style manual (you should find at least one that's to your taste listed in "Resources") On its simplest level, copy-editing style is what determines whether you use "blond" rather than "blonde," and no matter how complicated its prescriptions get, style's function is simply to ensure consistency in the interest of clarity.

Descriptions as well as spelling ought to be consistent throughout a manuscript (it's distracting or worse, for instance, to present readers with a character who's dainty and petite on page 16 and a strapping Amazon on page 92), and what you choose to stick to matters less than choosing to stick to something.

If you imagine, all the while you're copy-editing, that your manuscript is the work of a slipshod and possibly feeble-minded soul, you'll find it easy to adopt the most effective copy-editing attitude: suspicion. Go slowly and question everything: Is Wales correctly described as a peninsula; could anyone really fly to Rome in daylight all the way; does that say "dilemmma"; is "accurrate" spelled right; doesn't that plural verb refer back to a singular subject; and wouldn't the thought be clearer if it were presented in two sentences rather than one?

Many copy editors work with pencil on paper even when material has been composed on a computer and all good copy editors mark all changes, no matter what their purpose, with standard proofreading symbols (see the relevant "Tools" in "Resources" or use the list you'll find in your dictionary).

Though a thorough job means checking every proper noun, every fact (even in fiction) and every word that looks the slightest bit odd, the most important statements to verify are those that might lead to legal difficulties. If you are writing anything that is derogatory and/or untrue about living people or functioning businesses, you may face a libel suit or a suit for invasion of privacy. Additional legal pitfalls open up when writers quote too extensively from other people's material, or when they print matter that might be adjudged obscene. Moreover, a new legal danger zone has arisen as a result of our culture's increasing emphasis on self-help; a reader with vertigo who falls off a branch and is seriously hurt while following the advice in your "Blueprints for a Tree House" may think about holding you responsible.

This last trouble spot is the hardest to deal with, but common sense may be of some help (don't assume that your readers will realize they should unplug the toaster before they start fiddling with its innards, for example; or that they'll think to consult their doctors before embarking on a strenuous diet or exercise program).

Otherwise, your best course is to get hold of one or more of the legal guides mentioned in "Resources"; after you've read them you'll have a better sense of whether you need to call in a literary property lawyer or take any other measures to protect yourself from legal action. Just remember that even those people who win lawsuits find litigation expensive and aggravating. Consequently, it's sound policy to recast all potentially dangerous material in your manuscript unless doing so involves violating your principles.

When all changes are finally in place and your work is as correct, consistent and clear as you can make it, be sure to claim your own legal rights and the status your work deserves in the eyes of librarians, booksellers and reviewers by getting an ISBN or ISSN (aka International Standard Book Number and International Standard Serial Number), a Library of Congress Catalog Number and a Cataloging in Publication Data block for your book's copyright page, and by registering your copyright. Use "Resources" to get forms and detailed instructions for these—and start early.

Design and Production

Thanks to computers and laser printers, self-publishers can now get books, magazines, newsletters and promotional pieces ready to be printed without going through several costly production steps that used to be mandatory.

But there's a catch. The ability to use a page layout program doesn't make you a designer any more than the ability to use a word-processing program makes you a writer. Then too, you may not be interested in graphic arts or you may not have time to learn them.

Cover design is especially risky for amateurs, both because it requires special skills and because the cover is the single most important sales stimulator your work will ever have. It's a good idea, therefore, to think of your cover as an ad and to hire a professional to create it.

Cover copy, which either you or a copywriter you hire might create, should focus on benefits to the consumer. Since people need a good strong reason to pause in their busy lives and pay attention to something new, you'll want the title, the subtitle, the blurbs, the bio and any other information the cover presents to reveal a payoff, a reason or reasons they'll be glad if they stop long enough to read this.

When you're done with the descriptive copy, add your URL if you have a Web site; a use the relevant entries in "Resources" to choose the category label or labels that will simplify handling for wholesalers and retailers (thus increasing accessibility for readers), and get the machine-readable identifiers that your markets rely on (without a BISAC category, your book may not pop up in the computer databases that potential buyers use; without a Bookland EAN bar code it will be a turnoff for bookstores). Finally, decide on copy for the spine, bearing in mind that this is all most potential book buyers will see—unless and until the copy printed on it is legible and attractive enough to make them pull a volume off the shelves and learn more about it.

Then look for cover designers who'll do justice to your copy (and maybe create a logo for your press as well). Browse through your own shelves and at stores and libraries in your area; select several covers that you like and that have the look and the tone you need, and get in touch with their designers through the publishers' art departments.

Cover designers, who often charge between $1,000 and $3,000, usually suggest a flat fee plus expenses, offer more than one option and build one round of fine-tuning into their fees. If you hire wisely and make your own goals and preferences clear up front, you shouldn't need more than that.

The cover aside, you might be perfectly safe in handling design yourself. If what you're publishing is a book that consists of straight text, consult one or more of the design and production guides listed in "Resources" and absorb the elementary advice that follows. When you've formulated a tentative design/production plan, talk briefly with a few promising printers (see below) and make sure it's a good plan from the printers' point of view. Then proceed to create electronic files and/or camera-ready copy (i.e., pages ready to be printed) using your computer and a good-quality laser printer.

As you work, keep two principles firmly in mind: (a) What written material looks like will have a good deal to do with how it's received; if it's sloppy or jumbled, if the body type is too small to read easily or the headings are so big and black that—no matter what they say—they always seem to be threats, then the power of your carefully assembled words will be vitiated, and (b) beginners do best by keeping things standard and simple.

One standard to adhere to is that of page size. You'll save money by choosing the dimensions that both paper companies and printers are accustomed to. For books and pamphlets, this generally means a page that's roughly 5½ by 8½ inches or 6 by 9 inches; and for magazines, journals and newsletters, one that's 7 by 10 inches or 8½ by 11 inches. Check with printers you're considering to see exactly what sizes their equipment handles most economically.

Having chosen a size for your page, you then must decide on margins (use your own books or magazines as models, and make the bottom margin bigger than the top so your pages won't look droopy) and on how to arrange text, headings and white space effectively (avoid the short lines known as widows at the top of a page, and remember that empty space contributes a good deal to beauty and readability; if you don't leave enough of it or you don't arrange it well, you'll end up with dense, uninviting pages).

For beginners symmetrical and centered layouts pose the fewest problems. For designers at all levels, the fundamental unit of design is the spread—or pair of facing pages—that the reader's eyes take in with a single glance. Again, a printed work that you admire will make a fine model, and you can't go far wrong by sticking with a couple of conventional typefaces and varying type size and degree of boldness to indicate relative importance.

"People unfamiliar with graphic design tend to make the text's type size larger than necessary," Deborah Rust notes. Rust, who designs book covers as well as periodicals and books, recommends using 10- or 11-point type for books and making the leading (i.e., the space from the baseline of one line of type to the baseline of the line below) at least two to four points more than the type size. Type with serifs (look for little handles on the letters) is easier to read than sans serif type, and headings register best when they're upper and lower case—rather than all capital letters—with no punctuation at the end. Heads for parts of a book might work well in 36- or 30-point type with 30- or 24-point chapter heads and 18- or 14-point for the subheads within chapters.

Some self-publishers have artwork that's integral to their projects. Others go in search of pictures to illustrate or decorate text, and sometimes they have trouble finding good ones. If you're in this category, try the public relations departments of large organizations involved with work that's relevant to your subject (what they supply will be free), appropriate governmental agencies (through their PR departments); the picture sources listed in *LMP* and picture sources on the Internet. Be sure to get permission in writing to use copyrighted artwork and photographs of people. Perhaps you can copy the release form your local newspaper uses.

When all your pages are laid out, summon up your copy-editing personality and view each spread with a jaundiced eye. Is all the right front and back matter just where it should be (examine current books to see the proper deployment)? Are the section heads all the right sizes? Are the running heads in place? Did you remember to provide page numbers? Also known as folios, page numbers can be centered below the text or placed in outside corners; they are always odd on right-hand pages and even on the left. (Page 1 is the right-hand page facing the inside front cover in a periodical and the first page of chapter one or the first part-title page in a book; pages that precede a book's page 1 should get Roman rather than Arabic numerals or not be numbered at all.)

Then take a few minutes to consider whether using colored paper or ink would be desirable. Sepia stock might give a family chronicle just the right nostalgic look; dollar-bill green headings might enhance the message of a personal finance pamphlet; a gray screen might set off a book's sidebars to best advantage.

Because color gives you a relatively cheap way to add life and interest to your book or periodical—and because it makes promotional materials far more noticeable—it's worth exploring the options and incurring some extra expense. Ask your printer about incremental costs and check to see that any colors you choose for a cover will reproduce well together in black-and-white since that's how the cover is likely to appear in reviews and promotional materials.

If you're publishing something more complicated than an all-text book, or if getting involved with graphics has no appeal, you can, of course, avoid all this work by hiring a designer to do it for you. See "Resources" for leads to graphic artists, and consider using your cover designer, your printer, a print broker (see "Resources" again) or one of the production companies with a menu of publishing services for you to choose from.

These companies are relatively new on the publishing scene, spawned partly by the expanding small-publisher universe. No matter what they call themselves—co-publisher and book producer are common labels—they differ from the vanity presses in terms of their fees, which are significantly lower; and their attitude toward the writers they work with, whom they view as customers rather than patsys.

Different production companies offer different services. Some menus extend from editing all the way through to fulfillment and marketing, while others are limited to functions relating to printing. Whatever you want to buy, explore the basis for billing (hourly vs. project vs. page), be clear about expectations and rights, and take all the other—and by now usual—precautions.

Printing

Printers star often in publishing horror stories. Poor quality, late delivery, short shipments, mix-ups too peculiar to predict—even large firms run up against such snags. To avoid as many headaches as possible, study the sections on printing in the design and self-publishing manuals listed in "Resources" and profit by other people's current experiences.

If you're working with a freelance designer, ask for recommendations. Pinpoint several books or periodicals whose looks you like and call their art directors or their production managers to find out which printers they use and whether they'd advise you to use them too. And then send a Request for Quotation to at least six firms. Don't hesitate to approach giant firms as well as smaller printers (and, for very modest projects, local copy shops). Technology now enables even huge printers to do short runs (i.e., print relatively few copies) economically and well.

In hopes of having a solid basis for comparison, you should send the same Request for Quotation form to each printer you contact (sample forms are available from books listed in "Resources"). Be prepared, though; some will respond with their own forms, and variations in price may be enormous. Even when all specifics are the same, bids on 3,000 copies of a 256-page, 8½" by 11" paperback that's delivered camera-ready may range from something like $8,000 or $9,000 up to twice that or more.

As Donna Fulner explained at Thomson-Shore, this is partly because different printers have different equipment in-house. For example, some can be competitive for small softcover editions but priced out of the market on hardcovers because they don't have the necessary binding equipment. Fulner advises, therefore, that you ask each printer "the all-encompassing question: 'What is the most economical way to produce my book?'" and that you consider changing certain specifications to keep expenses down. Unit costs will decline, of course, as print orders rise, and those who order thousands of copies rather than hundreds should be able to get as good a deal as an established publisher would.

Factors other than price are important, though, so the lowest bid may not be the one to accept. Before you hire anybody, examine samples and references; look for evidence of pride in the work that the printer does; ask how their equipment meshes with yours; establish clearly what changes will cost at various points and what you'll be paying for proofs and for the cover over-runs you'll need for reviewers and other media people; think about whether you really need a printer nearby so that you can oversee operations; and arrange to get the particulars of your agreement in writing.

Most printers gladly offer suggestions about paper and ink and produce samples on request. Moreover, plenty of leads to information on these subjects appear in "Resources." You won't go wrong, though, if you pick 30-pound newsprint for a newspaper, 50- or 60-pound stock for a book and 80- to 100-pound stock for soft covers, and you're safe in letting your printer choose ink for you.

"Soft covers?" you say. "Don't I want to produce a real (i.e., hardcover) book?" Until recently, the answer would have been a qualified yes; binding some copies (though not all) in hardcover was mandatory, because reviewers were reluctant to write about paperbacks and libraries wouldn't buy them. Today, however, the cover composition of a book is increasingly, and often totally, irrelevant in the minds of both librarians and critics. Your markup on the hardcover may be better but softcovers are favored in most stores and schools, and often preferred by readers who've been conditioned to think of them as bargains. Besides, because they're lighter they're cheaper to mail, which will mean a lot when you start sending out the promotional copies and filling the orders that the next chapter tells you how to generate.

Hard covers or soft, you can rely on a carefully selected printer to handle binding for you. Just remember that when printers talk about "perfect" binding they're not promising flawless work; instead, they're referring to the popular method of gluing pages together inside a square-backed cover.

Material that's ready for final printing should be submitted the way your chosen printer wants it—which might be hard copy produced on a 600 dpi laser printer, film from a service bureau or electronic files in a specified format. Whatever you send, don't forget to keep copies.

Print Runs and Pricing

Even economic simpletons know that what you'll net on sales of your work will be the difference between what you get for it and what you spend for it. What you get, however, will be largely determined by what you spend (on production, promotion and distribution) and by what you charge (too high a price can cut down on sales, but so can a price that's too low, which will signal readers that this product isn't worth much); while what you spend and what you charge may be largely determined by what you think you can get.

Leading publishing firms, which have been thrashing around inside this vicious circle for centuries, have developed a system for determining the major getting and spending variables: cover price and print order. They carefully assess unit costs for assorted quantities (which they estimate fairly accurately) in the light of projected sales (which they estimate with wildly varying degrees of success) and of current dogma about cover-price ranges. Then, when the book in question is one they really want to do, they crunch the numbers until the bottom line looks appealing.

A more rational way to proceed is by focusing first on your market. Identify the people who are most likely to want your work and then try to figure out how many of them there are, how you might reach them, how important your book could be in their lives and how much they'd pay for it (how much do they pay now for comparable sources of information and/or entertainment? what do they tell you they'd pay for your material?).

"My principal advice is: Do not be afraid to charge top dollar," says James J. Brodell. When Brodell self-published *How to Purchase a Newspaper and Succeed* he thought about pricing in terms of "what I would charge someone for a consultancy involving a newspaper property they sought to purchase." Then he decided on $22.50, "not bad," as he points out, "for a slim paperback." Using two trade publications that "reach everyone who is thinking about purchasing a newspaper," Brodell sold 900 copies and got feedback that the book was well worth what it cost.

Whatever price you set on your published work, it must, of course, be high enough to let you (1) recoup your production and marketing expenses, remembering that booksellers and other intermediaries may swallow 70% or more of the amount a reader shells out; (2) cover your other expenses, for such things as rent and labor; and (3) produce at least a modest profit. If readers won't pay that high a price, however, you'd better know it early on; and if they'll pay more, that's surely a useful bit of knowledge.

Similarly, you'll want to be clear on how soon you need to recover your investment (as this chapter indicates, you'll probably be spending a few thousand dollars on creation processes, even if you hire nobody but a printer, and maybe $20,000 or more with lots of hired help). Many self-publishers are content to wait for second and subsequent printings to cover the heavy one-time costs of the first—and of the initial marketing campaign, which is also relatively expensive (see the next chapter). Profit per book sold will rise once you've got things going. But well-heeled or not, what's required of you at this stage is a small but sprightly leap of faith in your project, cushioned by a sensible marketing program that will make it bring money in—as soon as possible, as often as possible and as much as possible.

Managing Sales

IF THE BIG, established publishers—with all their money, personnel and media connections—have a tough time getting most of their books and periodicals off the ground, what chance do self-publishers have? Though you may be surprised to hear it, they have a good one, and it's getting better every day.

Self-publishing writers have three important advantages over writers who are conventionally published when it comes to selling their work.

❖ Self-publishers get closer to their readers. Conventionally published authors are separated from their audiences by two sets of people: the publishing-company staff members, whom the author relies on; and the wholesalers, retailers, librarians and media personnel, whom the staff members rely on.

Working through double ranks of intermediaries is seldom the most efficient way to accomplish anything, and it's especially inefficient when the goal in view is person-to-person communication, as it is for writer and reader. It is a definite plus, therefore, to eliminate intermediaries, particularly if you have the option of getting them to work for you when you want them—which self-publishers now do. (In fact, if their budgets permit, self-publishers can hire someone to assist with or execute almost every selling task they'll confront; see "Resources.")

❖ Self-publishing writers don't have to sell thousands of copies in order to have their work survive in print; editions numbering in the low hundreds make splendid economic sense so long as expenses can be kept down. Often, you can select a size for your first printing that will virtually ensure that you break even on it. And because a small first edition can serve as a trial run, later, and perhaps larger, print orders will be less risky.

❖ Self-publishers can sell through a synergistic mix of markets over a lengthy period of time. Instead of being exhausted and frustrated by promotional activities, they're generally stimulated. Selling makes a nice change of pace from writing (which you can do for only a part of the day anyway), and it's financially and psychologically rewarding besides. Unlike conventionally published authors (who must deal, on their good days, with grueling tour schedules, interviewers who haven't read their books and booksellers who don't have copies in stock), self-publishers can go where they know they're wanted, arrange to coordinate supply and demand and stick with a project long enough to maximize sales.

Long enough, it's crucial to remember, is almost always at least a year, although some projects do take off fast and some need two years or more to be profitable.

Wise self-publishers bear two truths in mind throughout the lengthy marketing process.

1. For publishers of every size, getting people to want a book or periodical is only half the battle. Arranging to give them what they want is the other half. Even bestselling books are sometimes not really "Available at your bookstore," and it's a lot to expect that all interested parties will get to a bookstore anyway. It pays, therefore, to encourage orders whose fulfillment you control. Ideally, all reviews, all other coverage and all promotional materials will include easy and relatively foolproof

ordering information. Your toll-free number and/or your URL would be fine.

2. The people who can make your marketing campaign successful have agendas quite different from yours. Even though selling vast quantities of your work would help them too, they must focus first on pleasing their employers and their customers within the context of institutional and industry constraints. These constraints cause problems, and those problems can easily become your problems. Approaches to media people, retailers and wholesalers should, therefore, take account of their setups and goals.

Because these two truths, and other basics noted below, affect the fate of conventionally published work and self-published work alike, all writers can use the same techniques in reaching out to readers, and self-publishers should read "Why and How to Be Your Own Best Sales Force" (in "The Sale and Its Sequels"). A mental blend of the information from that chapter with the self-publishing framework outlined below should then yield a fine base for marketing campaigns.

Publicizing and Promoting

Some of the first people a self-publisher should become acquainted with are the editors and publishers at small publishing companies (they're reachable through their associations and various "Foot in the Door Resources," and in many cases they're eager to share their experience). And one of the first things a self-publisher will discover in conversations and correspondence with established independents is that they're often self-publishers too (though they may publish other writers' work as well as their own). Which leads to a reminder: Don't flaunt the fact that you and your publisher are one and the same. Certain people—some in powerful positions—still consciously or unconsciously equate self-publishing with vanity publishing, and people in general also often confuse these very different publication processes.

Blurbs

Like a conventional publisher's staff, a self-publisher should begin marketing efforts well in advance of publication. When galleys are ready, or in some cases even before that, it's time to go forth and get blurbs. Endorsements from famous and/or well-credentialed people will encourage the media to pay attention and booksellers to buy.

The famous-name blurb tactic is worth a try if (a) you have access to any well-known personalities whose praise might help attract reviewers' attention, or (b) you think that if particular celebrities read your work they'd find it valuable, perhaps even exciting, and agree to be quoted to that effect. For names and addresses of potential blurb writers, consult *Who's Who in America, Contemporary Authors* and relevant specialized directories. And if you send your work out for advance comments, accompany it with a covering letter that explains why you think it will interest the particular person you're addressing.

Whether or not you succeed in getting quotable comments from superstars, you should request advance quotes from leading lights in your work's field whose credentials will give force to what they say. "These insights will actually help us avoid future wars" may do as much for sales if it's signed by Prof. John Doe, Chairman of the Political Science Department, Such-and-Such U., as it would if it had come from the Secretary of State.

Celebrities and authorities alike are often happy to help a good project along and deterred from providing comments mainly because reading anything and deciding what to say about it takes so much time. You may wish, therefore, to offer a short-cut by phrasing blurbs busy people can adopt or adapt.

Reviews

Once you have copies and comments to distribute, be careful not to mail them out too early or too late. Check lead times for the review organs you hope will cover your work, and arrange to deliver it a month or more before the editors finalize the issue whose pub date coincides with yours. (Be sure to include information on pub date, price, format, page count, distribution and ordering.)

As to where to send review copies, you needn't be reluctant to approach prestigious national media, which sometimes cover new magazines in feature stories and which will be hospitable to any book if it's professionally produced and submitted and if it suits their readers' needs. Publications with short lead times— daily papers, for instance—like their review copies close to pub date and in the form of finished material. It's important to remember, though, that you need to send galleys—not bound books—to trade media such as *Publishers Weekly* and *Kirkus Reviews* and to powerful monthlies and weeklies that pride themselves on running reviews either before a book comes out or right around its publication date. If editors there get a finished book, they're likely to ignore it because they'll assume (a) that pub date is imminent or past and (b) that they therefore don't have the three to four months they need to get a review into print.

"Yeah, yeah," you might think, "major media aren't going to cover my work no matter how I submit it." Well, you'd be wrong. While self-publishers shouldn't count on reviews in mass-market magazines and papers (any more than conventionally published authors should), coverage is common. This is especially true in *Publishers Weekly*. "Much of the best writing in America is going on in the small presses," *PW*'s Forecasts editor, Sybil Steinberg, believes. As long as self-publishers have the distribution its subscribers want, *PW* treats them like everybody else.

"*PW* reviews for the trade and exists to inform booksellers, libraries, movie industry people and others about books that they may wish to order," Steinberg explains. "Since space in the magazine is tight, we must serve our audience by running reviews of books they can acquire though the usual channels. Therefore, we cannot run reviews of books with inadequate distribution or a tiny print run." Does this mean that commercial success is the major criterion? Not according to Steinberg. Her threshold quesion is, "Is it good?"

Self-publishers can target the appropriate reviewers at *PW* and other standard media from mastheads or from the lists in the latest *Literary Market Place* and the latest *Book Publishing Resource Guide*. The non-standard media, though—the media that are particularly right for your particular project—are even more important and, as a rule, far more responsive. Getting them on your review-copy list means combing through *Bacon's* and other media directories, checking relevant groups in the *Encyclopedia of Associations* to find those with periodicals that do reviews, and exploring Web sites that cover books. Periodicals in your geographic area as well as periodicals in your subject area should be included.

By the time it's done, a review-copy list may have a couple of hundred entries or more (if yours has fewer than 50, keep looking). For the smallest or the most peripheral publications, it's fine to send only a descriptive announcement—the small firm's version of the big publisher's catalog—instead of your book itself, with a note saying that review copies are available on request and a reply card that makes requesting them simple.

Since libraries can be a strong and supportive market for independently published books and periodicals (see below), *Library Journal, School Library Journal* (if that's appropriate) and *Booklist* should also get galleys at least three months before pub date, and *Choice* should get a copy of your finished product. It's helpful to send a covering letter that explains why you think library patrons will want your work, and it's wise to follow up with polite reminder letters as necessary.

Reviews can spur sales, of course, but other kinds of coverage do that too, often faster and better. So target feature story writers and editors as well as reviewers at selected periodicals; think about setting up a Web site if you don't already have one; pitch talk shows about appearances and explore additional on-the-air opportunities. A Web site will serve you best when it's crosslinked to many other sites that already attract your audience and that can, thanks to hypertext, put interested individuals immediately in touch with you. You can reach talk-show producers via services like *Radio-TV Interview Reports* or media lists you rent or compile from directories (see "Resources"), and get them interested by focusing on newsworthy, controversial and colorful things you'd say on the air, rather than on the work you're plugging per se. TV home shopping channels may also be hospitable, in which case you can pretty much count on selling thousands of copies directly through them and still more from the echo effect of those sales.

Listings

Booksellers, librarians and members of the reading public rely on a number of standard reference works, and it's to the advantage of all published authors to be mentioned in as many as the nature of their work allows. Make sure you're included in the Bowker directories (especially the *Books in Print* volumes and/or *Ulrich's International Periodicals Directory*), the *Cumulative Book Index* and the Dustbooks skein of small-press information; go through the Bowker, Dustbooks, Gale Research and H.W. Wilson catalogs to identify all publications from these houses that should mention what you're publishing (addresses appear in "The Self-Publishing Option Resources"; see the "Foot in the Door Resources" for additional relevant directories).

Nonfiction on your subject can also serve to publicize your work. As you come across books with appropriate bibliographies, write to acquaint their authors with the work you're doing in the field, and ask them to mention it when they lecture and when they do revised editions.

Sales Channels

Because more marketing opportunities exist for every project than anyone can uncover or pursue, and because new marketing opportunities spring up all the time, advice from experienced small and self-publishers is extremely valuable. Fortunately, it's on tap through associations around the country. Both regional publishers' groups (you'll find lists in *Literary Market Place*) and national organizations such as PMA (for Publishers Marketing Association) let you share a wealth of hard-won knowledge through their newsletters and their meetings, and sometimes also give you access to productive sales channels through their programs.

But other kinds of intermediaries will also give you access. In fact, many make their living by helping small and self-publishers reach readers through retail outlets.

Bookstores

Most writers—and for that matter, most publishers—think "bookstores" when the topic is sales. They're an important sales channel, for sure, but by no means the only one, and for many books by no means the best, especially in the beginning, before word-of-mouth recommendations funnel demand to them.

Self-publishers who sell through bookstores are generally advised to work with distributors, which generally service accounts by sending sales reps to visit with catalogs and book covers in hand, just as the large houses do.

The main advantages a good distributor offers are one-stop shopping and operational expertise. Putting it simply, booksellers are more inclined to buy from a distributor than directly from the many, many imprints the distributor may represent because it's easier. (Also, it's important to note, booksellers are more inclined to pay distributors than individual imprints because business with them is ongoing.)

Not long ago, a self-publisher's chief problem with respect to reaching bookstores was the dearth of distributors. Today, the basic quandaries are whether they're worth the money (most distributors charge between 25% and 32% of what they get from wholesalers and booksellers, who usually buy at discounts of 40%–55%, which means there's not much left for you) and which ones it seems safe to sign with (book distribution is a risky business in which companies all too often go belly up, with damaging—sometimes disastrous—consequences for publishers).

Your best bet, if you're interested in working with a distributor, is to judge each one you consider according to its strengths and what it can do for you.

To narrow the field, ask congenial publishers to tell you what distributors they've found reliable and effective; look to fellow members of PMA and area publishers' groups for recommendations; talk with local booksellers about which distributors they prefer to deal with, and consult "Resources." After you have a list of names and addresses, write to each distributor you're interested in and ask for a catalog and for information about services, fees and timetables. Among other things, you want to know:

❖ Does this distributor have its own sales force, hire independent sales reps or rely exclusively on a catalog?
❖ What size cut does the distributor take?
❖ What territory does the distributor cover and how many accounts does it service? How does it deal with bookstore chains and wholesalers? Can you also hire Quality Books and/or Unique Books (see "Resources") to distribute to libraries? Will this distributor reach nonbook outlets and/or sell to consumers via direct mail? Which accounts does it insist on covering exclusively and which ones can you serve or control yourself?

Every catalog you read should give you a good feel for the kind of book that distributor represents best. Some will strike you as clearly inappropriate (if yours is a how-to title, a catalog in which page after page describes experimental literature is not for you). Once you have a final roster of likely candidates, you should design a proposal to get the distributor interested. Since distributors in general are unenthusiastic about one-book enterprises, this is a hard sell. But not impossible, as long as you answer the basic question in their minds: If we get this onto bookstore shelves, is the publisher going to get it off? To convince them that you will, you'll have to provide specifics about your marketing plans.

Some larger publishers can also function as distributors if the fit is right. But because it's expensive to work through any proactive distribution operation, many self-publishers choose to use wholesalers (who are primarily reactive) instead, or try selling to chains and individual stores themselves. This can work well if demand for a book is already strong or predictable (it's a title about the area this wholesaler serves; it's a travel guide and this store aims for comprehensive travel coverage)

Self-publishers who decide to approach booksellers on their own should begin by settling down in the library to study the *American Book Trade Directory*. A Bowker publication, it lists thousands of bookstores and hundreds of wholesalers in North America by state (or Canadian province) and then by city and specialty, and it has a list of bookstore chain headquarters too.

Step two is compiling your own list of booksellers and wholesalers in your area and/or in the locations or with the specialties appropriate for your book. And step three is getting in touch with the buyers at every place on that list (the manager or owner, whose name you'll usually find in the directory, can steer you to the proper person in a large and departmentalized operation).

Try to schedule a talk with each buyer—over the phone or, if possible, face-to-face—when things aren't too busy, and be prepared to explain why your book will sell once it's in stock. Since booksellers rely on publishers to promote, you'll make more headway if you can talk about the publicity you'll be getting locally, the public speaking you'll be doing in the region and the in-store events you could present that will draw a crowd.

Often it makes sense to suggest a program or display that will highlight several books; for example, you might select a dozen automotive titles (including yours on preventing car accidents), arrange them in the bookstore window with illustrative charts and models and demonstrate prevention techniques at the store one day from 4 to 6 P.M.; or you might make common cause with another author who disagrees with your book's position on mandatory retirement, create a window display featuring both books and placards revealing the crux of the argument and invite the public to an open debate on the issue inside the store.

Since one order from a large chain or wholesaler can make your book widely available throughout the country, you'll want to contact the giants (like Ingram and Baker & Taylor, among wholesalers, and Barnes & Noble and Borders, among the chains) as well as selected independent booksellers, smaller chains and appropriate local, regional or specialized wholesalers.

Be prepared for all of them to start by saying you must use a distributor or some other vendor they deal with all the time (it's easier for them, remember), and if you end up selling to wholesalers and retailers on your own, get payment in advance or resign yourself to giving away a lot of copies for nothing. Also try as hard as you can to sell on a nonreturnable basis. This will mean offering a bigger discount than normal—perhaps over 50 percent—but it's sound practice, because unless store managers have paid for your book, they'll have little, if any, incentive to sell it.

Most sales forces are still stuck to fully returnable policies for most titles on the dubious—and incorrect—grounds that the industry has to do business this way. But that doesn't necessarily mean you have to get hamstrung by the full-right-of-return rule too.

Better Stores and Other Nontraditional Outlets

Although book distributors are apt to insist on exclusive rights to sell to bookstores, self-publishers of both books and periodicals can do plenty of selling themselves to nonbook stores of all kinds. In fact, in imaginative marketing to nonbook outlets, small and self-publishers have taken a definite lead over big firms. What began as a necessity (because there was no effective way for little houses to get what they published into bookstores) has thus become an asset (because bookstores are such bad places to launch anything but bestsellers). Today, health food stores, craft shops, hardware stores, warehouse clubs and variety stores are all accustomed to selling written work along with their other merchandise.

Some books succeed handsomely in outlets like these without ever penetrating the bookstore market, and some succeed first in such "nontraditional" or "special sales" channels and then, once word of mouth has begun to build, they find favor with book-sellers. Whatever the pattern, unconventional approaches to marketing serve self-publishers well.

Take the first step in exploring special sales opportunities for your work by listing the kinds of nonbookstore retail outlets your readers are likely to frequent. Next, prepare a selling speech, explaining how your book will help selected retailers move their basic (nonbook) stock and try the speech out on the managers of appropriate stores nearby. If one or more of them will take some books on consignment and customers buy those books, you can set your sights on national distribution.

Let's say, for example, that the local sporting goods store proves a fine outlet for your *Backpacking With Kids* guide. They're making money on each copy they sell and they're making more money on backpacks, whose sales are up 30%. Ask the manager which distributors service the store, contact those distributors, explain your experience with the Acme Sports Center in Home-town, Kansas, and declare that other sporting goods stores would profit by stocking your book too. Then offer to sell them as many copies as they want at a large discount—you may have to go well over 50 percent—nonreturnable.

Next, make a list of mail-order catalogs that might offer your book in their pages ("Resources" will lead you to likely candi-dates), and send for copies of the ones that sound promising to see if they carry books like yours and/or other products that would appeal to your readership. Mail-order catalogs of all kinds are increasingly apt to include books; so far, how-to, novelty, gift and educational titles have been particularly successful.

Third, look into premium sale possibilities. The hardest kind of special sale to make, a premium sale is also often the most lucrative kind. Premiums—in the form of pens, mugs and a wide variety of other goods besides books—are items businesses offer to attract new customers and to prompt current buyers to buy more. Since a premium sale may involve tens or even hundreds of thousands of copies—and dollars—it's worth trying for if you can make a connection between your book and a product or service. One self-publisher persuaded a company that makes fondue pots to package a copy of her fondue cookbook with each order. Perhaps you can arrange for a moving company to buy your moving manual in bulk for its clients, or work a deal with a magazine whose subscribers might renew more readily if they got your book free when they signed on for another year.

To spot companies that favor premium ploys, examine your junk mail and keep your eyes peeled when you shop. And when you have a prospect list, see the *Thomas Register of American Manufacturers* (listed in "Money Resources"); you'll find company names and addresses there.

Because the list of good nontraditional sales channels for your work can be very long indeed, it pays to exercise your imagination. In the first few months after publication, Dale Smith sold *What the Parrot Told Alice*—a young people's novel that illuminates today's key environmental issues—through a review in *Bird Talk* (which included telephone ordering information and produced hundreds of sales), through attendance at conventions (including the American Federation of Aviculture, whose past president bought one copy there and 12 copies later, at which point he offered to use his connections to facilitate a premium sale), through pet shops (having found a distributor who sells them bird books) and through the Chinaberry catalog (which, incidentally, got him a nibble from a movie producer).

Direct Routes to Readers

Although conventional publishing houses often classify mail-order campaigns and other direct approaches to readers as "special sales," they shouldn't be special for you. Instead, they should form the core of your sales campaign.

Selling to readers is, after all, the purpose and the promise of all publishing. Every writer's efforts are directed, in the final analysis, to reaching them.

Self-publishers have four primary ways to get directly in touch with the people they want as readers—via the mail, advertising, the Internet and personal appearances. In planning each approach, be sure to include provisions for feedback—in the form of orders, with payment, as well as in the form of verbal give-and-take—and when you begin to get results, keep a record of the names and addresses of everyone who places an order from any source. In the event that you publish another book or periodical or issue a revised edition, you'll have a powerful, free mailing list at your fingertips.

Direct Mail

A popular sales channel for small publishers, direct mail offers the best way to appeal, one-to-one, to groups of people around the country who are likely to want your work and who might not ordinarily hear about it or be able to get hold of it.

Getting a direct-mail package together can be an elaborate and expensive proposition (and it is in the hands of most sizable houses), but a self-publisher can keep costs down by simply preparing a description of the benefits a book or periodical provides, a collection of enthusiastic (and preferably prestigious) comments and a tear-off order blank with a toll-free number and/or an Internet address for placing orders easily. When a table of contents says best what the work is like, it might accompany the description, and the author's relevant experience and credentials should be mentioned as well. Whatever its specific content, however, mail-order copy must always answer the question potential readers will be asking themselves: What's in it for me?

You may want to use slightly different approaches to reach slightly different segments of your public, but whether you mail one letter or a variety, choosing wisely where to send them is essential. As you'll discover when you explore mailing lists, every imaginable interest is represented. You can rent a list of people who've bought inflatable chairs as easily as you can rent one of full professors of economics (direct mail is, you should know, a favorite way of reaching academics). Prices start at about $50 for 1,000 names, and the more narrowly you can define your market the better your chances will be of getting your money's worth.

If your work focuses on a very precise subject—like directing a summer camp, say—and you know there's an association of camp directors, you can go straight to that group and ask for the use of their membership roll (you may even get the list free if you're on it yourself).

In the event that neither your background nor your subject matter leads you directly to ideal lists, you should consult "Tools" in "Resources"; see especially *LMP, Book Publishing Resource Guide* and Standard Rate and Data Service.

Before renting a mailing list, ask the broker what response rate other people have gotten with it (2 percent is considered very good), and solicit the broker's advice on your project. Then, using common sense mixed with courage, you'll have to decide for yourself whether a mailing will be cost-effective. Remember, expenses will include preparation of copy and purchase of paper, envelopes and postage—unless you can persuade a group whose list you're using to stuff your piece in with its regular mailing (in which case they'll not only foot the postage bill but also give you an influential, if implicit, endorsement). In addition, you may need to budget money for return envelopes (possibly also with postage). And of course there are those list rental fees.

Starting with a small test mailing to just part of a list will let you keep some of these costs down. Even the pros test before they "roll out" with a major direct mail campaign because it's all but impossible to tell in advance what the response will be. If your test pulls well, mail to more of that list and test others. If it doesn't, keep testing or refocus on alternative marketing channels.

Direct-Response Advertising

Nobody in the industry has any hard knowledge as to whether ads without ordering information sell books. Given the inadequacy of most publishers' distribution efforts, however, it seems unlikely that they do, so use ads *with* order information— a coupon for sales by mail, your URL or the address of an online bookstore and a toll-free number for telephone sales (self-publishers who don't have toll-free numbers sometimes link up with local booksellers who do and who'd be happy to fill telephone orders). That way, it'll be easy for readers to buy and for you to measure the success of your advertising.

There's no better place to run a direct response ad than in a periodical that's printing a review or an excerpt of your work. Logical advertising outlets also include magazines, newsletters and newspapers that share your area of interest. *National Wildlife*, for example, might provide a good environment for an ad about a photographic essay on a prairie-dog town; while the *Vassar Quarterly* could pull orders for a history of higher education for women.

Ask the advertising departments of local newspapers, magazines and radio stations where you want to run an ad for advice on how to prepare copy (it's in their interest that your ad succeed, so don't be shy). Or hire an agency. And if you plan to advertise in more than one place, key each order form (on the coupon in the *Hometown Gazette*, for instance, instruct people to address their orders to Dept. HG, and use Dept. AW as part of the address cited on the coupon in *Airways*); that way, when only three orders come in on the HG blank but you get 150 marked AW, you can keep running *Airways* ads until the response tapers off, and pull out of your local paper.

Classified ads, which are cheap, may work for some books and periodicals. Per inquiry ads are relatively inexpensive too; since you pay for space for a PI ad by splitting your revenues from it with the periodical that runs it, your only up-front costs are for production. And exchange ads are free. Magazines often swap advertising, so if you're putting one out you ought to see what kind of a deal you can arrange with kindred publishing spirits. How much room you'll be accorded in someone else's periodical will depend upon relative circulation figures and/or upon good will.

The Internet

When talk turns to sales and publicity on the Internet, publishers agree: It's too soon to tell. Nobody knows. That's uncharted territory. But some observations based on current experience figure to hold up, among them:

❖ The Internet is likely to do more for self-publishers and authors published by small, specialized houses than for most authors without sites of their own who are published by the giant firms. If you had a book coming from a large trade publishing house that didn't figure to be a bestseller (most of their books aren't) and if the house's Web site featured bigbooks and celebrity authors (most of them do), your work would be all-but-invisible rest-of-the-list in this context as in others. By contrast, Web sites for niche publishers, including self-publishers, feature information, advice and interaction on a particular subject, just the sort of things that surfers value. And they feature easy ordering information besides.

❖ Basic questions about using the Web—should I have my own site and if so who should create it and host it and what should happen there?—need up-to-date answers, which are most accessible on the Net and through leads supplied there.

❖ As with other media, self-publishers can take advantage of a variety of opportunities online. Think, at a minimum, in terms of cross-linking with as many related sites as possible, hosting a chat group, participating on bulletin boards and moderating a list, as well as informing, advising and conversing with people who visit a site you've set up. When these people are or become your readers, they can give you valuable critiques, powerful word-of-mouth recommendations and insights into your marketing strengths.

❖ Bestsellers can be born here. *Drums of Autumn* by Diana Gabaldon, for instance, became the "first surprise blockbuster hit of 1997," in the words of the *Wall Street Journal*, "thanks in large part to the author's cultlike following on the World Wide Web." Gabaldon, who posted portions of her developing novel on her Web page for two years, reportedly uses the Net to answer "a stream of questions from fans" and to offer free inscribed bookplate stickers and maps relating to her book as well as autographed copies for sale.

Personal Appearances

Each group you can reach electronically, by mail and through advertising you can probably also reach in person, with exciting results. Refer back to "Why and How to Be Your Own Best Sales Force," and please remember that schools are a fine place to meet young readers (and their teachers) and that almost every one of this country's thousands of organizations has scheduled meetings and fund-raisers. Check the *Encyclopedia of Associations* and selected Web sites to see what's coming up in your area or might be worth traveling to.

But neither events nor the examples in this book exhaust the avenues for selling a book in person, so strive for impromptu, innovative strategies. "Sometimes, when I don't have anything pressing to do," says Russell M. Genet, a self-publisher who's an authority on astronomy, "I'll go through the journals in my field and write individual authors short notes on their papers (probably the only responses they ever get) and also pop in flyers for my books. I get about a 90 percent order rate from this."

With drive and ingenuity, maybe you can even top that.

Libraries

Have you sent review copies to the magazines librarians trust? Have you visited the Midwest Book Review Web site and taken advantage of its links? Have you told librarians in your area about what you've published and about your skill and availability as a reader or a speaker? If you got a good review in one of the library journals, have you reprinted it on a postcard and sent it to librarians around the country? Have you explored using Quality Books and Unique Books to handle distribution to libraries for you?

If so, then take one additional step. As orders come in, either directly from librarians or via a wholesaler like Baker & Taylor, fill them promptly and make your paperwork exemplary. Many small publishers already have excellent relationships with libraries, and you'll benefit by joining their ranks.

More Markets

When marketing tasks begin to seem never-ending, self-publishers have two options: Keep plugging, which is undoubtedly the key to success, or pass the project on to a bigger publisher, which can result either in so many more sales that everyone will exult or in so many fewer sales that the new publisher will kill the project.

Connie Evers provides encouragement to those who favor Option #1. Evers, an award-winning registered dietitian, believes strongly in niche marketing. She sells her book *How to Teach*

Nutrition to Kids to nutritionists, teachers, PTA members, cooperative extension agents and state departments of education. Other sales channels include catalogs and a Web site.

Surfing one day, Evers visited a Simmons College site that described a nutrition project involving Massachusetts educators and school nurses. "I sent them info on my book and they ordered a single copy," Evers recalls; months later a professor called to order copies for all the teachers in their grant. While this sale was gestating, Evers was working—as she constantly does—to generate others. She had "significant success," for instance, with a mailing to food editors a year after pub date. "Although many had received my basic, boring release when the book came out," she reports, "I decided to re-angle the piece to correspond to current events. The new release has the feel of a news story," with "A Giant Step for School Nutrition" as its headline and a reportorial lead: "Along with new notebooks, teachers, and back-to-school clothes, kids throughout the U.S. will also face a 'new and improved' lunch period," it announces, going on to explain that this is because of "the biggest program overhaul in 50 years," a new requirement by the United States Department of Agriculture that participants in the National School Lunch and Breakfast Program serve "healthful meals in line with the Dietary Guidelines for Americans." Although the fact-packed release mentioned the book almost by-the-way, coverage ensued—in *Child* magazine, the *Richmond Times-Dispatch,* the *Miami Herald,* the Milwaukee *Journal Sentinel, The Orange County Register* and *The Kansas City Star,* which did a major story—and sales increased.

Those interested in Option #2, shedding load, also have inspiring examples to follow, including the self-published books that have snagged the prize big houses value most—space on the national bestseller lists. But books below the stratosphere of *The Celestine Prophecy, Mutant Message Down Under* and *The Christmas Box* are also attractive to the large houses. In fact, big firms try hard to acquire self-published titles with impressive sales in nontraditional and/or trade channels and sometimes offer rewards for reps who discover them.

Like well-established publishers, well-established book clubs are receptive to submissions from self-publishers. Be bold, therefore, and try your book on any clubs listed in *Literary Market Place* and *Book Publishing Resource Guide* that seem right for it, either at the manuscript stage or after you can demonstrate audience enthusiasm or both.

If you think you have a book that a bigger publisher, a book club, a foreign publisher, an audiotape producer or anybody else ought to buy rights to, but you find that potential buyers are psychologically unprepared to deal with an author, try getting an agent to represent you. And in any case, consider hiring a literary property lawyer to advise you on contract provisions and prepare to ride herd on payments (see "Getting What's Coming to You"). Friendly small publishers may be willing to recommend agents and lawyers who'll help with sub rights sales. The "Money" chapter called "Spin-offs" will tell you more about how to generate them.

Money

Finding Funding

BEFORE YOU CAN begin a major piece of writing you'll need to know how you're to support yourself while you work on it. If you're otherwise employed and writing part-time, you may not have a problem. If you're rich, there's no problem, of course. And if your publisher has provided an enormous advance, it may tide you over until you're ready to launch your next project. But if you're among the vast majority of writers, you'll have to scramble to make ends meet.

To supplement whatever income you derive directly from writing, tap any or all of the money sources outlined below.

Grants

Browsing through the directories that list grants available to struggling writers should prove heartening, both because you'll see how many people and groups are trying to help, and because you'll find at least one program, and probably more, for which you're eligible. Even unknown authors have grants earmarked especially for them; for instance, Delacorte Press (a part of the Bertelsmann empire) gives a prize to a first young adult novel and PEN's Ernest Hemingway Foundation Award goes to writers having first books of fiction published.

You can find out who's giving what by sending for *Grants and Awards Available to American Writers*, which is put out by the PEN American Center branch of the international writers group, and by checking books listed in "Resources." In addition, read *Poets & Writers Magazine* for announcements of new awards (and reminders about deadline dates for old ones); look at prefaces and acknowledgments sections of books in your field to see whether one foundation or another is especially receptive to your kind of project; contact your state council for the arts to ask for information about financial aid; check phone books of cities nearby for local and regional foundations, and visit the National Endowment for the Arts and the National Endowment for the Humanities Web sites (see "Resources") to find out what they have to offer.

As a rule, grants are designed either to support a writer's work in general—to advance the writer's "career" is the usual language—or to fund a particular project. Those who apply for career-advancement money are generally judged on the basis of samples of their strongest work. Barry Targan, whose fiction was selected for Martha Foley's prestigious anthology *Best American Short Stories* for three years running, said of a National Endowment for the Arts grant that he won: "The application form itself is quite simple and straightforward, and even though it asks what you will use the grant for (you can only honestly answer— to continue to write, for support while you do write), still I think what matters most is the feeling the judges have for the samples of writing that you submit. In my own case, the fact that I'd won the Iowa School of Letters Award for Short Fiction may have helped, but many other people who received grants have published very little."

Those who want grants for particular projects have to satisfy more complicated requirements. In addition to filling out application forms, they will probably be asked to write project descriptions, estimate the budgets necessary for their execution and solicit letters of recommendation. All this takes a good deal of time, but it's worth doing well since you're shooting for thousands of dollars.

To discover what the right approach is for any specific grant, try talking with people who've won it. The roster of previous winners that generally comes along with each application form may seem intimidatingly star-studded at first, but because many of the famous names on it got their grants while they were still unknown, they should be willing to empathize with you now. So explore the winners list for clues about what level of achievement is expected and what types of projects have been funded in the past, and then muster the courage to call a couple of successful grant-getters and ask for advice. Tell them about your proposal and admit it if this is your first foray into the grants game.

Susan Jacoby—who got several grants, including an Alicia Patterson Foundation fellowship, to help finance her book about new immigrants—found this to be a productive practice, as do other writers who've tried it. "Talking with someone who's recently won a grant from the foundation you're applying to gives you an insider's edge," Jacoby explained. "Each foundation has its own style: some like polysyllabic, academic presentations; others prefer it straight and simple. What's desirable and what's not changes as the composition of the selection board changes, so it's important that you talk with someone who won recently."

To go with whatever firsthand advice you can get, here are some general rules of grant-seeking:

❖ Incorporate selected elements of the effective book proposal (as described in "Procedures") in your project description. Emphasize the credentials and expertise you bring to your work. Explain why your project is worth undertaking and what its significance is in relation to other work in the field. If you've received an advance from a publisher, mention it, and say why you need additional funding.

❖ Once you've drafted a proposal you're satisfied with, circulate it among friends for suggestions; include at least one writer who has already won a grant, if you can.

❖ Make up a professional-looking budget. This means estimating your living expenses as accurately as possible, and in general using hard figures whenever you can, instead of guessing.

❖ Contact the leading authorities in your field for letters of recommendation, and try to set up meetings with them individually. If you can't arrange meetings, write and describe your project; explain what you've accomplished thus far; and ask each authority if they'd be willing to recommend you for the grants you need. When you make it clear that your work will constitute a real contribution to their field, they'll probably agree to support your application.

In follow-up correspondence with sponsors who seem truly interested in your work, you might ask whether they can suggest any other foundations you ought to try. And you should be sure, of course, to thank every sponsor and to apprise them of the outcome of your efforts. Whatever grants you win—or fail to win—this time around, you may need their help again.

❖ Don't assume that you're limited to holding one grant at a time. Getting money from X rarely precludes a writer from applying for more from Y and Z.

❖ If there's anything on the application form that you don't understand, call and ask for clarifications and explanations.

Prizes

Prize money, often awarded after a book is published, may be big enough to amortize over lean times to come. Consider, for example, the $50,000 Kingsley Tufts Award for the most worthy book of poetry published the preceding year and the $75,000 Lannan Literary Awards for poetry, fiction and nonfiction. Prizes also help writers earn more from current books because the credential impresses potential readers and the money can be used partly for marketing; in fact, half the $30,000 Kiriyama Pacific Rim Book Prize goes to the winning book's publisher, which has to spend it on publicity and promotion. And of course prizes can boost future revenues by impressing editors, who then offer better terms.

So explore the PEN directory and other resources mentioned above to find whatever prizes you might win.

Writers Colonies

Scarcely a writer alive hasn't felt at one point or another that a little peace and quiet was the key to getting some real work done. At writers colonies scattered throughout the United States, peace and quiet are abundantly available, along with free room and board in most cases (at some colonies writers are asked to contribute by buying their own groceries and preparing their own meals).

Colonies come in a wide variety of styles, from Yaddo, outside Saratoga Springs, New York (with its mansion, woodland trails, tennis courts and swimming pool) to The MacDowell Colony in Peterborough, NH (where studios have electricity and heat but no telephones, "no one may visit a studio without invitation" and "messages are delivered in emergencies") and The Wurlitzer in Taos, New Mexico (where residents get adobe houses and there aren't any rules about anything).

Some colonies actively encourage beginners to apply but all say that writers with talent—published or not—will be welcomed, and most accept both fiction and nonfiction writers on the basis of samples of their work. See this section's "Resources" for help in figuring out where you might best apply.

For some writers, time in a colony is not just productive; it's almost magical. Louise Smith used recent stays to finish a story that won the Antietam Review Prize, polish a story that the *Virginia Review* took and write 20-odd chapters of a memoir, among other things, but she values colony life also because "You get to step across a boundary and exist in another world," a world composed almost entirely of artists. "They may be picky," she says, "but they're with you and you feel it. What misses really misses and what succeeds really succeeds. An audience like that makes you keener and more critical about your own work."

For others, though, there's little magic and even productivity is a problem. Having your own cabin in the woods will free you from the distractions of kids at home, phones in the office and other assorted turmoil, but it won't necessarily activate your muse. As one writer who has stayed at a number of colonies put it: "You don't get inspiration by looking at the trees." Nor is the problem of self-discipline any easier to handle at a colony than it is at home, although some writers do find that living in a community composed exclusively of artists shames and/or encourages them to buckle down. Those who get the most from colony life usually arrive with a specific goal in mind: five poems; the first three chapters; a rough draft. The goals you set for yourself will naturally depend in part on how long you plan to stay (some colonies ask that you spend no less than a month on the premises, while others have flexible residence requirements), but even if you don't have time to get a great deal of writing done, you may find colony conditions just right for making valuable discoveries, as Anne Grant, a documentary writer and director, did when she stayed at the Millay Colony for the Arts in Austerlitz, New York, for 10 days to work on her study *Elizabeth Cady Stanton's Quarrel with God*.

"I had imagined I could finish my book," she said, looking back on the experience, "but I completed only twenty pages and a lengthy outline. I accomplished something else, though. For the first time in my adult life, I discovered my natural rhythms of waking, eating and sleeping, my flow of energy and thought when I am not interrupted. At home, whenever I failed to accomplish as much as I had planned, I would reproach myself and resent my family. At the Millay Colony, I found that even under the best conditions it takes time to develop an idea and even more time to create art."

With colonies as with grants, don't be dismayed if at first you don't succeed. Understandably, the waiting lists at most retreats are long, so you may very well have to try and try again.

Economic Ingenuity

Let's say you desperately need to get away right now in order to pull your manuscript into shape, and there's no room to be had at any of the colonies you applied to. What do you do? Well, you could decide that the world's an unfair place, shelve the manuscript, and sulk; or you could choose to abandon dependence on other people's largesse and substitute reliance on your own wits. One good way to keep yourself in funds, after all, is to devise clever ways to avoid giving up those you've got.

Do some friends of yours have second homes that they're not using and that they might allow you to live in for a couple of weeks if you volunteered to paint the kitchen during your stay? Can you afford to have a neighborhood teenager sit for your preschoolers between three and six o'clock while you work in the empty apartment of a friend who's at her office?

Most writers become experts at cash-conserving improvisations of this sort out of sheer necessity. But devising money-saving moves can be pleasurable as well as practical if you enjoy the idea of outwitting such capitalist evils as inflation and planned obsolescence by reviving secondhand clothing and furniture, for instance, or by using a barter system; maybe the electrician will fix your stove for nothing if you teach his kid grammar.

Or maybe you'd like to save money by forming or joining a publishing co-op, where members share all the work the publication process entails. The Fiction Collective in New York and Alice James Books in New England provide excellent models to follow, and their histories show that the benefits aren't just economic. "Alice James poets have achieved substantial personal empowerment," Marie Harris wrote recently in *Poets & Writers Magazine*. "We have wandered off to found new presses and liter-

ary magazines . . . been accorded teaching jobs, academic promotions, tenure. We have brought our expertise to bear in the
world of commerce. Those of us who now deal with New York
publishing houses participate in the production and marketing
of our books in ways we have earned and which we might otherwise never have dared to insist upon."

One other thing all writers can do to improve their economic
situation is keep tax bills down. Get hold of the IRS pamphlets
for self-employed workers (your local office will have a list);
remember that you're personally responsible for making Social
Security payments, and put yourself in a favorable position at
tax time by keeping an expenses diary. Simply carry a pocket
calendar with you and record any money you spend on work-
related matters (including transportation to and from editors'
offices, postage and supplies, copying costs, phone calls, magazine subscriptions necessary for your project, professional membership dues and the like). Keep all receipts; mark clearly what
each one is for, unless it's self-evident; and in dealing with businesses that don't normally issue them, bring your own form (you
can buy a pack at any stationery store) and get it signed. Faith-
fully recording your expenses should help you take full advantage of applicable tax deductions and keep the costs of tax
preparation down.

Some writers organizations help their members save money
by offering informational seminars, charter flights, group insurance plans and the like. And they may also provide an incidental
financial benefit: Membership in a major writers group indicates
to the IRS that you are indeed a professional writer and therefore
entitled to all the tax breaks attendant on that occupation.

Wages

For many men and women, writing is a sometime thing, an avo-
cation they pursue to further their goals in business or the professions. But even people whose main ambition is to write can

hold down full-time nonwriting jobs that give them economic security along with other benefits.

Look at the poet Dana Gioia, for example. The author of *Can Poetry Matter? Essays on Poetry and American Culture*, which made *Publishers Weekly*'s Fifty Best Books list the year it came out, Gioia has been profiled in *Esquire*, published in *The New Yorker* and *The Hudson Review*, and employed by General Foods. Managing new business development for a major corporation didn't just let him put bread on the table and a roof over his head, he found. It also opened up new perspectives by immersing him in workaday concerns and large-scale business decisions, and it boosted his confidence besides. "Nothing, I assume, not even the Nobel Prize, would keep a real writer from feeling some anxiety about his work," Gioia has observed, "but making some visible progress in a career does help give a writer, especially a beginning writer, a base of security to work from." Writers who work for software manufacturers, life insurance companies, stockbrokers and law firms report similar benefits.

Prepublication Sales

Riffle through the pages of the glossy magazines and you'll notice before long that products featured in the editorial departments tend to come from the very same companies that fill the advertising columns. Almost all magazines depend on advertising revenues for economic viability, although some are more fussy than others about the nature of the links between ads and editorial attention, and a few manage to run plenty of ads that relate to articles without relinquishing control over content in any way.

A similar system exists to get funding for books and pamphlets from businesses, charitable organizations or entities of any other sort that would benefit from a published work. What the funder gets out of the deal is publicity, promotion and perhaps additional revenue. What the writer gets is a sponsor, except that instead of the Medicis or the Ford Foundation, this time it's a camera company for your book of photographs of cats, a car-rental company for your blue highways atlas of America or a paint store chain for your guide to redecorating on a tight budget.

Established book publishers often make tie-in deals of this sort, but they're not well known among writers, most of whom discover prepublication funding by accident, if at all, the way Ann Reed and Marilyn Pfaltz did as they were making the rounds of New York houses with their cookbook, *Your Secret Servant.*

When a friendly editor who didn't want the book for her list suggested that it might make a good premium, Reed and Pfaltz asked her what she meant by that, and then switched targets. Instead of offering their manuscript to publishing houses, they began offering it to advertising agencies, and fairly soon they found one that wanted to use it as an incentive to draw new accounts to a banking client's offices. The bank paid enough for its copies of *Your Secret Servant* so that the authors could print and bind 5,000 extra books for their own purposes. With the finished work in hand, selling publishers was simpler. Scribner's bought the 5,000 copies and kept the book in print for a number of years.

To find the organizations that might subsidize you, figure out what institutional aims your work might serve (maybe a company that manufactures luggage would like to fund your anthology of expeditions and distribute the book as its Christmas gift this year, for instance; or maybe the NHL would underwrite your history of hockey). Then contact potential sponsors themselves, or match companies with appropriate books by using the leads you'll find in "Money Resources."

Like all forms of patronage, sponsorship may raise moral issues. But if you're honest with yourself, your sponsor and your public, there's nothing to stop you from having clean hands, a pure heart and a healthy bank balance all at the same time.

Spin-offs

THE SINGLE BEST key to financial success in writing is recycling. Both the materials and the skills that go into creating a piece of written work can be reused in a great variety of profitable ways, and while those who've written books have the widest range of recycling options, everyone who has written anything should be able to make it do at least double duty for pay. Or triple. Or more.

Check any contracts you've signed, though, before you start the recycling processes to see which rights you control and which you'll need to clear.

Transforming the Whole

To switch from worrying about how to keep the wolf from the door to worrying about whether to be bullish or bearish with your surplus funds, get your story made into a successful movie or television program. TV and movie people prefer to buy best-sellers, of course, because they want presold audiences for their products, but they also transform little-known books for large and small screens.

Movie deals are largely a matter of luck. An aggressive and talented agent who specializes in dramatic properties can be a great asset (you might start a data bank, like the one outlined for editors and literary agents in "Openings," in order to figure out which Hollywood agents would be good for, and receptive to, what you've written). The affection approach (see "Openings" again) may be worth trying with a producer, a director or an actor whose work strikes you as similar in significant ways to your own. And who you know can be crucial, as the saga of *Dances with Wolves* demonstrates. Its author, Michael Blake, described the story to Jim Wilson and Kevin Costner, his friends in the film business, back in the mid-'80s. Costner urged him to get it published as a book first. Endorsing that strategy, Wilson persuaded a literary agent to represent it. After a string of turn-downs and a period of severe poverty, Blake got a buyer. Fawcett issued his book as a paperback original in 1988. That deal didn't solve Blake's poverty problem—the advance was $6,500—but then, sure enough, Costner and Wilson made the story into a phenomenally successful movie, with Blake's screenplay. The film then spawned a tie-in title (from Newmarket Press) that outsold every previous illustrated movie book.

Now, you probably don't know Kevin Costner personally. But you don't have to. The lesson here is that you should look for personal connections in the film world and work them hard. Is your cousin's sister-in-law an editor at Paramount? Ask him to ask her to call your book to the attention of a producer or two. It probably won't lead to big bucks and glitzy awards. But it might.

In case it does, you'll want to brace yourself. Writers often recoil from the Hollywood versions of their work. Subplots get lost or added; ideas vanish or mutate. As the director and screenwriter Paul Schrader once explained, in adapting a book for the screen, you "crack" it—i.e., "you reach into it and pull out the movie . . . . You can't crack a book by telescoping or condensing it. You have to decide what story you're going to tell, and what the theme is . . . . When you go from book to movie, you excise everything that doesn't adhere to the movie form, and you're left with a handful of scenes."

Writing a screenplay is "like composing an elephantine, one-hundred-twenty-page haiku," Richard Rhodes observes in his splendid book *How to Write*. Rhodes, who has tried it, says he found the pay good but "the work is lousy. If you've been independent, work for hire is a shock. Anyone up the hierarchy, including a twenty-two-year-old snot fresh out of Princeton who happens to gofer your producer, is allowed to tell you how to fix your first or second or third or infinituple draft. 'I know! Let's make the main character a serial killer!' 'I know! Let's make the love interest a frog!' If you've invested any heart at all in your screenplay," Rhodes concludes, "you'll find it breaking."

With other transformations, surprises should be fewer, luck will play a smaller part and you can depend upon energy and intelligence to help you toward goals you'll be glad you reached. Among the many possibilities worth exploring, several stand out. For example:

Export

Some books travel well, and if you think hard about what sorts of people in which foreign countries would respond to what you've written, perhaps yours will be one of them. To get a sense of what's currently selling abroad, read *Publishers Weekly's* articles on publishing overseas, visit the Publishers Marketing Association's Virtual Rights Fair on the Web, and then consult your publisher or your agent or, if you've self-published, consider hiring a foreign rights agent listed in *LMP* about effecting foreign sales.

Great Britain, of course, provides a promising market for many American titles because language is no barrier, but scientific and even semiscientific writing may draw English-speaking audiences around the world, and so might essentially visual works for both children and adults and nonfiction books of various sorts, as long as they're written by experts and the content doesn't focus relentlessly on the author's homeland or include too much local language.

Foreign publishers may buy copies of the American book, or buy rights to publish an edition of their own.

Special Editions

"Proprietary publishing," which involves creating a book or an edition of a book for one big buyer, is attractive both because of the numbers (figure 15,000 copies and up, though the profit per unit is low) and because of the terms (no returns allowed). Good candidates are successful single titles in new formats (Candlewick produced a board book edition of *Guess How Much I Love You* exclusively for the Target outlet chain) and related titles bunched together (like the HarperCollins Mrs. Piggle-Wiggle collection).

Browse in bookstores to spot current omnibus offerings and in other retail outlets for specially imprinted books. Maybe you'll find examples you can follow.

Special editions of a different sort consist of a book and a related product, which might be a tape or a disk or even more print on paper, such as a teacher's guide. Again, study current offerings for insights into what's selling and who might work with you to produce and/or distribute the same sort of thing.

Audio

Audio is a growth area in publishing today. Driving, walking, riding the bus and the train or just sitting on a park bench, Americans in more than 11 million households now listen to books on tape that are produced by companies founded expressly for the purpose and by booksellers, publishers and special-interest concerns that make cassettes as a sideline. Check your contractual rights and your publisher's capabilities and intentions in this area, and see the cassettes in stock at nearby bookstores for leads to companies you might approach.

Whoever buys audio rights, you'll want to make the term of license somewhere between five and ten years, limit the buyer to one recording (perhaps plus the right to include it in anthologies) and arrange to approve cuts, added material and, if possible, the choice of narrator. Ideally, the producer will use only one voice (sit still for two at most so your audio deal won't interfere with other licensing agreements for dramatic rights). Because the power of the reading sells the tape, using a professional actor is generally wise. If you have acting talent and training, though, you might be able to do the narration yourself and get a bigger share of the gate.

Video and Multimedia

Translating words on paper into visual images with sounds attached is a tricky task but it can pay off handsomely—as witness the durable video versions of Jane Fonda's exercise books—so it's worth investigating for certain kinds of nonfiction. Suppose, for example, that you've written a book about living with a handicapped child; the techniques and attitudes it explains would probably be clearest if they were visually depicted as well as verbally described. Visual presentations could obviously be at least as useful with instruction manuals of various sorts—how to refinish your antique furniture, care for your houseplants, understand body language.

To find likely prospects for sales of video rights, check video directories at your library, your local video rental store and online, and canvass companies that already reach appropriate audiences. Organizations that serve nurses might adapt a book on touch therapy, for instance, and large corporations might adapt one that explains how to get the most out of meetings.

A similar process will lead you to prospects for multimedia. Because production is expensive and complicated, though, you may also want to consider approaching one or more of the multimedia specialists listed in *LMP* to see whether they'd like to license rights. Although early euphoria about the prospects for this format has now been tempered by reality, it works admirably for some material, particularly content aimed at kids.

TV and Radio

Paralleling the growth of small, special-interest operations in book and periodical publishing, small, special-interest television channels have been multiplying. In general, their need for new material is insatiable, their budgets are small, and their reliance on print materials for program ideas is marked.

Check out channels and their various program slots in your area to identify possible showcases for you and your work; and when you find a likely prospect, try to come up with a proposal that meets the demands of television by remembering that people want lots of action and entertainment when they click on a TV set.

Local radio may provide possibilities too. Could you do a regular one-minute spot about stress reduction on a drive-time show, for instance, or read a chapter a week of your picaresque novel about a local industry on the NPR station that serves your area? Conceivably, there's money in this. Certainly, if it happens, there's publicity and ammunition for approaching national media.

The Internet

If your contract didn't strip you of electronic rights, or if you own all rights because you're your own publisher, income can come from the Internet. You might sell your whole book or periodical through your own Web site and through chat groups and lists you participate in or host. You might present stand-alone excerpts or individual articles at your site—either for sale or as inducements to buy the primary product. You might offer selections from your work to relevant Web stores willing to display them and make ordering easy. And for sure you'll want to keep attracting potential customers (wherever they might end up buying) by linking your site to all sites you can find that feature related information, products or services.

Re-producing the Parts

Offline, too, sections of books and magazines can be lifted out, sometimes virtually intact, and stood firmly on their own feet. In which case, the next task is figuring out where they might run and maximizing the chances that they will.

Often, however, books refuse to disassemble neatly, and carving articles or stories from their pages takes careful craftsmanship.

Once you've decided which parts of your story merit publication on their own (perhaps you'll have to supply a new lead or a few passages of transition or a local news peg before any of them does), you can approach magazines, newspapers and syndicates with your selections (see "Resources" and, if you feel the need of a refresher course, "A Foot in the Door"). You should offer to sell either first serial rights (that is, the rights to the first appearance in print of this work) or second serial rights (i.e., the rights to republish, perhaps in a slightly different form). For obvious reasons, first serial rights go for more money.

Send as many different adaptations of your material as you can prepare to as many appropriate outlets as you can find, and use the biographical note that runs with them to identify yourself as the author of their parent work. You'll want readers who are enthusiastic about an excerpt to know they can easily get a copy of its source, so try hard to get periodicals to print full ordering information—including a toll-free number and an URL—along with your pieces.

Don't stop, though, when you've gotten a bunch of excerpts into print and a bit of action going. Fan the flames by developing reprint possibilities. Should the *Reader's Digest* see the chapter of your book that appeared in *Essence*? Would airline magazines or trade journals or special-interest newsletters or local papers pick up your piece from *Inc.*?

The effort involved in querying periodicals that might reprint is minimal, and likely to be fully repaid even if all you get is additional exposure. There can be big money in the offing, though, for anyone who does win the vote at the *Digest*.

Deploying Writing Skills

If you decide to use your writing skills in order to earn enough money to use your writing skills the way you really want to use them, you have several interesting options.

One thing you can do is write other people's books. Celebrities and executives and experts of various sorts with good stories to tell often lack the time and talent to tell them well. As a result, they and their agents and editors frequently go looking for ghostwriters and collaborators.

When you're tapped to write for or with somebody else, you may get a flat fee or a percentage of the royalties or both. Try for a nonreturnable fixed payment up front in addition to, or as an advance against, the percentage, and expect to work hard for your money however it's paid. There's no such thing as "an easy book," according to William Novak, who has done autobiographies with celebrities such as Lee Iacocca, Nancy Reagan and the "Mayflower Madam" as well as books, including *The Big Book of Jewish Humor*, on his own.

Novak reports that he enjoys writing as part of a team. If you think you'd also like that, ask your acquaintances in publishing about assignments, and then, once you're hired, arrange to be billed as a co-author if you can, and be absolutely certain you get credit somewhere. (Drawing up a written agreement at the outset about the terms of a collaboration is a good way to ensure that these and other focuses for dissension don't cause trouble later.)

Expending less effort (and no doubt earning less in the way of psychic rewards), you can take up writing fillers, short features, booklets and greeting-card verse. Successful practitioners of these and comparable minor arts have, predictably, written books that tell how you too can cash in on them, and although you can sneer if you want to, this may be a good way to pay the bills.

Other opportunities to write for money exist in organizations that need newsletters, companies that need house organs, government bodies that need speech-writing staffs and myriad other concerns. Let your own ingenuity be a guide to the ones that will work well for you.

Book packagers also hire writers. Sometimes known as book producers or book developers, packagers come up with ideas for books, find people to write them and sell the finished products—in the form of fully edited manuscripts, sets of camera-ready pages or thousands of bound volumes—to publishing houses. Authors who work for packagers can negotiate a variety of deals involving flat fees and/or shares of earnings.

To get packagers to think about hiring you, write to tell them about your special expertise and your writing credits, and enclose brief samples of your best work. See "Resources" for leads to particular book producers and send for descriptive literature from those you find appealing.

Purveying Publishing Know-How

Instead of working for a packager, you may want to consider becoming one, as scores of people have done in the recent past.

Packagers often, but not always, have editorial experience and contacts. And packaged books are usually nonfiction, with titles like *The Baseball Timeline* (Stonesong Press) or *The Audubon Society Nature Guides* (Chanticleer Press) or *The Nitpicker's Guide for X-Philes* (Ettlinger Editorial Projects) or *Theme Gardens* (Regina Ryan Publishing Enterprises, Inc.). Novels get packaged, too, though, especially genre fiction like historical sagas, mystery series, action/adventure stories and romantic tales for women.

With a fund of ideas, a flair for selling and the ability to stay calm and efficient under pressure, a writer can also succeed as a packager. Those of you who like the idea of turning your ideas for fiction and nonfiction into proposals and then getting other people to write, produce and distribute the books you've dreamed up might seek advice from book producers in your area. Review "The Self-Publishing Option" if you decide to be the kind of packager who sells finished books, not just finished manuscripts.

Arguably, of course, if you're going to produce finished books, you might as well handle distribution too, and create your own publishing company.

Your safest move in that case is to specialize. By concentrating on one subject area or one kind of writing that appeals to a particular group of people, a publisher can build a following and eventually instill a strong brand-name loyalty that will help draw readers to new books from the house.

Some firms specialize successfully in books about a geographical region; *50 Hikes in New Hampshire's White Mountains* went through two editions and four printings in its first six years and spawned a series of related books at New Hampshire Publishing Company, for instance.

Other companies focus on a topic or two. Examples run the gamut from advertising and assertiveness training to yeast infections and Zen masterpieces, and any subject can work as long as you know your way around it, identify its devotees and devise reliable, cost-effective ways to reach them.

Whatever you publish, you'd be wise to search for out-of-print books on your topic that you can simply reissue and for related books other publishers may be glad to grant you licenses for, either because they can't penetrate the markets you get to or because their sales are minimal. Add these to your list and you're likely to find that it reaches critical mass much faster than it would with new releases only.

But you needn't stop there. Out-of-print and underappreciated books can themselves constitute a publishing program. A number of publishers specialize in such hidden treasures. Consider Phil Zuckerman's Applewood Books Americana Reprints, for example. That line's many titles include work by Benjamin Franklin, George Washington and Walt Whitman, early versions of selected volumes in the Nancy Drew and Hardy Boys series and the original version of *Rudolph the Red-Nosed Reindeer*. When you can re-issue a book in a facsimile edition, you incur no costs for typeset-ting and layout, and when you can publish one whose copyright has lapsed, you won't have to pay royalties. Even works still copy-righted can usually be had for modest fees, though, when no one has been paying much attention to them for a while.

Experienced authors can also sell certain publishing skills and services. If you've become adept at using a page layout program, by all means make your expertise generate extra income (see "Resources" for specific guidance). If you've developed editing, copy-editing or proofreading skills, you ought to tap the ready market for them as well; try publishing houses, newspapers, ad agencies and almost any other business that involves the prepa-ration of materials to be printed (which almost any business does). If you've developed the ability to design and maintain Web sites, people might pay you to do that for them. And if you've amassed as much marketing know-how as self publishers Dan Poynter of Para Publishing, Tom and Marilyn Ross of Com-munication Creativity and John Kremer of Open Horizons, you might follow their lead by creating books, newsletters, work-shops and all manner of other goods and services geared to help-ing small publishers. See "The Self-Publishing Option Resources" for a better idea of their various approaches.

And look to independent publishers on the PMA List and in your geographic area for more advice on selling publishing expertise (and publishing artifacts as well, like your mailing list).

Lecturing

Lecturing is lucrative; in fact, it's what supports a good many well-known writers. For months every year, these prominent authors crisscross the country to speak before civic and corpo-rate groups and on college campuses, and many of them earn thousands of dollars per speech. (The take for beginners is lower, of course.)

The lecture bureaus that schedule celebrities' talks (*LMP* has a list) are prepared to welcome new clients, but as in any other business, a recommendation from a respected source and a strong presentation will improve the odds for acceptance.

Both in approaching lecture agents and in fulfilling the engagements they'll get you if they take you on, you should be aware that what works when you write won't necessarily work when you talk. What people in groups want is entertainment and/or the voice of authority. You should concentrate, therefore, not on your writing but on its substance; stress your theme, your colorful examples, your useful knowledge and your credentials.

Teaching

Though it doesn't pay as well as lecturing, teaching also makes a good sideline for writers and draws on many of the same skills. Writing and journalism classes and assorted continuing-education programs in your area may well be hospitable to new courses. If you're interested in teaching, explore opportunities at prisons and rehabilitation centers as well as at schools and universities in your region; and send for catalogs. Perhaps one of the instructors listed will agree to advise you about drafting and submitting a course proposal.

Teaching has several attractions. Serious writers report that helping others learn writing techniques gives them new insights into their own creative processes, and that contact with both students and fellow instructors is often stimulating. Furthermore, the pay is steady, at least as long as the semester lasts, and much longer than that in most cases.

Never Say Die Department

Out-of-print books can be revived. Publishers reissue neglected titles from time to time. Authors resell books to other publishers after rights have reverted. Furthermore, new kinds of rights deals crop up as new media develop (less than a decade ago, Web site sales were unknown) and old media seek content (a recent deal provides for Judith Rossner's novel *Emmeline* to become an opera). And even when it looks as if the end has come for sure, when piles of unsold copies haunt your dreams, more routes to readers exist. Hospitals, facilities for the poor and other non-profit organizations may be delighted by donated books that could get you a tax break (consult your accountant). At reduced prices, books may move fast at your Web site (half off meant twice as many orders, one self-publisher found). At drastically reduced prices, they may sell at the annual Chicago International Remainder and Overstock Book Exposition (CIROBE). And, once remaindered, books sometimes sell so well that they go back to press time and again and bring in more money than the original editions ever earned.

Endnote

Righting the Scales of Success

OWN DEEP WHERE it matters—on some subrational level—
it's natural for authors to suspect that pub date constitutes
the publishing industry's equivalent of the theater's opening
night. And it would be nice if it did. After the long and lonely
work of writing and the petty aggravations of production, there
ought to come a time when the audience cheers and the critics
dole out stars and a person knows for sure whether to pop open
the champagne at a party or slink off to suffer alone.

In the normal course of events, however, a writer's audience is
apt to remain silent (people seldom volunteer comments on what
they've read unless it made them mad); potential critics will
probably pay no attention (reviewers ignore periodical pieces
and the vast majority of new books); and any responses that do
come an author's way are liable to be hell on the impulse that
wants certainty because they'll straggle in over such a long
period of time and be so liberally sprinkled with waffle words
("Despite its flaws, . . ."; "Despite its promise, . . ."; "Despite its
very real merits, . . .").

But if random reactions are imperfect indicators of accomplishment, the supposedly scientific polls known as bestseller
surveys are even worse. Credited by the public with mirroring its
response to what's published, all the bestseller lists actually aim
to reveal is which trade books are selling well in bookstores, and

they rank even that small fraction of what people read more in terms of rate of sale than in terms of sales per se. As a result, a book that sells 2,500 copies in one week through a particular set of stores may make the list, while another book that sells 250,000 copies—or, and this does happen, 2,500,000 copies—over a longer period of time will never get near it.

Worse still, and more important, bestseller lists don't generally rank anything right. The bookstore managers who supply data to compilers have learned over the years that the bestseller label stimulates demand, and they're not above reporting inflated sales figures for a specific book simply because—having been persuaded to order large quantities of it—they want it hyped.

On at least one memorable occasion, booksellers cited a book that hadn't been written yet, let alone published and sold, as a current bestseller, and although their motivations may have been a bit obscure in that instance, it is clear enough on the whole that bookstore managers (and publishers too) can and do regularly skew bestseller standings, so that nobody knows just what they may mean.

Given this set of circumstances, most writers find that publication day comes and goes and leaves in its wake nothing but a gnawing sense of anticlimax that can lead eventually to a debilitating conviction of failure. In fact, only two kinds of authors are likely to get a fair share of pleasure from getting published: (1) those whose books catapult to commercial success (no matter what your personal hierarchy of values is, almost everybody in our culture gets a warm feeling at some level from winning fame and money); and (2) those who've learned from this book, or from any other source, how to go where readers they respect will appreciate them and how to appreciate themselves.

Techniques for reaching appropriate and appreciative audiences have already been outlined—in "Why and How to Be Your Own Best Sales Force" and in "Managing Sales"—but techniques for arranging to appreciate yourself are harder to explain, partly because the subject is fraught with tension. In the light of our Puritan heritage, it's hard not to believe that to appreciate yourself is to be proud, and to be proud is to be vain, and to be vain is to be threatened by comeuppance.

Forget that. If you got your work published and read, you have plenty to be proud about, and the more parts of the publishing process you completed successfully, the more plaudits you've earned. Furthermore, nobody's in a better position than you are to evaluate the extent and nature of your accomplishments.

The Achievement Awards list that follows is designed as a playful first step to help people who write learn to sing their own praises. At the outset, you may feel uncomfortable claiming credit for anything on it but the items that you can recite with a faintly self-mocking air. In the end, however, perhaps you'll abandon all pretense of sophistication, add freely to the list in your mind, and accept all legitimate commendations—whatever their cultural authority—with unselfconscious joy.

Start by assuming that you're fully entitled to applause if you have:

❖ Had a manuscript—or still another manuscript—accepted (the vast majority of submissions to publishing houses are turned down).

❖ Discovered a way to issue a book or periodical on your own.

❖ Produced an aesthetically pleasing piece of work.

❖ Elicited congratulatory letters and phone calls from family and friends (who may or may not have read whatever it was you wrote).

❖ Elicited congratulatory letters and phone calls from total strangers who've not only read your work but liked it enough to comment on it.

❖ Earned out your advance at a large house (90 percent of their books don't, a knowledgeable source has revealed).

❖ Gotten enthusiastic and insightful reviews.

❖ Gotten bad reviews with good lines in them. ("*Catch–22* has much passion, comic and fervent," said *The New York Times*, "but it gasps for want of craft and sensibility.")

❖ Created a tangible literary object with your name on it that snuggles on the shelf between James and Kafka.

❖ Built friendships—with your editor, agent, art director, readers, booksellers, distant colleagues.

❖ Mastered a new skill (page layout, proofreading, public speaking).

❖ Become eligible for membership in the Authors Guild and for all the grants and prizes only published writers can win.

❖ Found and informed the audience that will benefit by your work, even though it numbers only 2,000 readers and they're scattered all over the country.

❖ Furthered a cause.

❖ Generated interest in whatever you do next.

❖ Managed to escape the 9-to-5 rat race without descending to a subsistence standard of living.

❖ Learned a new language ("let's trap the picture and make that a 9-point caption; this is the wrong font").

❖ Established or embellished a track record (getting published is always easier when you have past achievements to parade as well as a future to promise).

❖ Completed what you started. Now, instead of a wistful interior monologue—"Someday I've got to write that up"—you can be party to a spirited public dialogue: "Your piece [magazine, book] made me think [laugh, weep, see more clearly, want to tell you that...]."

And if ever you lose sight, for a moment, of the mysterious force that prompted you to sit down and write to begin with, listen to R.V. Cassill: "Writing is a way of coming to terms with the world and with oneself. The whole spirit of writing is to overcome narrowness and fear by giving order, measure, and significance to the flux of experience constantly dinning into our lives." And that's no small achievement.

Resources

❖   ❖   ❖

How to Use Resources

The five intertwined "Resources" sections that follow are designed to function as a giant supply closet, stocked with items that will serve almost any purpose you dream up as long as you use them creatively and with care.

If you keep "Resources" somewhere handy, you'll benefit by browsing back and forth among the listings in your spare moments, picking out different ones to use at different times in somewhat different ways and allowing your mind to play with a range of possibilities.

Before you make a sizable commitment to anyone or anything mentioned here, please investigate with your own aims in view. Obviously, you'll have to determine not only what you need but also whether, when you need it, it still fits the description it merited when its write-up went to press.

Because prices are unstable, they're not listed but every recommended book and periodical was available in libraries and/or on the Internet and/or for sale at a reasonable cost when it was selected as a Resource.

The diamonds indicate goods or services that are exceptionally valuable.

Getting the Words Right
Resources

THE LISTINGS BELOW will help you uncover fresh material and find the time, the temerity and the talent to write it up successfully.

Advice, Analysis and Reportage

Alberti, Robert E. *Your Perfect Write: The Manual for Self-Help Writers*. Impact Publishers, PO Box 1094, San Luis Obispo, CA 93406. 1985.

Alberti knows what he's talking about; he heads Impact Publishers, which specializes in self-help books.

American Poetry Review, 1721 Walnut Street, Philadelphia, PA 19103; 215-496-0439. Published bimonthly.

Poetry and prose for poetry lovers and practitioners.

Barzun, Jacques. *On Writing, Editing, and Publishing: Essays Explicative and Hortatory*. University of Chicago Press, 5801 South Ellis Avenue, Chicago, IL 60637. Second edition, 1986.

Writer's block, jargon and style are among the topics Barzun's classy lectures address.

Beinhart, Larry. *How to Write a Mystery*. Ballantine Books, 201 East 50th Street, New York, NY 10022. <http://www.randomhouse.com>. 1996.

Just what the title says, and skillfully done.

The Best Writing on Writing. Edited by Jack Heffron. Story Press/Writer's Digest, 1507 Dana Avenue, Cincinnati, OH 45207; 513–531–2690; fax: 513–531–7107. 1994.

Though this title seems to call for a qualifier (the Netspeak IMHO would do), the anthology does offer pieces by many fine writers, including Edna O'Brien, Adrienne Rich and Carolyn Heilbrun.

Bly, Carol. *The Passionate, Accurate Story: Making Your Heart's Truth into Literature.* Milkweed Editions, 430 First Avenue North, Suite 400, Minneapolis, MN 55401. 1990.

It's rare and refreshing to find a writer who not only believes in fiction with moral force but can illuminate the process of creating it.

Bogen, Nancy. *How to Write Poetry.* Prentice Hall Press, 1230 Avenue of the Americas, New York, NY 10020. 1991.

Challenging and enlightening exercises make this a valuable guide for poets who are not afraid of hard work.

Boston, Bruce O. *Language on a Leash.* EEI Press, 66 Canal Center Plaza, Suite 200, Alexandria, VA 22314–5507; 800–683–8380 or 703–683–0683; fax: 703–683–4915; e-mail: info@eeicom.com. <http://www.eeicom.com>. 1988.

A stylish collection of essays for people who care about the English language, by a writer who stakes out an attractive middle ground between the purists and the overly permissive.

❖ Brande, Dorothea. *Becoming a Writer.* Jeremy P. Tarcher, 200 Madison Avenue, New York, NY 10016. <http://www.putnam.com/>. 1981.

This book aims to "teach the beginner not how to write, but how to be a writer." Focusing mainly on fiction, Dorothea Brande asserts that there really is a magic about writing and that it can be taught. What she has to say is as eye-opening today as it was when it first appeared in 1934.

Brown, Rita Mae. *Starting from Scratch: A Different Kind of Writers' Manual.* Bantam Doubleday Dell, 1540 Broadway, New York, NY 10036. Reissue edition, 1989.

The author of *Rubyfruit Jungle* and *High Hearts* (among other novels) has definite ideas about how writers should live and learn. Her ebullient, bossy book includes imaginative exercises.

Browne, Renni, and Dave King. *Self-Editing for Fiction Writers: How to Edit Yourself into Print*. HarperCollins, 10 East 53rd Street, New York, NY 10022. <http://www.harpercollins.com>. 1993.

"Self-editing is the only kind of editing your manuscript will ever get," say the authors, summing up experiences with big book publishers. But even if you're aiming at houses where editing is still SOP, you can benefit from the discussion in here.

Burnett, Hallie. *On Writing the Short Story*. HarperCollins, 10 East 53rd Street, New York, NY 10022. <http://www.harpercollins.com>. 1983.

Teacher, editor and writer Hallie Burnett presents essays about plot, character, style and the other elements of good short fiction along with six stories that illustrate her points.

Burnham, Sophy. *For Writers Only*. Ballantine Books, 201 East 50th Street, New York, NY 10022. <http://www.randomhouse.com>. 1994.

Graceful observations and apt quotations about the passions of creation, especially the dark ones like fear and self doubt. Burnham is the author of the bestselling *A Book of Angels*.

❖ Burroway, Janet. *Writing Fiction: A Guide to Narrative Craft*. Watson-Guptill, 1515 Broadway, New York, NY 10036. Fourth edition, 1995.

A creative writing textbook that's a joy to read. Janet Burroway, whose own prose is a delight, focuses on stories by 21 leading modern writers—including Jamaica Kincaid, Bobbie Ann Mason, Peter Taylor and Raymond Carver—to explore form and structure, the writing process, methods of character presentation and other essential aspects of fiction.

Calderazzo, John. *Writing from Scratch: Freelancing*. Littlefield Adams Quality Paperbacks, 4720 Boston Way, Lanham, MD 20706. 1990.

Friendly first-person prose about creating and placing periodical pieces.

Cantor, Jeffrey A. *A Guide to Academic Writing*. Praeger Publishers/Greenwood Publishing, 88 Post Road West, PO Box 5007, Westport, CT 06881–5007. 1993.

Guidance on getting articles and books into print for the publish-or-perish population.

Carroll, David L. *A Manual of Writer's Tricks*. Marlowe & Company, 632 Broadway, 7th Floor, New York, NY 10012. Second edition, 1995.

Taken as suggestions rather than directives, Carroll's "tricks" will be helpful, particularly the procedural ones like "Don't attempt serious rewriting when you're tired or in a bad mood."

Cart, Michael. *From Romance to Realism: 50 Years of Growth and Change in Young Adult Literature*. HarperCollins, 10 East 53rd Street, New York, NY 10022. <http://www.harpercollins.com>. 1996.

A thoughtful, in-depth analysis of changes in YA fiction over the years.

❖ Cassill, R.V. *Writing Fiction*. Prentice Hall, One Lake Street, Upper Saddle River, NJ 07458. Second edition, 1975.

Cassill, who's written some highly acclaimed fiction himself, advocates learning to write by reading the best writing available and by comparing your writing with that by more experienced hands. He includes readings along with his text and explains how to analyze the ways writers produce their effects. Although difficult to find, this fine book is worth hunting for.

❖ *Children's Books and Their Creators*. Edited by Anita Silvey. Houghton Mifflin, 222 Berkeley Street, Boston, MA 02116. <http://www.hmco.com/trade/>. 1995.

A beautiful encyclopedia covering 20th-century children's and young adult books in words (including first-person pieces by writers and illustrators) and in enchanting, evocative pictures. This is not only a treasure trove of information for those who write for children; it's a delight for former children, especially but not only those who now have children of their own.

Christianson, Gale E. *Writing Lives Is the Devil! Essays of a Biographer at Work*. Archon Books/The Shoe String Press, PO Box 657, 2 Linsley Street, North Haven, CT 06473–2517; 203–239–2702. 1993.

Good background if you write, or might write, biographies, and interesting even if you just like to read them.

Cormier, Robin A. *Error-Free Writing: A Lifetime Guide to Flawless Business Writing*. Prentice Hall, One Lake Street, Upper Saddle River, NJ 07458. 1995.

A four-step procedure designed to let you produce perfect copy.

Crawford, Tad, and Tony Lyons. *The Writer's Legal Guide.* Allworth Press, 10 East 23rd Street, Suite 400, New York, NY 10010; 212–777–8395. Revised edition, 1996.

Crawford covers a wide range of legal issues that writers must confront.

Creed, Jack. *Capturing the Magic of Fiction Writing.* Glenbridge Publishing, 6010 West Jewell Avenue, Lakewood, CO 80232. 1991.

Designed for high-school English teachers as well as beginning writers, Creed's analysis focuses on fiction categories, elements and techniques.

Dickey, James. *Self-Interviews.* Recorded and edited by Barbara and James Reiss. Louisiana State University Press, PO Box 25053, Baton Rouge, LA 70894–5053. Reprint edition, 1984.

A fascinating tour of the mind of a poet. In an appealing conversational voice, Dickey interweaves observations about writing poems with reportage about his life.

Digregorio, Charlotte. *You Can Be A Columnist: Writing and Selling Your Way to Prestige.* Civetta Press, PO Box 1043, Portland, OR 97207–1043; 503–228–6649. 1993.

A friendly overview that's more about writing columns than selling them.

❖ Dillard, Annie. *The Writing Life.* HarperPerennial, 10 East 53rd Street, New York, NY 10022. <http://www.harpercollins.com>. 1990

Annie Dillard writes magnificently about writing (and every other topic she's tackled, as witness her Pulitzer Prize–winner, *Pilgrim at Tinker Creek*). Give yourself a treat; read this, soon and often.

❖ Eco, Umberto. *Six Walks in the Fictional Woods.* Harvard University Press, 79 Garden Street, Cambridge, MA 02138–1499. 1994.

Dazzling insights into reading and writing fiction. Eco explains the Model Reader, the Model Author, the collaboration between them and "the reason people tell stories."

The Editorial Eye. EEI Press, 66 Canal Center Plaza, Suite 200, Alexandria, VA 22314–5507; 800–683–8380 or 703–683–0683; fax: 703–683–4915; e-mail: eye@eeicom.com. <http://www.eeicom.com>.

A monthly publication for pros packed with lively, varied pointers.

Field, Syd. *The Screenwriter's Workbook.* Dell, 1540 Broadway, New York, NY 10036. 1984.

Based on Field's workshops, this is a step-by-step program for creating a screenplay. He's a friendly, well-informed, clear-headed guide.

First Person Singular: Writers on Their Craft. Compiled by Joyce Carol Oates. Ontario Review Press (dist. by George Braziller, Inc.), 171 Madison Avenue, New York, NY 10016; 212–779–7668. 1983.

Illuminating essays by, and interviews with, more than two dozen leading writers, including Gail Godwin, Anne Tyler, Mary Gordon and E. L. Doctorow.

Fishman, Stephen. *The Copyright Handbook: How to Protect and Use Written Works.* Nolo Press, 950 Parker Street, Berkeley, CA 94710. <http://www.nolo.com>. Third edition, 1996.

Copyright nitty-gritty for written work—a thorough discussion.

Fontaine, André, and William A. Glavin, Jr. *The Art of Writing Non-fiction.* Syracuse University Press, 1600 Jamesville Avenue, Syracuse, NY 13244–5160. Second edition, 1991.

A more accurate title for this helpful handbook would have been *The Art of Writing the Interpretive Story,* "interpretive journalism" being the authors' term for the "new journalism" pioneered by Tom Wolfe and others.

Friedman, Bonnie. *Writing Past Dark: Envy, Fear, Distraction, and Other Dilemmas in the Writer's Life.* HarperCollins, 10 East 53rd Street, New York, NY 10022. <http://www.harpercollins.com>. 1993.

The darker, scarier aspects of a writer's life, illuminated by Friedman's intellect and emotions. And beautifully written.

Gach, Gary. *Writers.Net: Every Writer's Essential Guide to Online Resources and Opportunities.* Prima Publishing, 3875 Atherton Road, Rocklin, CA 95765. <http://www.primapublishing.com/>. 1997.

An enormous annotated list (entries vary in terms of usefulness, of course) coupled with helpful information for beginners about navigating and understanding the Internet.

❖ Gass, William H. *Finding a Form.* Alfred A. Knopf, 201 East 50th Street, New York, NY 10022. <http://www.randomhouse.com>. 1996.

Exemplary essays. You'll revel in the power of the language, the ideas and the analyses. Subjects include Pulitzer Prizes for fiction, use of the present tense and "the music of prose."

Gaudet, Marcia, and Carl Wooten. *Porch Talk with Ernest Gaines: Conversations on the Writer's Craft.* **Louisiana State University Press, PO Box 25053, Baton Rouge, LA 70894–5053. 1990.**

The author of *The Autobiography of Miss Jane Pitman* and other fine fiction shares his ideas and experiences in an engaging series of interviews.

Goldberg, Natalie. *Writing Down the Bones: Freeing the Writer Within.* **Shambhala Publications, Horticultural Hall, 300 Massachusetts Avenue, Boston, MA 02115. 1986.**

Natalie Goldberg, a teacher of writing and a student of Zen Buddhism, offers practical advice about writing and "about using writing as . . . a way to help you penetrate your life and become sane."

Gutkind, Lee. *Creative Nonfiction: How to Live It and Write It.* **Chicago Review Press, 814 North Franklin Street, Chicago, IL 60610. 1996.**

When you write creative nonfiction, you're "teaching or informing a reader about a person, place, or situation . . . filtered almost exclusively by your own experience." Gutkind, editor of the journal *Creative Nonfiction,* uses readings and exercises to explain the genre here.

The Happiness of Getting It Down Right: Letters of Frank O'Connor and William Maxwell. **Edited by Michael Steinman. Alfred A. Knopf, 201 East 50th Street, New York, NY 10022. <http://www.randomhouse.com>. 1996.**

No matter what your own relationship with editors may be, you can experience author-editor teamwork vicariously here. Maxwell was O'Connor's editor at *The New Yorker* for a great many years.

Hatcher, Jeffrey. *The Art & Craft of Playwriting.* **Story Press/Writer's Digest, 1507 Dana Avenue, Cincinnati, OH 45207; 513–531–2690; fax: 513–531–7107. 1996.**

This extraordinarily clear analysis is designed to find "the tools, methods and strategies held in common by plays we like, plays that work, plays that delight and move us." Exercises add to its practical value.

Higgins, George V. *On Writing: Advice for Those Who Write to Publish (or Would Like To)*. Henry Holt & Company, 115 West 18th Street, New York, NY 10011. 1990.

Professor and prolific novelist, Higgins has written a lengthy lecture that's both entertaining and educational, although the Olympian tone may put some readers off.

Holzer, Burghild Nina. *A Walk between Heaven and Earth: A Personal Journal on Writing and the Creative Process*. Bell Tower/Harmony, 201 East 50th Street, New York, NY 10022. <http://www.randomhouse.com>. 1994.

Holzer created this journal about journal writing to help her students and others "trust their own writing quest."

Horowitz, Lois. *Knowing Where to Look: The Ultimate Guide to Research*. Writer's Digest Books, 1507 Dana Avenue, Cincinnati, OH 45207; 513–531–2690; fax: 513–531–7107. 1988.

This is a meaty, comprehensive and thoroughly readable guide. Sections on indexes and on looking for addresses, statistics and other particular kinds of information are especially valuable.

How to Write an Uncommonly Good Novel. Edited by Carol Hoover. Ariadne Press, 4817 Tallahassee Avenue, Rockville, MD 20853. 1990.

Members of the Writers Mentors Group based in Washington, DC, cover a range of topics, including point of view, humor, foreshadowing, rhythm and revising.

Hughes, Elaine Farris. *Writing from the Inner Self*. HarperCollins, 10 East 53rd Street, New York, NY 10022. <http://www.harpercollins.com>. 1991.

Delightful as well as practical, this guide to stimulating creativity and overcoming writer's block is an ingenious blend of writing and meditation exercises.

Jacobi, Peter P. *The Magazine Article: How to think it, plan it, write it*. Indiana University Press, 601 North Morton Street, Bloomington, IN 47404–3797; 800–842–6796. 1997.

A journalist's riffs on excerpts from a wide variety of pieces.

Jassin, Lloyd J., and Steven C. Schechter. *The Copyright Permission and Libel Handbook: A Step-by-Step Guide for Writers, Editors, and*

Publishers. John Wiley & Sons, 605 Third Avenue, New York, NY 10158. 1997.
In addition to explaining copyright and libel isues, these two lawyers tell how to locate the people who hold the rights you want.

Jerome, John. *The Writing Trade: A Year in the Life*. Lyons & Burford, 31 West 21st Street, New York, NY 10010. Reprint edition, 1995.
John Jerome's year-long journal shows "how a writing life works." A specific story that will resonate for writers in general.

❖ Jerome, Judson. *The Poet's Handbook*. Writer's Digest Books, 1507 Dana Avenue, Cincinnati, OH 45207; 513–531–2690; fax: 513–531–7107. 1986.
A remarkably deft tutorial for everyone who wants to write "effective comprehensible poetry."

Joselow, Beth Baruch. *Writing without the Muse: 50 Exercises for the Creative Writer*. Story Line Press, 3 Oaks Farm, Brownsville, OR 97327–9718. 1995.
Based on Joselow's writing classes, and drawing on her skills as a poet, these exercises should get your creative juices flowing.

Kelton, Nancy Davidoff. *Writing from Personal Experience: How to Turn Your Life into Salable Prose*. Writer's Digest Books, 1507 Dana Avenue, Cincinnati, OH 45207; 513–531–2690; fax: 513–531–7107. 1997.
Laugh while you learn. Drawing on her talents as a humorist as well as on her experiences as a writer and a teacher of writing, Kelton deftly weaves stories into instruction.

❖ Keyes, Ralph. *The Courage to Write: How Writers Transcend Fear*. Henry Holt & Company, 115 West 18th Street, New York, NY 10011. 1995.
A thoroughgoing pro, Keyes offers practical and positive advice, drawn from the real-life struggles of many professional writers, that should help you capitalize on anxiety instead of knuckling under to it.

Killien, Christi, and Sheila Bender. *Writing in a New Convertible with the Top Down: A Unique Guide for Writers*. Blue Heron Publishing, 24450 NW Hansen, Hillsboro, OR 97124; 503–621–3911. Revised edition, 1997.
In letters back and forth, Killien and Bender comment wisely and constructively on writing as a process. You may want to follow their

lead by creating your own intimate, long-distance writers group with someone you admire and trust, and in any event you'll enjoy sitting in on theirs.

Kilpatrick, James J. *The Writer's Art.* **Andrews and McMeel Publishing, 4520 Main Street, Suite 700, Kansas City, MO 64111–7701. 1984.**

What to do and what not to do to become a better writer. Kilpatrick is an opinionated and engaging instructor who provides wonderful examples to prove his points.

Kirby, David. *Writing Poetry: Where Poems Come From and How to Write Them.* **The Writer, Inc., 120 Boylston Street, Boston, MA 02116–4615; 617–423–3157. <http://www.channel1.com/thewriter/>. New edition, 1997.**

An energizing discussion by English professor and poet David Kirby, who believes in poetry as a route to fresh, original thinking, a path to the "back door of knowledge."

❖ **Kirsch, Jonathan.** *Kirsch's Handbook of Publishing Law for Authors, Publishers, Editors and Agents.* **Acrobat Books, PO Box 870, Venice, CA 90294. 1995.**

A standout in its field, *Kirsch's Handbook* is not just thorough, knowledgeable and helpful; it's actually fun to browse through because of the boxed tidbits that jump out from the text.

Klauser, Henriette Anne. *Writing on Both Sides of the Brain: Breakthrough Techniques for People Who Write.* **HarperSanFrancisco, 353 Sacramento Street, Suite 500, San Francisco, CA 94111–3653. <http://www.harpercollins.com>. 1987.**

First you use the right side of your brain to create; then you use the left side to edit. According to Henriette Anne Klauser, who runs Writing Resource Workshops, it's when we try to write and edit simultaneously that we run into problems. Her incisive manual explains just how you can separate the two functions and why you'll be glad you did.

Kozak, Ellen M. *Every Writer's Guide to Copyright and Publishing Law.* **Owl Books/Henry Holt, 115 West 18th Street, New York, NY 10011. Second edition, 1996.**

A short, readable introduction.

Kupfersmid Joel, and Donald M. Wonderly. *An Author's Guide to Publishing Better Articles in Better Journals in the Behavioral Sciences.* **John Wiley & Sons, 605 Third Avenue, New York, NY 10158. 1994.**

Interaction among university personnel, journal editors and reviewers, and scientist authors has produced "a plethora of irrelevant studies," say the authors, whose prescription for change might also apply to other academic fields.

Lamott, Anne. *Bird by Bird: Some Instructions on Writing and Life.* **Anchor Books/Doubleday, 1540 Broadway, New York, NY 10036. 1994.**

Funny and personal, Lamott's report on her life as a writer and on her workshops for writers shows why "publication is not all that it is cracked up to be. But writing is."

Leader, Zachary. *Writer's Block.* **The Johns Hopkins University Press, 2715 North Charles Street, Baltimore, MD 21218–4319. 1990.**

A "theoretical and historical enquiry" that's stimulating scholarly reading.

Lehman, John. *The Writer in You.* **Weekend Seminars, 315 East Water Street, Cambridge, WI 53523; 800–7-TO–KNOW. 1996.**

Six steps to better writing presented on six audio cassettes. Lehman, who also publishes the literary magazine *Rosebud* (address above) and gives weekend workshops, puts the aural medium to very good use. Listening to these tapes—whenever and wherever—is a fine alternative or supplement to reading about writing.

❖ **Lipsett, Suzanne.** *Surviving a Writer's Life.* **HarperSanFrancisco, 353 Sacramento Street, Suite 500, San Francisco, CA 94111–3653. <http://www.harpercollins.com>. 1995.**

So beautifully written that you'll want to read it again and again, *Surviving a Writer's Life* is by turns funny, scary and exhilarating. Using her personal "raw material," Lipsett illuminates the amazing web of connections between life and art.

Maggio, Rosalie. *The Dictionary of Bias-Free Usage: A Guide to Nondiscriminatory Language.* **Oryx Press, 4041 North Central Avenue, Suite 700, Phoenix, AZ 85012–3397; 800–279–6799. 1991.**

Use this admirably comprehensive dictionary to check on sexist overtones and undertones in your language, and to get rid of them.

Mairs, Nancy. *Voice Lessons: On Becoming a (Woman) Writer.* Beacon Press, 25 Beacon Street, Boston, MA 02108. 1994.

An incandescent writer and an indomitable human being, Mairs found her own voice partly by trying on different styles—romantic anguish, guy talk, muteness, critical bombast—as she learned to "speak plainly out of my own experience to an audience I liked and trusted." It'll be worth your while to listen.

Matkin, Ralph E., and T. F. Riggar. *Persist and Publish: Helpful Hints for Academic Writing and Publishing.* University Press of Colorado, PO Box 849, Niwot, CO 80544. 1991.

Two much-published academic authors discuss the requirements and benefits of various kinds of scholarly publishing.

McCormack, Thomas. *The Fiction Editor, the Novel, and the Novelist.* St. Martin's Press, 175 Fifth Avenue, New York, NY 10010. Reissue edition, 1995.

McCormack, who headed St. Martin's Press, offers conceptual tools that both writers and editors can use to diagnose and solve problems with fiction manuscripts. Pungent, persuasive, engaging and edifying.

Meyer, Herbert E., and Jill M. *How to Write: Communicating Ideas and Information.* Storm King Press, PO Box 2089, Friday Harbor, WA 98250; 206–378–3910. 1993.

The authors analyze and illustrate the decisions, steps, skills and techniques that go into writing any kind of prose, and they come up with a tidy prescription. Brisk, clear, sound advice that's most easily applicable to nonfiction.

Meyrowitz, Joshua. *No Sense of Place: The Impact of Electronic Media on Social Behavior.* Oxford University Press, 198 Madison Avenue, New York, NY 10016. 1986.

Professor Meyrowitz's masterly analysis includes a fascinating discussion of the powers (and limitations) of print.

Moffat, Mary Jane. *The Times of Our Lives: A Guide to Writing Autobiography and Memoir.* John Daniel & Company, PO Box 21922, Santa Barbara, CA 93121; 800–662–8351. Third edition, 1996.

A little book of practical wisdom for people who want to create written legacies rather than publishable manuscripts.

Newlove, Donald. *First Paragraphs: Inspired Openings for Writers and Readers; Painted Paragraphs: Inspired Description for Writers and Readers;* and *Invented Voices: Inspired Dialogue for Writers and Readers.* Henry Holt & Company, 115 West 18th Street, New York, NY 10011. 1992, 1993, 1994, respectively.

Each of these small volumes analyzes and exemplifies its subject in a long, incisive, spirited essay.

Noble, William. *Make That Scene: A Writer's Guide to Setting, Mood and Atmosphere.* Paul S. Eriksson, PO Box 62, I–54 Dunmore, Forest Dale, VT 05745. 1988.

Noble, who's also done books for writers on such subjects as dialogue, structure and plagiarism, offers advice generously sprinkled with examples.

Noble, William. *Show, Don't Tell: A Writer's Guide.* Paul S. Eriksson, PO Box 62, I–54 Dunmore, Forest Dale, VT 05745. 1991.

The subject here is "the art of keeping the story on stage and its audience emotionally involved."

Norwick, Kenneth P., and Jerry Simon Chasen. *The Rights of Authors, Artists, and Other Creative People.* Southern Illinois University Press, PO Box 3697, Carbondale, IL 62902–3697. Second edition, 1992.

A remarkable thing happens when you read what Jerry Chasen and Ken Norwick have to say here. You actually begin to understand how the law works and how it might apply to your particular situation. This is an excellent guide for all writers, and especially useful for anyone who's been deluded into thinking that legal rules are hard, fast, mysterious and totally unpredictable.

O'Conner, Patricia T. *Woe Is I: The Grammarphobe's Guide to Better English in Plain English.* Grosset/Putnam, 200 Madison Avenue, New York, NY 10016. <http://www.putnam.com>. 1996.

No-nonsense guidance on grammar that's lively and funny enough to stick with you and prevent those embarrassing mistakes.

Page, Susan. *The Shortest Distance Between You and a Published Book.* Broadway Books, 1540 Broadway, New York, NY 10036. 1997.

Although the tone is engaging, Page overgeneralizes on the basis of limited experience. Some useful tips appear in the chapters on working with large publishers.

Parting the Curtains: Interviews with Southern Writers. Interviews by Dannye Romine Powell. Photographs by Jill Krementz. John F. Blair, 1406 Plaza Drive, Winston-Salem, NC 27103. 1994.

Wide-ranging conversations with nearly two dozen writers—including Reynolds Price, Maya Angelou and Peter Taylor—accompanied by detailed bios and evocative photos.

Patterson, Benton Rain. *Write to Be Read: A Practical Guide to Feature Writing.* Iowa State University Press, 2121 South State Avenue, Ames, IA 50010; 800–862–6657. 1986.

Good solid advice from a pro. Pointers on finding an angle and organizing a piece are especially helpful.

Pearlman, Mickey, and Katherine Usher Henderson. *A Voice of One's Own: Conversations with America's Writing Women.* Houghton Mifflin, 222 Berkeley Street, Boston, MA 02116. <http://www.hmco.com/trade/>. 1990.

Interviews with Josephine Humphreys, Gail Godwin, Susan Fromberg Schaeffer and 25 other writers emphasize memory, myths, family and the relationships among them.

Plotnik, Arthur. *The Elements of Expression: Putting Thoughts into Words.* Henry Holt & Company, 115 West 18th Street, New York, NY 10011. 1996.

Ebullient and thorough.

Poets & Writers Magazine.

See "Advice, Analysis and Reportage" in "A Foot in the Door Resources."

❖ *The Portable Writers' Conference: Your Guide to Getting and Staying Published.* Edited by Stephen Blake Mettee.

See "A Foot in the Door Resources."

Poynter, Dan, and Mindy Bingham. *Is There a Book Inside You?* Para Publishing, PO Box 8206-R, Santa Barbara, CA 93118–8206; 800–PARAPUB; e-mail: Orders@ParaPublishing.com. <http://www.ParaPublishing.com/>. Fourth revised edition, 1996.

If you're intrigued by the question the title poses and not sure what the answer is in your case, use the exercises here to find out.

Priest, Susanna Hornig. *Doing Media Research: An Introduction.* Sage Publications, 2455 Teller Road, Thousand Oaks, CA 91320; e-mail: order@sagepub.com. 1996.

Written by a journalism professor, this lucid introduction to social science research is designed to help even beginners "ask interesting and important questions" and use suitable methods and techniques to find and present answers.

Rae, Colleen Mariah. *Movies in the Mind: How to Build a Short Story.* Sherman Asher Publishing, PO Box 2853, Santa Fe, NM 87504. 1996.

Thanks to Rae's take-charge tone and inventive exercises, you may feel you're getting instruction in person from this exceptionally energizing book. It's "about getting out of your own way so that the story-maker inside of you can tell its stories."

Rainer, Tristine. *Your Life as Story: Writing the New Autobiography.* Jeremy P. Tarcher, 200 Madison Avenue, New York, NY 10016. <http://www.putnam.com/> 1997.

A graceful and persuasive presentation of tools you can use "to see story in your life" and then "give it shape in writing so it can be shared."

The Reporter's Handbook: An Investigator's Guide to Documents and Techniques. Edited by **Steve Weinberg.** St. Martin's Press, 175 Fifth Avenue, New York, NY 10010. Third edition, 1995.

Investigative reporters share hard-won know-how. This authoritative, admirably organized volume is packed with information.

❖ **Rhodes, Richard.** *How to Write: Advice and Reflections.* William Morrow, 1350 Avenue of the Americas, New York, NY 10019. 1995.

Rhodes makes you believe he's talking quietly to you, sharing his experiences as a writer and the lessons drawn from them. Though the prizes he's won put him way up in the ranks, he treats his readers as colleagues.

Rico, Gabriele Lusser. *Writing the Natural Way: Using Right-Brain Techniques to Release Your Expressive Powers.* Jeremy P. Tarcher, 200 Madison Avenue, New York, NY 10016. <http://www.putnam.com/>. 1983.

Gabriele Lusser Rico offers undergraduates and others a system designed to foster self-expression.

Roseman, Janet Lynn. *The Way of the Woman Writer.* Harrington Park Press/The Haworth Press, 10 Alice Street, Binghamton, NY 13904–1580. 1995.

Like attendees at her autobiography workshops for women, Roseman hopes, her readers will discover themselves, heal themselves and learn "to trust their writing as guides back to themselves."

Rule, Rebecca, and Susan Wheeler. *Creating the Story: Guides for Writers.* Heinemann, 361 Hanover Street, Portsmouth, NH 03801–3912. 1993.

The "guides" are wise and encouraging essays, covering all steps between the idea stage and publication and accompanied by intelligent exercises.

Saltzman, Joel. *If You Can Talk, You Can Write.* Warner Books, 1271 Avenue of the Americas, New York, NY 10020. 1993.

Short, exuberant chapters with invigorating examples and quizzes.

Saltzman, Joel. *If You're Writing, Let's Talk: A Road Map Past Writers' Blocks from Page One to The End.* Prima Publishing, 3875 Atherton Road, Rocklin, CA 95765. <http://www.primapublishing.com/>. 1997.

A better subtitle would have been *Notes from a Writers' Workshop.* Saltzman offers snippets from one he led, along with relevant generalizations and stories that participants ended up producing.

Schwartz, Marilyn, and the Task Force on Bias-Free Language of the Association of American University Presses. *Guidelines for Bias-Free Writing.* Indiana University Press, 601 North Morton Street, Bloomington, IN 47404–3797; 800–842–6796. 1995.

Directed to the scholarly publishing community but usable by everyone who wants to avoid putting people down for no good reason.

Science and Technical Writing: A Manual of Style. Edited by Philip Rubens. Henry Holt & Company, 115 West 18th Street, New York, NY 10011. 1992.

Comprehensive, well conceived and well executed.

Seuling, Barbara. *How to Write a Children's Book and Get It Published.* Macmillan, 1633 Broadway, New York, NY 10019. Revised and expanded edition, 1991.

Knowledgeable, encouraging, step-by-step guidance for beginners.

Shelnutt, Eve. *The Writing Room: Keys to the Craft of Fiction and Poetry.* Longstreet Press, 2140 Newmarket Parkway, Suite 102, Marietta, GA 30067. 1989.

An accomplished writer and teacher interweaves essays, stories and poems by "writers in the process of development and change" to illuminate useful ways of thinking about writing.

Storey, Valerie. *The Essential Guide for New Writers: From Idea to Finished Manuscript.* Dava Books, 513 Bankhead Avenue, Suite 194, Carrollton, GA 30117. 1995.

The aptly named author gears most of her advice to beginners who want to write fiction.

❖ Strunk, William, Jr., and E. B. White. *The Elements of Style.* Allyn & Bacon, 160 Gould Street, Needham Heights, MA 02194. <http://www.abacon.com>. Third edition, 1995.

By now this collection of clearly and amusingly written "rules" of style is considered virtually sacrosanct. A valuable and thoroughly enjoyable classic.

Thomas, Francis-Noël, and Mark Turner. *Clear and Simple as the Truth: Writing Classic Prose.* Princeton University Press, 41 William Street, Princeton, NJ 08540. 1994.

Explaining and exemplifying the "classic style," Professors Thomas and Turner start from the conviction that "writing is an intellectual activity, not a bundle of skills" and argue that "classic" style "adopts the stance that its purpose is presentation; its motive, disinterested truth." Heavy-duty analysis, unfortunately riddled with sexist pronouns.

The True Subject: Writers on Life and Craft. Edited by Kurt Brown. Graywolf Press, 2402 University Avenue, Suite 203, St. Paul, MN 55114. 1993.

Talks originally delivered at writers conferences by Gary Snyder, Donald Justice, Jane Smiley and others, on topics including failure, the art of memoir and a writer's sense of place.

Ueland, Brenda. *If You Want to Write: A Book About Art, Independence and Spirit.* Graywolf Press, 2402 University Avenue, Suite 203, St. Paul, MN 55114. Third edition, 1997.

"Everybody is talented, original and has something important to say." That's Brenda Ueland's position, based on her experiences as a writer and a writing teacher. First published in 1938, *If You Want to Write* dispenses courage as well as advice. Most useful for fiction.

Vargas Llosa, Mario. *A Writer's Reality.* **Syracuse University Press, 1600 Jamesville Avenue, Syracuse, NY 13244–5160. 1991.**
Eight incisive lectures by the author of *Aunt Julia and the Scriptwriter* and other acclaimed novels.

Venolia, Jan. *Write Right! A Desktop Digest of Punctuation, Grammar, and Style.* **Periwinkle Press/Ten Speed Press, PO Box 7123, Berkeley, CA 94707. Third edition, 1995.**
A chatty, well-organized handbook.

Wallace, Robert. *Writing Poems.* **Watson-Guptill, 1515 Broadway, New York, NY 10036. Fourth edition, 1995.**
This rich, inventive book is designed to provide an environment that fosters learning for poets. Focusing on form, content and process, Wallace writes with grace and sophistication about work by many contemporary poets, including himself and some of his students.

Weiss, Jason. *Writing at Risk: Interviews in Paris with Uncommon Writers.* **University of Iowa Press, University of Iowa, 100 Kuhl House, Iowa City, IA 52242–1000. 1991.**
Julio Cortazar, Eugene Ionesco, Milan Kundera and Nathalie Sarraute are among Weiss' subjects, and they have something important in common, he believes: "Public approval placed a distant second for these artists compared to the stages of understanding achieved."

Welty, Eudora. *One Writer's Beginnings.* **Belknap Press/Harvard University Press, 79 Garden Street, Cambridge, MA 02138–1499. Reprint edition, 1995.**
Eudora Welty's charming memoirs illuminate a fiction writer's mind-set.

Wilson, Lee. *The Copyright Guide.* **Allworth Press, 10 East 23rd Street, Suite 400, New York, NY 10010; 212–777–8395. 1996.**
Not just friendly, but also clear and confidence-inspiring.

Woolley, Catherine. *Writing for Children.* **Plume/Penguin, 375 Hudson Street, New York, NY 10014. 1989.**
Lessons from a lifetime of writing children's books. Woolley has had dozens published, some under her own name and some as Jane Thayer.

The Writer. The Writer, Inc., 120 Boylston Street, Boston, MA 02116–4615; 617–423–3157.<http://www.channel1.com/thewriter/>. **Published monthly.**

This venerable magazine features instructive essays by published writers along with news tidbits and market lists. The Writer also publishes books for beginning writers. Send for information.

The Writer on Her Work, Volume II: New Essays in New Territory. **Edited by Janet Sternburg. W.W. Norton, 500 Fifth Avenue, New York, NY 10110. 1991.**

Kaye Gibbons, Harriet Doerr, Ursula Le Guin and 16 other contributors illuminate "what is central to the creative lives of women."

Writer's Digest.

See "Advice, Analysis and Reportage" in "A Foot in the Door Resources."

❖ *A Writer's Guide to Copyright.* **Poets & Writers, Inc., 72 Spring Street, New York, NY 10012; 212–226–3586. <http://www.pw.org>. Second edition, 1989.**

A clear, concise, inexpensive guide, complete with a copyright checklist and sample forms, including a Random House contract.

The Writer's Handbook. **Edited by Sylvia K. Burack. The Writer, Inc., 120 Boylston Street, Boston, MA 02116–4615; 617–423–3157. <http://www.channel1.com/thewriter/>. 1997.**

A comprehensive compendium of essays by established writers about fiction, nonfiction, poetry, playwriting and more, plus sections on markets for a wide variety of written work and other useful information.

The Writer's Journal: 40 Contemporary Authors and Their Journals. **Edited by Sheila Bender. Delta/Dell, 1540 Broadway, New York, NY 10036. 1997.**

You get two pleasures here for the price of one. It's fun to read what are normally private scribblings, and it's exhilarating to see how writers use their journal entries as they work.

Writing for Your Life. **Edited by Sybil Steinberg. Pushcart Press, PO Box 380, Wainscott, NY 11975. Volume 2, 1995; Volume 3, 1997.**

The interviews with dozens and dozens of writers that appear in each volume generally focus on dealing with agents, editors and publishers, as well as on writing. Steinberg, who wrote some of them, runs *PW*'s powerful "Forecasts" (i.e., book review) section.

Writing It Down for James: Writers on Life and Craft. **Edited by Kurt Brown. Beacon Press, 25 Beacon Street, Boston, MA 02108. 1995.**
A collection of lectures given at writers conferences. This is the second in a series and it focuses on travel.

❖ **Zinsser, William.** *On Writing Well: An Informal Guide to Writing Non-fiction.* **HarperCollins, 10 East 53rd Street, New York, NY 10022. <http://www.harpercollins.com>. Sixth revised edition, 1998.**
Zinsser is not only a good teacher; he's wonderful company as he explains and exemplifies style, audience, interviews, business writing and other aspects of the writer's craft.

Zinsser, William et. al. *Speaking of Journalism: 12 Writers and Editors Talk About Their Work.* **HarperCollins, 10 East 53rd Street, New York, NY 10022. <http://www.harpercollins.com>. 1994.**
Thoughtful, personal reports designed to help aspiring writers. Contributors have worked for top-notch papers and magazines.

Tools

AcqWeb. <http://www.library.vanderbilt.edu/law/acqs/acqs.html>.
Affiliated with AcqNet, an electronic newsletter for librarians and others interested in acquisitions and collection development, AcqWeb links to an excellent, well-organized collection of international resource sites. Its Directory of Publishers and Vendors and General Reference Resources sections are particularly useful.

Acronym and Abbreviation List. <http://www.ucc.ie/info/net/acronyms/index.html>.
Type in an acronym or abbreviation (including ones that aren't pronounceable as a word) and get back its meaning, as well as its expansion.

All-in-One Search Page. <http://www.albany.net/allinone/>.
From this single interface, you can use more than 200 search forms, including the Internet Law Library and the Globewide Network

Academy Course Catalog, though you have to enter your queries into each engine or directory separately.

The Argus Clearinghouse. <http://www.clearinghouse.net/>.
A browsable and searchable directory of online guides to assorted subjects, fairly rigorously rated by the librarians who run this site.

ASJA Membership Directory. **American Society of Journalists and Authors, 1501 Broadway, Suite 302, New York, NY 10036; 212–997–0947; fax: 212–768–7414; e-mail: asja@compuserve.com. <http://www.asja.org>. Updated annually.**
An alphabetical, annotated, pricey list of writers who belong to the American Society of Journalists and Authors. It's indexed by subject specialties, areas of expertise and geography. Try ASJA's Dial-a-Writer service (see this section's "People, Places and Programs") first.

The AWP Official Guide to Writing Programs. **Edited by D. W. Fenza and Gwyn McVay. Dustbooks, PO Box 100, Paradise, CA 95967; 800–477–6110; e-mail: len@dustbooks.com. <http://www.dustbooks.com>. Updated periodically.**
Indexed by degrees offered, among other things, the *Associated Writing Programs Guide* covers hundreds of institutions and groups that "provide the time, place, learning, and the fellow spirits with which a writer may learn to master a difficult and lonely craft."

Bernard, André. *Now All We Need Is a Title: Famous Book Titles and How They Got That Way.* **W.W. Norton, 500 Fifth Avenue, New York, NY 10110. 1996.**
A delicious little book that may help you phrase possible titles and will certainly amuse you and add to your fund of literary trivia.

Book Stacks Unlimited. <http://www.books.com>.
Although Book Stacks doesn't have nearly the breadth of Amazon.com, it's a cozier source for books you need to use as you write.

Casey's Snow Day Reverse Dictionary (and Guru). <http://www.c3.lanl.gov:8064/>.
"Finally, the remedy for that tip-of-the-tongue feeling . . . type in a definition, and Casey's dictionary will tell you which word you are trying to think of!" Be sure to read the "How it works" section before you get started.

Children's Literature Web Guide.
<http://www.ucalgary.ca/~dkbrown/index.html>.
   Lively and packed with material on children's and young adult books, this site lists resources for teachers, parents, storytellers, writers and illustrators, and includes book reviews, discussion forums, recommended books and an Internet guide to children's book awards.

❖ Croteau, Maureen, and Wayne Worcester. *The Essential Researcher.* HarperPerennial, 10 East 53rd Street, New York, NY 10022. <http://www.harpercollins.com>. 1993.
   Look here for answers to those factual questions that keep cropping up as you write. (Who won the most Cy Young Awards? What's a reverse annuity mortgage? When are the Pleiades visible? Where are the nuclear power plants in North Carolina?) Like *A Writer's Companion,* edited by Louis Rubin (below), this is an amazingly rich compendium, conceived and structured especially for authors. Getting both would be a smart move; there's surprisingly little overlap.

dictionary.com. <http://www.dictionary.com>.
   Links to a number of reference tools available online, including *Roget's Thesaurus, Bartlett's Quotations,* Strunk's *Elements of Style,* Webster's *Dictionary, The Free On-line Dictionary of Computing* and *The New Hacker's Dictionary.*

Directory of Accredited Institutions. Distance Education and Training Council, 1601 18th Street NW, Washington, DC 20009–2529; 202–234–5100. Updated periodically.
   Before you sign up for a home study program, write for this free list.

A Directory of American Poets and Fiction Writers. Poets & Writers, Inc., 72 Spring Street, New York, NY 10012; 212–226–3586. <http://www.pw.org>. Updated periodically.
   Good for contacting professional writers on your wavelength and, unlike most directories of contemporary authors, inexpensive enough to own. More than 7,000 entries (e.g., Alice Adams, Garrison Keillor, John Irving) include addresses and phone numbers.

Directory of Special Libraries and Information Centers. Gale Research, Inc., 835 Penobscot Building, Detroit, MI 48226–4094; 800–877–4253; fax: 800–414–5043. <http://www.gale.com>. Updated periodically.

Check the index for troves of information on the subject(s) you're researching.

Dogpile: A Multi-Engine Search Tool. <http://www.dogpile.com>.
Dogpile queries 25 engines that search the Web, Usenet, FTP and News Wires and lets you customize the order of the search engines.

"Editorial Services," *Literary Market Place* **(see below).**
Plenty of professional writers are ready to give you a hand in expressing what you have to say, and this list will lead you to a number of them. In approaching a potential collaborator, be sure to ask for an estimate and to check references. See also Editorial Freelancers Association, below.

Encyclopedia of Associations. **Gale Research, Inc., 835 Penobscot Building, Detroit, MI 48226–4094; 800–877–4253; fax: 800–414–5043. <http://www.gale.com>. Updated periodically.**
The roughly 23,000 organizations and reference centers listed here can supply information and leads on almost any topic. Indexed in terms of geography as well as area of interest, entries are extremely informative.

FedStats. <http://www.fedstats.gov>.
Come here to find the statistics that will support whatever argument you're trying to make.

Filez. <http://www.filez.com>.
This search engine "gives users access to the important data on FTP servers," such as files on major corporate sites and in freeware and software archives. An excellent research tool.

Gale Research, Inc. Catalog. **Gale Research, Inc., 835 Penobscot Building, Detroit, MI 48226–4094; 800–877–4253; fax: 800–414–5043. <http://www.gale.com>.**
Gale's free catalog will familiarize you with a wide variety of reference books that will help you in all kinds of research.

Glasser, Selma. *The Analogy Book of Related Words: Your Secret Shortcut to Power Writing.* **Communication Creativity, PO Box 909, 425 Cedar Street, Buena Vista, CO 81211–0909; 800–331–8355. 1990.**
A thesaurus of sorts, this book is arranged by subject (Acting to Zodiac) with lists of relevant words for each.

Gonick, Larry, and Woollcott Smith. *The Cartoon Guide to Statistics*. HarperCollins, 10 East 53rd Street, New York, NY 10022. <http://www.harpercollins.com>. 1993.

For those whose research does—or should—deal with statistical data and whose knowledge of phenomena like standard deviations and confidence intervals is rudimentary, at best.

Idea Catcher: An Inspiring Journal for Writers. Story Press/Writer's Digest, 1507 Dana Avenue, Cincinnati, OH 45207; 513–531–2690; fax: 513–531–7107. 1995.

Clean pages topped by quotes and exercises that should help words flow onto them.

The Independent Study Catalog. Peterson's for the National University of Continuing Education Association, PO Box 2123, Princeton, NJ 08543–2123. <http://www.petersons.com>. 1995.

Entries cover 10,000 correspondence courses and are indexed by subject.

Inference Find. <http://www.inference.com/ifind/>.

First Inference Find sends "parallel" queries to what it considers to be the six best search engines on the Internet—AltaVista, Excite, Infoseek, Lycos, WebCrawler and Yahoo (although it can be configured to use any search engine). Then it groups similar items together instead of sorting results by how well the query is matched.

Inkspot. <http://www.inkspot.com>.

The WWW Virtual Library's Writers' Resource (see below for WWW VL). Well-organized information on the nuts and bolts of writing, with links to a multitude of related resources, discussion forums for writers and a free, bimonthly e-mail newsletter.

The Internet Sleuth. <http://www.isleuth.com>.

The 1,800 searchable databases here include many that are very specialized.

iTools! <http://www.itools.com>.

A tripartite site consisting of Research-It! and Find-It! (which let you search using selected tools such as Webster's Dictionary, the Universal Translator and AltaVista without leaving the site itself) and Promote-It! (which lists sites where you can list your site free).

Journalism. <http://www.cais.com/makulow/vlj.html>.

The WWW Virtual Library's Journalism Resource (see below for WWW VL). This extremely thorough site covers the journalism subcategories of broadcasting, communications, media and news and includes associations, news bureaus, research services, grants and other resources.

The Library of Congress Experimental Search System.
<http://lcweb2.loc.gov/resdev/ess/booksquery2a.html>.

Search selected material from the Library of Congress by subject, author, number (e.g., LC call, ISBN, Dewey), and then by type of collection (e.g., Books, Maps, Prints and Photographs, Film, Music), publication date, language, etc.

***Literary Market Place.* R.R. Bowker, 121 Chanlon Road, New Providence, NJ 07974; 888–BOWKER2; fax: 908–464–3553; e-mail: info@bowker.com. <http://www.bowker.com>. Updated annually.**

As subsequent "Resources" entries will show, *LMP* has many virtues. In connection with writing, its most useful sections are "Courses for the Book Trade" (which lists programs that teach publishing skills along with programs that teach writing) and "Writers' Conferences & Workshops" (which provides a small list of the perennials that you should supplement; see relevant entries above and below).

Magazine and Newsletter Editors' Resource List.
<http://www.tfs.net/personal/tgoff/erlist.html>.

A "modest" but handy collection of Web links for writers and editors, to (among other things) photography, advertising, journalism and circulation sites. Goff, the site's overseer, also offers a searchable online catalog of Cartoons for Newsletters and Magazines.

❖ **My Virtual Reference Desk. <http://www.refdesk.com>.**

A friendly, first-rate collection of reference links whether you want to dig deep for information or get quick access to it.

❖ *The New York Public Library Writer's Guide to Style and Usage.*
HarperCollins, 10 East 53rd Street, New York, NY 10022.
<http://www.harpercollins.com>. Updated periodically.

Remarkably user-friendly, as well as comprehensive and authoritative.

On-Line Resources for Writers.
<http://webster.commnet.edu/writing/writing.htm>.
Excellent useful material, including a Proofreading and Symbols Abbreviations chart, a Guide to Grammar and Writing and links to various sites run by good-hearted academics, such as The Purdue University On-Line Writing Lab.

OneLook Dictionaries: The Faster Finder. <http://www.onelook.com>.
Its searchable database includes more than 100 dictionaries.

***Readers' Guide to Periodical Literature.* H.W. Wilson Company, 950 University Avenue, Bronx, NY 10452; 800–367–6770. <http://www.hwwilson.com>. Updated periodically.**
The leading bibliography of articles from mass-circulation and other fairly general magazines, the *Readers' Guide* is useful for tracking down a piece you read some time ago that's relevant now to your work; for finding out what has appeared in the periodical press about a subject you're investigating; and for introducing yourself to varied angles on the same topic (see "What the Pros Know"). To get the most mileage from this guide, be sure to look under every subject heading that might possibly pertain to your needs.

***Research Centers Directory.* Gale Research, Inc., 835 Penobscot Building, Detroit, MI 48226–4094; 800–877–4253; fax: 800–414–5043. <http://www.gale.com>. Updated periodically.**
A guide to university-related and other nonprofit research organizations, this directory supplies excellent leads to experts and expertise. Use the subject index.

***Rising Voices: A Guide to Young Writers' Resources.* Compiled by Heather Blakeslee. Poets & Writers, Inc., 72 Spring Street, New York, NY 10012; 212–226–3586. <http://www.pw.org>. Second edition, 1997.**
Listings cover conferences, camps, prizes, periodicals, Web sites and more in terms of what they offer kids who want to write.

Roget's Internet Thesaurus of English Words and Phrases.
<http://www.thesaurus.com/?/>.
Search for that perfect word or phrase, browse the alphabetical index or skim the Six Main Classes of Words.

SavvySearch. <http://cage.cs.colostate.edu:1969/>.

A metasearch Web site that lets you search multiple databases simultaneously and get the results on one page (with no duplication). A Search Plan, based on your search terms and other factors, ranks and groups the 25 search engines listed here in order of usefulness for your query.

Scientific Style and Format: The CBE Manual for Authors, Editors, and Publishers. **Cambridge University Press, 40 West 20th Street, New York, NY 10011–4211. Sixth edition, 1994.**

An admirable example of a specialized style manual, this one, issued by The Council of Biology Editors, aims to cover all scientific disciplines.

**Search Engine List.
<http://www.nic.fr/~ouin/Private/html/search.html>.**

Links to more than three dozen search engines and 10 online white page and yellow page directories, with explanations of how they differ.

Search Engine Watch. <http://searchenginewatch.com>.

How search engines work; which to use when and why; tips on using them effectively and submitting your site(s) successfully, and where to go for more information.

Statistics Sources. **Gale Research, Inc., 835 Penobscot Building, Detroit, MI 48226–4094; 800–877–4253; fax: 800–414–5043. <http://www.gale.com>. Updated periodically.**

Arranged by subject, *Statistics Sources* will tell you where to find organizations and publications that can supply data you need.

Subject Guide to Books in Print. **R.R. Bowker, 121 Chanlon Road, New Providence, NJ 07974; 888–BOWKER2; fax: 908–464–3553; e-mail: info@bowker.com. <http://www.bowker.com>. Updated annually.**

To get a good idea of what's already been written about your subject, consult this compilation. Useful for a style survey as well as for research leads, the *Subject Guide* is available in libraries.

Swidan, Eleanor A. *Reference Sources: A Brief Guide.* **Enoch Pratt Free Library, Publications Office, 400 Cathedral Street, Baltimore, MD 21201–4484. 1988.**

Well-organized annotated listings that will help you select what you need from your library's shelves.

Telephone Directories on the Web.
<http://www.contractjobs.com/tel/>.
Includes online white pages, yellow pages and fax directories for more than 40 countries. Also links to some of the most popular online e-mail directories.

Twentieth-Century Children's Writers **and** *Twentieth-Century Young Adult Writers.* **Gale Research, Inc., 835 Penobscot Building, Detroit, MI 48226–4094; 800–877–4253; fax: 800–414–5043.**
<http://www.gale.com>. Updated periodically.
Like *The Writer's Directory* (below), these volumes can be conduits to professional writers you want to reach.

21st Century Manual of Style. **Edited by the Princeton Language Institute. Laurel/Dell, 1540 Broadway, New York, NY 10036. 1993.**
A small-print paperback that lists words and terms that people often get wrong, and proper nouns and abbreviations the way they're supposed to be. Punctuation, suffixes and the like are covered too.

The Ultimate Black Book. **Compiled by Godfrey Harris and Kenneth L. Harris. The Americas Group, 9200 Sunset Boulevard, Suite 404, Los Angeles, CA 90069; 800–996–7716; e-mail: hrmg@aol.com.**
<http://www.worldprofit.com/maamer.html>. Second edition, 1997.
Phone and fax numbers for institutions and other sources of information on 30+ subjects (e.g., Agriculture, Labor, Transportation) in a pocket-size paperback.

Weinstein, David A. *The Complete Copyright Protection Kit: Information and Legal Forms You Need to Protect What You Create.* **Intellaw, 636 Gaylord Street, Denver, CO 80206. 1992.**
The subtitle says it.

whatis.com. <http://whatis.com>.
The site has a glossary of Internet terms that is both searchable and alphabetically browsable, along with general information on using and figuring out the Internet.

❖ *A Writer's Companion.* **Edited by Louis D. Rubin Jr. in association with Jerry Leath Mills. HarperCollins, 10 East 53rd Street, New York, NY 10022. <http://www.harpercollins.com>. 1997.**
Like Maureen Croteau and Wayne Worcester's *The Essential Researcher* (above), this is a delicious compendium of information

geared to writers' needs. Rubin concentrates more on literature and the arts, but the range here is wide and wonderful. There's even a section that tells you when a host of consumer products came into general use.

Writers Conferences. Poets & Writers, Inc., 72 Spring Street, New York, NY 10012; 212–226–3586. <http://www.pw.org>. Updated annually; issued in March.

Look here for information on more than 200 writers conferences in the U.S. and overseas.

The Writer's Directory. St. James Press/Gale Research, Inc., 835 Penobscot Building, Detroit, MI 48226–4094; 800–877–4253; fax: 800–414–5043. <http://www.gale.com>. Twelfth edition, 1995.

Brief biographies, with addresses, of more than 17,500 writers, indexed in terms of broad subject categories. The library's copy will help you track down professional writers you want to contact.

❖ **The WWW Virtual Library.** <http://www.w3.org/vl/>.

A "distributed subject catalogue" (different sites handle different subjects) with links to other, more specialized virtual libraries. An excellent research project tool created by the people who started the Web.

People, Places and Programs

Associated Writing Programs. Tallwood House, Mailstop 1E3, George Mason University, Fairfax, VA 22030; 703–993–4301; fax: 703–993–4302; e-mail: awp@gmu.edu. <http://web.gmu.edu/departments/awp/>.

A clearinghouse for information, AWP puts out a newspaper and a catalog of writing programs, presents awards and publishes work by outstanding student writers. See "Money Resources" for additional information.

❖ **Dial-a-Writer Referral Service,** American Society of Journalists and Authors, 1501 Broadway, Suite 302, New York, NY 10036; 212–398–1934; fax: 212–768–7414; e-mail: asja@compuserve.com. <http://www.asja.org>.

Ask for help in locating potential co-authors in your area if you feel sure that your own efforts at composition are bound to be inadequate for one reason or another. When writers surface whom you might like to work with, study what they've already published, ask for and check their references and get the terms of the deal with you down in writing.

Editorial Freelancers Association, 71 West 23rd Street, Suite 1504, New York, NY 10010; 212–929–5400; fax: 212–929–5439.

You may find just the right editor, collaborator or ghostwriter by using the EFA's Job Phone. As above, remember to ask for writing samples, to get and check references and to be clear about the deal you're making.

International Women's Writing Guild, PO Box 810, Gracie Station, New York, NY 10028; 212–737–7536; fax: 212–737–9469; e-mail: iwwg@iwwg.com.

"A network for the personal and professional empowerment of women through writing," IWWG aims to encourage and support both published and aspiring writers through (among other things) a newsletter and an annual conference at Skidmore College in upstate New York.

❖ **Poets & Writers, Inc., 72 Spring Street, New York, NY 10012; 212–226–3586. <http://www.pw.org>.**

The people at Poets & Writers have figured out lots of ways to improve the quality of a writer's life. The group's publications are designed especially for writers of fiction and poetry but they're helpful to writers of all sorts. Among them are *Poets & Writers Magazine* and the *Directory of American Poets and Fiction Writers*. Send for the informational brochure, and if you write fiction or poetry ask to be listed in the next edition of the directory.

Romance Writers of America, 13700 Veterans Memorial Drive, Suite 315, Houston, TX 77014; 713–440–6885; fax: 713–440–7510. <http://www.rwanational.com>.

Open to "all writers actively pursuing a career in romantic fiction" (and to industry pros they deal with), RWA provides a magazine and networking opportunities. Check for chapters in your area.

U.S. Government.

A prime source of information on countless subjects. Write to the public relations staff of appropriate departments to request help in getting the data you want, and check out Matthew Lesko's *Information U.S.A.* (see "Money Resources").

The Writers Room, Inc., 10 Astor Place, 6th Floor, New York, NY 10003; 212–254–6995.

More than 200 writers rent space in The Writers Room, which functions as a support system and a grapevine and houses a library as well as desks. If you don't live close enough to apply, think about asking the director for guidance on setting up something similar.

A Foot in the Door Resources

SINCE MAKING SALES to publishers depends on what you know, whom you know and how you present each project, many of the resources mentioned here are designed to serve as introductions not only to markets but to people and procedures you'll find helpful as you approach publishing firms.

Advice, Analysis and Reportage

Bly, Robert W. *Getting Your Book Published: Inside Secrets of a Successful Author.* Roblin Press, 405 Tarrytown Road, Suite 414, White Plains, NY 10607; 800–874–9083. 1997.
　　Bite-size chunks of advice from the author of many how-to titles.

❖ Curtis, Richard. *How to Be Your Own Literary Agent: The Business of Getting A Book Published.* Houghton Mifflin, 222 Berkeley Street, Boston, MA 02116. <http://www.hmco.com/trade/>. Revised and expanded edition, 1996.
　　A feisty guide to contracts and mores at large book publishing houses. Curtis, an eminent and experienced agent with an acid wit, can be laugh-out-loud funny while dispensing essential information.

Day, Robert A. *How to Write & Publish a Scientific Paper.* Oryx Press, 4041 North Central Avenue, Suite 700, Phoenix, AZ 85012–3397; 800–279–6799. Fourth edition, 1994.
　　Knowledgeable and readable.

❖ Derricourt, Robin. *An Author's Guide to Scholarly Publishing.*
See "The Sale and Its Sequels Resources."

Gach, Gary. *Writers.Net: Every Writer's Essential Guide to Online Resources and Opportunities.*
See "Getting the Words Right Resources."

Gage, Diane, and Marcia Coppess. *Get Published: 100 Top Magazine Editors Tell You How.* Owl Books/Henry Holt, 115 West 18th Street, New York, NY 10011. 1994.
Based on experience and on interviews with editors of national magazines. Some of this is dated but that shouldn't matter much as long as you're careful to read the periodicals you want to write for.

❖ Herman, Jeff. *Writer's Guide to Book Editors, Publishers, and Literary Agents.* Prima Publishing, 3875 Atherton Road, Rocklin, CA 95765. <http://www.primapublishing.com/>. New, revised edition, 1997.
Virtually the only place you'll find descriptive material about editor after editor, Herman's book also offers essays and generously annotated listings of selected agents. (Remember to find out whether people you target have moved since this book came out.)

Hinckley, Karen, and Barbara Hinckley. *American Best Sellers: A Reader's Guide to Popular Fiction.* Indiana University Press, 601 North Morton Street, Bloomington, IN 47404–3797; 800–842–6796. 1989.
A mother and daughter team not only list and describe bestsellers from the '60s to the '80s; they analyze the books in terms of authors, categories, characters and themes. A fascinating compilation.

❖ Kopelman, Alexander. *National Writers Union Guide to Freelance Rates & Standard Practice.* National Writers Union, 873 Broadway, Suite 203, New York, NY 10003; 212–254–0279. 1995.
Thanks to the 1,200 writers whose experiences are reflected here, even beginners can be savvy negotiators. And that holds true for deals with corporations as well as with newspapers, magazines and book publishers of many sorts.

Larsen, Michael. *How to Write a Book Proposal.* Writer's Digest Books, 1507 Dana Avenue, Cincinnati, OH 45207; 513–531–2690; fax: 513–531–7107. Revised edition, 1997.

Exhaustive instructions for writers who have big books to sell to big houses and who are planning to spend big bucks as well as immense amounts of time promoting themselves and their work.

Larsen, Michael. *Literary Agents.* **John Wiley & Sons, 605 Third Avenue, New York, NY 10158. 1996.**

An upbeat analysis of the work agents do and of ways to work with them. The colorful, detailed contents pages will lead you quickly to whatever aspects of the agent-author relationship interest you at a particular time.

Levin, Martin P. *Be Your Own Literary Agent: The Ultimate Insider's Guide to Getting Published.* **Ten Speed Press, PO Box 7123, Berkeley, CA 94707. 1995.**

Levin, who's held high-level jobs at huge publishing houses, corroborates the fact that agents aren't necessary; you can sell your work yourself.

Litowinsky, Olga. *Writing and Publishing Books for Children in the 1990s: The Inside Story from the Editor's Desk.* **Walker & Company, 435 Hudson Street, New York, NY 10014. 1992.**

This particular editor's desk was situated variously at Delacorte, Scribners, Viking Penguin and Macmillan. Her advice covers books for young people at all age levels and she offers interesting observations about trends that were running when she wrote.

Luey, Beth. *Handbook for Academic Authors.* **Cambridge University Press, 40 West 20th Street, New York, NY 10011–4211. Third edition, 1995.**

A comprehensive, comprehensible guide for anyone working on articles for scholarly journals or on textbooks and other books for the academic market.

❖ **Maass, Donald.** *The Career Novelist: A Literary Agent Offers Strategies for Success.* **Heinemann, 361 Hanover Street, Portsmouth, NH 03801–3912. 1996.**

An agent who specializes in fiction offers a remarkably interesting factual account of how the biggest publishers think and act. His typology of agents is especially telling.

My First Year in Book Publishing: Real-World Stories from America's Book Publishing Professionals. Edited by Lisa Healy. Walker & Company, 435 Hudson Street, New York, NY 10014. 1994.

Amusing and informative first-person essays.

Poet. Cooper House Publishing, PO Box 5646, Shreveport, LA 71135–5646. Published 4x/year.

Peggy Cooper's lively magazine includes how-to and reportorial pieces, interviews, criticism and book reviews, plus, of course, poetry.

❖ *Poets & Writers Magazine.* Poets & Writers, Inc., 72 Spring Street, New York, NY 10012; 212–226–3586. <http://www.pw.org>. Published bimonthly.

Along with timely, solid information (when and how to apply for grants and awards, what various writers colonies offer, where to find fellow writers in your area), *Poets & Writers Magazine* has feature stories that shed light both on creating prose and poetry and on attracting readers to written work.

❖ *The Portable Writers' Conference: Your Guide to Getting and Staying Published.* Edited by Stephen Blake Mettee. Quill Driver Books, 950 North Van Ness Avenue, PO Box 4638, Fresno, CA 93744–4638. 1997.

A commendably rich compendium, more like a whole bunch of writers conferences than just one. Writers of all sorts at all levels should look here for guidance.

Powell, Walter W. *Getting into Print: The Decision-Making Process in Scholarly Publishing.* University of Chicago Press, 5801 South Ellis Avenue, Chicago, IL 60637. 1985.

Focusing on two scholarly presses that he observed closely, Powell punctures publishing myths and reveals realities. His trenchant observations conclude with a skippable chapter on organizational theory.

Publishing Books. Edited by Everette E. Dennis, Craig L. LaMay, and Edward C. Pease. Transaction Publishers, Rutgers University, Building 4051, New Brunswick, NJ 08903; 908–445–2280; fax: 908–445–3138. <http://www.transactionpub.com>. 1997.

Observations on the book publishing process by insiders and educators who originally provided them for a 1992 issue of *Media Studies Journal.* An interesting play of perspectives.

Scribner, Charles, Jr. *In the Company of Writers: A Life in Publishing.* Scribner/Simon & Schuster, 1230 Avenue of the Americas, New York, NY 10020. 1991.

Derived from an oral history by Joel R. Gardner, this modest autobiography by a scion of the Scribner family provides glimpses of editors and writers in action.

❖ Smedley, Christine S., Mitchell Allen et al. *Getting Your Book Published.* Sage Publications, 2455 Teller Road, Thousand Oaks, CA 91320; e-mail: order@sagepub.com. 1993.

Friendly, down-to-earth tutelage from members of the editorial acquisitions and production staff at Sage Publications, Inc., for authors of scholarly monographs, advanced texts and other professional/scientific books.

Steinberg, Jacob. *I Never Had a Best-Seller: The Story of a Small Publisher.*

See "The Self-Publishing Option Resources."

Tebbel, John, and Mary Ellen Zuckerman. *The Magazine in America: 1741–1990.* Oxford University Press, 198 Madison Avenue, New York, NY 10016. 1991.

Readable and thorough, *The Magazine in America* concentrates on 20th-century periodicals—the people and purposes behind them and the trends they mirrored and fueled.

Thyer, Bruce A. *Successful Publishing in Scholarly Journals.* Sage Publications, 2455 Teller Road, Thousand Oaks, CA 91320; e-mail: order@sagepub.com. 1994.

The title is apt, and the writer is an honest, friendly, well-informed guide.

West, Michelle. *The No-Bull Guide to Getting Published and Making It as a Writer.* Winslow Publishing, PO Box 38012, 550 Eglinton Avenue West, Toronto, Ontario, Canada M5N 3 A8. 1986.

Advice full of energy on writing for magazines.

The Writer.

See "Getting the Words Right Resources."

Writer's Digest, 1507 Dana Avenue, Cincinnati, OH 45207; 513–531–2690; fax: 513–531–7107. Published monthly.

Geared primarily to beginners, the articles in *Writer's Digest* sometimes promise more than they can deliver. On the other hand, there's savvy guidance in here too. Read skeptically and you'll be able to separate the practical advice from the puffery.

The Writer's Handbook. Edited by Sylvia K. Burack.

See "Getting the Words Right Resources" and note especially its section on writers colonies.

Writer's Yearbook. Writer's Digest Books, 1507 Dana Avenue, Cincinnati, OH 45207; 513–531–2690; fax: 513–531–7107. Published annually.

The *Yearbook* is essentially a fatter-than-normal issue of the monthly *Writer's Digest*.

Tools

AAR information. Association of Authors' Representatives, Inc., 10 Astor Place, 3rd Floor, New York, NY 10003; 212–353–3709.

An organization of conscientious professionals. If you send them a #10 envelope with 55 cents postage and a check (to AAR) for $7, they'll send you a list of members, a copy of their Canon of Ethics, and an informative brochure about agents in general and the AAR in particular.

❖ **AcqWeb.**

See "Getting the Words Right Resources."

❖ **Amazon.com Books! Earth's biggest bookstore.**
<http://www.amazon.com/>.

Not just a huge bookstore. Amazon's enormous searchable database makes it also a great research tool: Find out what your competition is and what readers are saying about it.

The American Directory of Writer's Guidelines: What Editors Want, What Editors Buy. Compiled and edited by John C. Mutchler. Quill Driver Books, 950 North Van Ness Avenue, PO Box 4638, Fresno, CA 93744–4638. 1997.

Write-ups supplied by editors at a wide variety of periodicals and a narrower range of book publishing houses; indexed by subject.

❖ **ASJA Contracts Watch.** <http://www.asja.org/cwpage.htm>. **E-mail asja@compuserve.com for subscription information.**

News about negotiations between publishers and writers that can boost your courage as well as your income if you're about to make a deal.

The Bloomsbury Review, **1762 Emerson Street, Denver, CO 80218–1012; 800–783–3338. Published bimonthly.**

A "book magazine" that provides a wider window on writing and writers than more famous review media.

Booklist. **American Library Association, 50 East Huron Street, Chicago, IL 60611; 312–944–6780. Published twice monthly September–June, monthly July–August.**

Together with *Choice, Library Journal* and other review media listed below, *Booklist* exerts a great deal of influence on librarians as they ponder what books to buy. Skimming its reviews, you can begin to sense the patterns of public taste that libraries both reflect and help create.

Book Review Digest. **H.W. Wilson Company, 950 University Avenue, Bronx, NY 10452; 800–367–6770. <http://www.hwwilson.com>. Published periodically.**

Tidbits from reviews of some 7,000 books a year appear here. Check to see (1) how critics reacted to recent books like yours and (2) which of them might be especially receptive to your work.

Bowker Catalog. **R.R. Bowker, 121 Chanlon Road, New Providence, NJ 07974; 888–BOWKER2; fax: 908–464–3553; e-mail: info@bowker.com. <http://www.bowker.com>.**

Bowker codifies and disseminates a great deal of information about publishing. Simply looking at the products in the catalog should give you fresh ideas about placement. See descriptions of selected Bowker publications above and below and get hold of them and others as needed. Your library may have CD-ROM or online versions as well as bound volumes.

Burrelle's Media Directory: Magazines and Newsletters. **Burrelle's Information Services, 75 East Northfield Road, Livingston, NJ 07039. 1997 edition.**

Arranged in subject categories, 12,000 entries offer information about content, circulation, ownership, staff and how to get in touch.

Chase's Calendar of Events. NTC/Contemporary Publishing, 4255 West Touhy Avenue, Lincolnwood, IL 60646–1975; 800–323–4900. Updated annually.

Fun to read and useful for finding news pegs on which to hang pieces, the calendar created by William and Helen Chase will also alert you to upcoming fairs, conventions and exhibits that might be worth covering or simply attending. More than 10,000 entries in all.

The Chicago Manual of Style.

See "The Self-Publishing Option Resources."

Children's Literature Web Guide.

See "Getting the Words Right Resources."

Choice: Current Reviews for Academic Libraries. Association of College and Research Libraries, American Library Association, 100 Riverview Center, Middletown, CT 06457; 860–347–6933. Published monthly except combined in July and August.

See *Booklist,* above, and get hold of a copy.

Clardy, Andrea Fleck. *Words to the Wise: A Writer's Guide to Feminist and Lesbian Periodicals & Publishers.* Firebrand Books, 141 The Commons, Ithaca, NY 14850. Updated periodically.

If you've written anything for a feminist and/or lesbian audience, use this informative annotated guide. It covers more than 150 book and periodical publishers.

Directory of Literary Magazines. Asphodel Press/Moyer Bell, Kymbolde Way, Wakefield, RI 02879.

Prepared in cooperation with the Council of Literary Magazines and Presses, this directory covers roughly 600 periodicals around the country that publish fiction, nonfiction and poetry.

Directory of Poetry Publishers. Dustbooks, PO Box 100, Paradise, CA 95967; 800–477–6110; e-mail: len@dustbooks.com. <http://www.dustbooks.com>. Updated annually.

Detailed listings describe more than 2,000 magazines and publishing houses that welcome poetry, and there's a useful subject index.

Ecola Newsstand. <http://www.ecola.com/news/>.

A searchable and browsable index of more than 4,500 print publications with unrestricted access sites on the Web. Useful for getting articles and other information without having to buy a physical newspaper or magazine.

Editor & Publisher International Year Book. **Editor & Publisher, 11 West 19th Street, New York, NY 10011; 212–675–4380; e-mail: edpub@mediainfo.com. <http://www.mediainfo.com>. Updated annually.**

A directory of newspapers that names department heads and gives circulation figures and other valuable data for each entry. Useful for selling stories with a local slant.

❖ *Gale Directory of Publications and Broadcast Media.* **Gale Research, Inc., 835 Penobscot Building, Detroit, MI 48226–4094; 800–877–4253; fax: 800–414–5043. <http://www.gale.com>. Updated periodically.**

Annotated listings of thousands of newspapers, magazines, trade publications, radio and TV stations and cable companies, arranged by geographic location and indexed by keywords. One or more of these entries may make good targets for material with a special-interest focus or a pronounced local slant.

Gold, Jerome. *Publishing Lives: Interviews with Independent Book Publishers in the Pacific Northwest and British Columbia.*
See "The Self-Publishing Option Resources."

The Horn Book Magazine, **11 Beacon Street, Boston, MA 02108; 617–227–1555; fax: 617–523–0299; e-mail: magazine@hbook.com. Published bimonthly.**

Like *School Library Journal* (below), this is a major review medium for children's books.

Hudson's Subscription Newsletter Directory. **The Newsletter Clearinghouse, PO Box 311, Rhinebeck, NY 12572; 914–876–2081; e-mail: HPHudson@aol.com. Updated periodically.**

Browse through your library's copy to see if you can find markets for your work among the thousands of newsletters listed here and indexed by subject.

Samir Husni's Guide to New Consumer Magazines. **Oxbridge Communications (dist. by Gale), 150 Fifth Avenue, Suite 302, New York, NY 10011; 212–741–0231; fax: 212–633–2938; e-mail:**

info@oxbridge.com. <http://www.mediafinder.com>. Published annually.

Organized by subject category. It's well worth checking out the latest version because magazines are usually hungrier for material when they're new than they are after they've become known.

Independent Publisher. The Jenkins Group, 121 East Front Street, 4th Floor, Traverse City, MI 49684; 616–933–0445; e-mail: jenkins.group@smallpress.com. <http://www.smallpress.com>. Published bimonthly.

Articles and reviews can help you identify small publishing companies that might be right for your work.

Inkspot.
See "Getting the Words Right Resources."

Inter-Links. <http://alabanza.com/kabacoff/Inter-Links/>.
Created as a public service "Internet navigator, resource locator, and tutorial" all rolled into one, this well-thought-out site is both educational and efficient in helping you find what you need online.

International Directory of Little Magazines and Small Presses. Edited by Len Fulton. Dustbooks, PO Box 100, Paradise, CA 95967; 800–477–6110; e-mail: len@dustbooks.com. <http://www.dustbooks.com>. Updated annually.

Descriptions of more than 6,000 markets appear in this affordable paperback, and its geographic and subject indexes make appropriate people easy to target.

Internet Writer's Guideline Listing.
<http://wane5.scri.fsu.edu/~jtillman/DEV/ZDMS/>.
This free service of *In Vivo Magazine* offers a searchable listing of roughly 160 online publications with precise instructions for submitting your material to them.

Journalism.
See "Getting the Words Right Resources."

The Journalist's Road to Success: A Career and Scholarship Guide. The Dow Jones Newspaper Fund, Inc., PO Box 300, Princeton, NJ 08543–0300; 800-DOWFUND or 609–452–2820; e-mail:

newsfund@wsj.dowjones.com. <http://www.dowjones.com/newsfund>. 1996.
Information for those interested in studying journalism and/or working for newspapers.

Kremer, John. *Celebrate Today!* Prima Publishing, 3875 Atherton Road, Rocklin, CA 95765. <http://www.primapublishing.com/>. 1996.
Like *Chase's Calendar of Events* (above), this is a fine source of news pegs. Organized chronologically, it doesn't have a subject index.

John Labovitz's E-Zine-List.
<http://www.meer.net/~johnl/e-zine-list/index.html>.
A browsable directory of more than 1,500 electronic 'zines. Entries give general contact information and link to each e-zine's Internet site but don't include in-depth submission guidelines. Note the helpful page of links to other e-zine-related resources.

Library Journal, 245 West 17th Street, 6th Floor, New York, NY 10011–5300; 212–463–6819. <http://www.ljdigital.com/>. Published 22x/year.
See *Booklist,* above.

❖ *Literary Market Place.* R.R. Bowker, 121 Chanlon Road, New Providence, NJ 07974; 888–BOWKER2; fax: 908–464–3553; e-mail: info@bowker.com. <http://www.bowker.com>. Updated annually.
As noted in "Getting the Words Right Resources," *LMP* is an indispensable reference work. When you're working on getting your foot in the door, study the following sections: "U.S. Book Publishers" (note especially the subject listing, which, although general, is handy, and the geographical location listing, which is a gold mine of good leads, particularly for regional books); "Book Trade & Allied Associations" (which can point you toward local and national organizations useful for networking, selling in bulk and getting information you need); "Reference Books for the Trade" (where you'll find specialized titles that may be relevant to your current work, along with leads to books about the publishing industry); "Awards, Contests & Grants" (if you win, you'll have acquired credentials that editors will respect); "Writers' Conferences & Workshops" (a partial but useful listing); "Literary Agents" (with names, addresses, phone numbers and some annota-

tions); "Courses for the Book Trade," and "Employment Agencies" (specializing in publishing positions).

Magazines for Libraries. R.R. Bowker, 121 Chanlon Road, New Providence, NJ 07974; 888–BOWKER2; fax: 908–464–3553; e-mail: info@bowker.com. <http://www.bowker.com>. Updated periodically.

Although the annotations are designed for librarians, anyone can use them to target periodicals for submissions (and, later, for publicity).

Midwest Book Review.
See "The Sale and Its Sequels Resources."

New Marketing Opportunities. Edited by Sophia Tarila. New Editions International, PO Box 2578, Sedona, AZ 86339–2578. <http://infinite.org/newedit>. Fifth edition, 1996.

Covers the market often labeled "New Age." Lengthy listings include retailers, catalogs, associations, radio and TV shows, events, co-op mailings and quite a lot more.

Newsletters in Print. Gale Research, Inc., 835 Penobscot Building, Detroit, MI 48226–4094; 800–877–4253; fax: 800–414–5043. <http://www.gale.com>. Updated periodically.

One or more of the indexes should lead you to periodicals where you might get published.

The New York Times on the Web, Book Section. <http://www.nytimes.com>.

Book reviews since 1980. If you're doing a book that fits the *Times'* interest span, check here for information on your "competition" and/or on writers who might give you blurbs.

Noble, William. *The Complete Guide to Writers' Conferences and Workshops.* Paul S. Eriksson, PO Box 62, I–54 Dunmore, Forest Dale, VT 05745. 1995.

Listings are arranged by state and interspersed with profiles of conference directors.

Novel & Short Story Writer's Market: Where & How to Sell Your Fiction. Edited by Barbara Kuroff. Writer's Digest Books, 1507 Dana Avenue, Cincinnati, OH 45207; 513–531–2690; fax: 513–531–7107. 1997.

Descriptions, which cover a wide variety of magazines along with some 'zines and book publishing houses, are geared to neophytes and most useful for their "Needs" data.

Penn State Reprints in Book History. Edited by James L.W. West III and Samuel S. Vaughan. The Pennsylvania State University Press, 820 North University Drive, University Park, PA 16802.

This new series offering glimpses of publishers, editors and writers in action supports the theory that the more things in publishing change, the more they stay the same (in case you had any doubt). Send for a list of available titles.

PMA Newsletter. **Publishers Marketing Association, 627 Aviation Way, Manhattan Beach, CA 90266; 310–372–2732; fax: 310–374–3342; e-mail: PMAonline@aol.com. <http://pma-online.org/>. Published monthly.**

PMA's periodical will introduce you to many interesting publishers and publishing possibilities.

Poet's Market: Where and How to Publish Your Poetry. **Writer's Digest Books, 1507 Dana Avenue, Cincinnati, OH 45207; 513–531–2690; fax: 513–531–7107. Updated annually.**

Unusually informative listings cover 1,700 publications, with tips and advice from poets (both celebrated and those newly published), Internet opportunities, and information about poets' resources— contests, awards, grants, conferences, colonies, workshops and the like.

Publishers Directory. **Gale Research, Inc., 835 Penobscot Building, Detroit, MI 48226–4094; 800–877–4253; fax: 800–414–5043. <http://www.gale.com>. Updated periodically.**

Roughly 20,000 publishers are listed here, including those that are small and specialized. Try your library for a copy.

❖ *Publishers Weekly,* **249 West 17th Street, New York, NY 10011; 212–463–6758; fax: 212–463–6631. <http://www.bookwire.com/pw>.**

PW, as it's familiarly known, has no equal as a source of up-to-date information about book publishing facts, figures, ideas and individuals. You can arrange to join the insiders who read it regularly by using your library's subscription copies or by subscribing yourself. Although it's aimed primarily at people who work with books, it frequently announces new periodicals, which provide promising markets (see also *Samir Husni's Guide to New Consumer Magazines,* above).

Publishing Trends. Market Partners International, 232 Madison Avenue, #1400, New York, NY 10016; 212–447–0855; e-mail: mpi@mpipubtrends.com. Published monthly.

The price tag is high, but you won't find this sort of insider information anywhere else. Market Partners' partners revel in reporting on conventions, studies and what's happening in the big book publishing houses.

The Pushcart Prize: Best of the Small Presses. Edited by Bill Henderson. Pushcart Press, PO Box 380, Wainscott, NY 11975. Published annually.

Look to the latest volumes of Bill Henderson's anthology not only for fine poetry and prose but also for insight into what literary publishers are currently enthusiastic about.

Pushcart's Complete Rotten Reviews and Rejections: A History of Insult, a Solace to Writers. Edited by Bill Henderson and André Bernard. Pushcart Press, PO Box 380, Wainscott, NY 11975. 1998.

A great pick-me-up for those times when turndowns get you down, The Rotten Rejections entries show you what editors said as they spurned *The Clan of the Cave Bear, The Spy Who Came in from the Cold* and a host of other titles they must have gone on to kick themselves about.

Readers' Guide to Periodical Literature. H.W. Wilson Company, 950 University Avenue, Bronx, NY 10452; 800–367–6770. <http://www.hwwilson.com>. Updated periodically.

Available in libraries, this standard and invaluable reference tool covers a variety of popular magazines. Use the subject headings to identify those that are likely to want your work and then tap the library's resources again to read a few issues and familiarize yourself with their style and their slant.

Ross, Marilyn. *National Directory of Newspaper Op-Ed Pages.* Communication Creativity, PO Box 909, 425 Cedar Street, Buena Vista, CO 81211–0909; 800–331–8355. 1994.

Pieces on these pages can help you attract editors for your work in progress as well as readers for your work in print. When you're ready to submit, call the papers you've targeted for updates on their listings.

School Library Journal, 245 West 17th Street, 6th Floor, New York, NY 10011–5300; 212–463–6759. Published monthly.
An excellent way to get an overview of current children's books and what librarians think of them.

Search Engine Watch.
See "Getting the Words Right Resources."

ShawGuides. <http://www.shawguides.com>.
Look here for a searchable online guide to writers conferences.

Standard Periodical Directory. **Oxbridge Communications (dist. by Gale), 150 Fifth Avenue, Suite 302, New York, NY 10011; 212–741–0231; fax: 212–633–2938; e-mail: info@oxbridge.com. <http://www.mediafinder.com>. Updated periodically.**
Listings arranged by subject cover 85,000 periodicals in the U.S. and Canada.

Stony Hills: News and Reviews of the Small Press. **Stony Hills Productions, RR 1, PO Box 780, New Sharon, ME 04955; 207–778–4699.**
Diane Kruchkow's *Stony Hills,* published from time to time, illuminates the world most people think of when you say "small press" rather than "small publisher"—a world of fiction, poetry and politics.

Stuart, Sally E. *Christian Writers' Market Guide.* **Harold Shaw Publishers, 388 Gundersen Drive, PO Box 567, Wheaton, IL 60189. 1997.**
Admirably annotated and indexed, these lengthy lists of Christian book and periodical publishers are accompanied by other useful information, including lists of conferences and groups.

❖ *Subject Guide to Books in Print and Forthcoming Books.* **R.R. Bowker, 121 Chanlon Road, New Providence, NJ 07974; 888–BOWKER2; fax: 908–464–3553; e-mail: info@bowker.com. <http://www.bowker.com>. Updated annually.**
Try your local bookstore or library for copies of these volumes and the periodic supplements. They're excellent tools both for trend-spotting and for manuscript marketing.

❖ *Subject Guide to Children's Books in Print.* **R.R. Bowker, 121 Chanlon Road, New Providence, NJ 07974; 888–BOWKER2; fax:**

908–464–3553; e-mail: info@bowker.com. <http://www.bowker.com>. Updated periodically.

Thousands of titles—fiction and nonfiction—are indexed here. A good way to identify kindred spirits at publishing houses if you write for kids.

Ulrich's International Periodicals Directory. R.R. Bowker, 121 Chanlon Road, New Providence, NJ 07974; 888–BOWKER2; fax: 908–464–3553; e-mail: info@bowker.com. <http://www.bowker.com>. Updated periodically.

A huge compilation. Available in five volumes and/or online and/or on CD-ROM in libraries.

Utne Reader. LENS Publishing Co., 1624 Harmon Place, Minneapolis, MN 55403; 612–338–5040; e-mail: info@utnereader.com. Published bimonthly.

Selections in here from "alternative media" can introduce you to ideas that differ from, and perhaps foreshadow, what you'll find in mainstream periodicals.

Voice of Youth Advocates, 4720 Boston Way, Lanham, MD 20706; 301–459–3366. Published bimonthly.

Includes book reviews and articles for and about adolescents.

Working Press of the Nation. R.R. Bowker, 121 Chanlon Road, New Providence, NJ 07974; 888–BOWKER2; fax: 908–464–3553; e-mail: info@bowker.com. <http://www.bowker.com>. Updated periodically.

Listings cover newspapers, magazines, TV and radio.

Writers Conferences. Poets & Writers, Inc., 72 Spring Street, New York, NY 10012; 212–226–3586. <http://www.pw.org>. Updated annually; issued in March.

A guide to roughly 200 gatherings with terse, extremely informative listings. Once you've studied the descriptions, you can send for literature about the conferences that interest you most, and then—taking account of the topics, the speakers, the chances for getting criticism and the condition of your pocketbook—choose those that will serve your current needs best.

Writer's Digest Catalog. Writer's Digest Books, 1507 Dana Avenue, Cincinnati, OH 45207; 513–531–2690; fax: 513–531–7107.

Get hold of this catalog to find specialized guides not reviewed here that are relevant to your work.

Writer's Market: Where & How to Sell What You Write. **Writer's Digest Books, 1507 Dana Avenue, Cincinnati, OH 45207; 513–531–2690; fax: 513–531–7107. Updated annually.**

Writer's Market flags thousands of publishing opportunities. If you do a bit of extra investigating to learn more about the ones that seem relevant before you approach an editor, these leads should serve you well.

Writers Northwest Handbook. **Media Weavers, PO Box 86190, Portland, OR 97286–0190; 503–771–0428. Updated periodically.**

Essays and tips accompany a lengthy, informative list of book and periodical publishers in a region where lots of exciting publishing takes place. Media Weavers also has a newspaper: *Writers NW: News and Reviews for the Community of the Printed Word.*

"*Writer's Profit Catalog*™", 22 East Quakenbush Avenue, 3rd Floor, Dumont, NJ 07628; 201–385–1220.

Guidance for writers from Robert W. Bly, who focuses on marketing and moneymaking and produces books, short reports, cassettes and seminars. Send for his catalog to see which products might serve your needs.

❖ **Write Time. Grossman Development Company, PO Box 85732, Seattle, WA 98145–1732; 800–891–0962 or 206–789–6263; e-mail: gdc@earthlink.net. Updated annually.**

A comprehensive, easy-to-use software program for writers that lists more than 2,000 grants, scholarships, fellowships and the like. It tracks your submissions, lets you add and update entries, and generates a form letter for getting award information. Yearly updates can be merged with your current version.

Write Trak. Grossman Development Company, PO Box 85732, Seattle, WA 98145–1732; 800–891–0962 or 206–789–6263; e-mail: gdc@earthlink.net.

Organize and track your publishing submissions using this software program, which also lets you enter specific notes on each manuscript and/or submission and keep a record of your writing-related expenses and income.

People, Places and Programs

The Children's Book Council, 568 Broadway, Suite 404, New York, NY 10012; 212–966–1990; e-mail: staff@cbcbooks.org. <http://www.cbcbooks.org>.

Write to the CBC if you'd like a list of its members (publishers, editors and art directors) and brief descriptions of their publishing programs. You'll need to enclose a self-addressed envelope pre-stamped for 78 cents postage, along with $2 to cover the list fee.

Mystery Writers of America, 17 East 47th Street, 6th Floor, New York, NY 10017; 212–888–8171; fax: 212–888–8107.

Meetings and a newsletter are among the benefits MWA offers. If you write crime/mystery/suspense, you're eligible for membership. Send for the group's brochure.

Poets & Writers, Inc.

See "Getting the Words Right Resources."

Poets House, 72 Spring Street, 2nd Floor, New York, NY 10012; 212–431–7920; fax: 212–431–8131.

A place to make contact with poets (see "The Sale and Its Sequels Resources") and to become acquainted with the publishers who buy poetry. There's a sizable collection of books, periodicals and tapes too.

The Publishing Institute, 2075 South University Blvd., D–114, Denver, CO 80210; 303–871–2570; fax: 303–871–2501. <http://www.du.edu/pi>.

Run with zest and acumen by Elizabeth Geiser, this four-week summer program at the University of Denver offers much-praised workshops and lectures about varied aspects of book publishing, with a helpful dose of career counseling. Write for details and application forms.

Radcliffe Publishing Course, Radcliffe College, 77 Brattle Street, Cambridge, MA 02138; 617–495–8678; fax: 617–496–2333; e-mail: rpc@radcliffe.edu. <http://www.radcliffe.edu>.

Another well-regarded program for people interested in training for publishing jobs, this summertime course takes six weeks and covers both book and magazine publishing.

Sensible Solutions, Inc., 271 Madison Avenue, Suite 1007, New York, NY 10016; 212–687–1761; fax: 212–867–8641; e-mail: Sensibly@aol.com. <http://www.happilypublished.com>.

A consulting firm headed by Judith Appelbaum and Florence Janovic, Sensible Solutions grew out of *How to Get Happily Published.* Its marketing plans are designed to help writers approach (or become) book publishers and—once books are scheduled—to round up readers.

Sisters in Crime.

See "The Sale and Its Sequels Resources."

Small Press Reference Center, 20 West 44th Street, New York, NY 10036; 212–764–7021; fax: 212–354–5365; e-mail: smallpress@aol.com.

Those in the New York area can get acquainted with hundreds of small publishers by examining books in the Center's library, which also includes how-to titles about writing and publication.

Small Publishers' Associations.

You'll find some regional, local and national groups in the "Book Trade & Allied Associations" section of *Literary Market Place*, and via Web sites such as BookWire, BookZone and The Midwest Book Review (see "The Sale and Its Sequels Resources").

Society of Children's Book Writers and Illustrators, 22736 Vanowen Street, Suite 106, West Hills, CA 91307; 818–888–8771. <http://www.scbwi.org>.

Through its publications, gatherings, grants and other benefits of membership, SCBWI educates and supports authors and artists who work on books for kids.

The Sale and Its Sequels
Resources

T O HELP YOUR WORK reach its best audience, it's wise to proceed as though you were responsible for getting it out to
readers. Those of you who are ambitious, therefore, will want to
study and use "The Self-Publishing Option Resources" along
with books, periodicals, programs, people and Web sites
described below that meet your needs.

Advice, Analysis and Reportage

The ASJA Handbook: A Writers' Guide to Ethical and Economic Issues.
American Society of Journalists and Authors, 1501 Broadway, Suite
302, New York, NY 10036; 212–977–0947; fax: 212–768–7414;
e-mail: asja@compuserve.com. <http://www.asja.org>. Updated periodically.

A thoroughly practical pamphlet. Tips distilled from members'
reports focus on dealing with editors, agents, publishers, other writers
and the IRS.

Barzun, Jacques. *On Writing, Editing, and Publishing: Essays Explicative and Hortatory.* University of Chicago Press, 5801 South Ellis
Avenue, Chicago, IL 60637. Second edition, 1986.

Barzun's targets in these stylish pieces include over-reaching copy
editors and talk-show hosts. The essays on writing and writer's block
are especially interesting.

Bly, Robert W. *The Copywriter's Handbook: A Step-by-Step Guide to Writing Copy That Sells.* Henry Holt & Company, 115 West 18th Street, New York, NY 10011. 1990.

"A book of rules, tips, techniques and ideas" for writing the kind of copy that sells products and/or services. Crystal clear.

❖ Bly, Robert W. *Targeted Public Relations: How to Get Thousands of Dollars of Free Publicity For Your Product, Service, Organization, or Idea.*

See "The Self-Publishing Option Resources."

Bodian, Nat. *The Joy of Publishing: Fascinating Facts, Anecdotes, Curiosities, and Historic Origins about Books and Authors, Editors and Publishers, Bookmaking and Bookselling.* Open Horizons Publishing Co., 209 South Main Street, #200, PO Box 205, Fairfield, IA 52556–0205; 800–796–6130 or 515–472–6130; fax: 515–472–1560; e-mail: JohnKremer@aol.com. <http://www.bookmarket.com>. 1996.

A quirky compendium that's fun to dip into.

Brent, Stuart. *The Seven Stairs.* Touchstone/Simon & Schuster, 1230 Avenue of the Americas, New York, NY 10020. Reprint edition, 1989.

The legendary, literary Chicago bookseller's charming memoir. It's good to get to know him and enlightening to see the bookselling business through his eyes.

Bugeja, Michael J. *Poet's Guide: How to Publish and Perform Your Work.* Story Line Press, 3 Oaks Farm, Brownsville, OR 97327–9718. 1995.

Particularly useful for published poets, this helpful handbook also includes advice on working with editors.

Bunnin, Brad, and Peter Beren. *The Writer's Legal Companion.* Addison-Wesley Publishing, One Jacob Way, Reading, MA 01867–3999. 1994.

A self-help guide designed to alert you to legal issues and help you figure out what action, if any, to take about them. Keep in mind, especially if you write for magazines, that it was written before the advent of electronic publishing.

Callenbach, Ernest. *Publisher's Lunch.* Ten Speed Press, PO Box 7123, Berkeley, CA 94707. 1989.

The form is fiction—about a man/woman, editor/author relationship portrayed through lunch-hour conversations—but you can learn a lot here about the facts of publishing life.

Crawford, Tad, and Tony Lyons. *The Writer's Legal Guide.* **Allworth Press, 10 East 23rd Street, Suite 400, New York, NY 10010; 212-777-8395. Revised edition, 1996.**

Comprehensive and readable, Crawford's book covers copyright, contracts, collaborations, new media and taxes, among other things.

Cuddihy, Michael. *Try Ironwood: An Editor Remembers.* **Rowan Tree Press, 124 Chestnut Street, Boston, MA 02108. 1990.**

Memoirs by the poet who became founder and editor of *Ironwood,* the literary magazine.

Curtis, Richard. *How to Be Your Own Literary Agent: The Business of Getting Your Book Published.*

See "A Foot in the Door Resources" and remember that understanding contract provisions in context is necessary but not sufficient; if you're dealing with a big firm and a complicated contract you need a literary agent or a literary property lawyer.

Curtis, Richard. *Mastering the Business of Writing.* **Allworth Press, 10 East 23rd Street, Suite 400, New York, NY 10010; 212-777-8395. 1996.**

Based on pieces that ran in *Lucas,* the science fiction trade publication, these urbane essays demystify a good many publishing processes and practices.

❖ **Derricourt, Robin.** *An Author's Guide to Scholarly Publishing.* **Princeton University Press, 41 William Street, Princeton, NJ 08540. 1996.**

Letters to assorted authors from "R.M.D." explain the whole scholarly publishing process with charm and clarity. Derricourt's background includes 12 years as publishing director for Cambridge University Press in England and Australia.

Dobkin, Jeffrey. *How to Market a Product for Under $500! A Handbook of Multiple Exposure Marketing.* **Danielle Adams Publishing, PO Box 100, Merion Station, PA 19066; 610-642-1000. 1996.**

Dobkin deals with publicity, direct mail and ads in considerable detail.

Editors on Editing: What Writers Need to Know About What Editors Do. Edited by Gerald Gross. Grove Press, 841 Broadway, New York, NY 10003–4793. Third edition, 1993.

The subtitle says it all. A word of caution, though: Don't be surprised if your editor isn't as talented or devoted as those represented here; they're an outstanding group.

Fletcher, Tana, and Julia Rockler. *Getting Publicity.* Self-Counsel Press, 1704 North State Street, Bellingham, WA 98225; e-mail: selfcoun@pinc.com. Second edition, 1995.

Subtitled "The very best book for your small business," this upbeat, energizing manual is packed with practical tips.

Gaughen, Barbara, and Ernest Weckbaugh. *Book Blitz: Getting Your Book in the News: 60 Steps to a Best Seller.* Best-Seller Books, 7456 Evergreen Drive, Santa Barbara, CA 93117; 805–968–8567. 1994.

The 60 steps include intelligent pointers and interesting case studies. Ignore the chronology and the promise of bestsellerhood.

Glenn, Peggy. *Publicity for Books and Authors: A do-it-yourself handbook for small publishing firms and enterprising authors.* Aames-Allen Publishing, 18281 Gothard Street, #105, Huntington Beach, CA 92648–1205. 1985.

Glenn, who began publishing her own books in 1980, realized there was a need for this one shortly thereafter. Because she's a smart and engaging tutor, you can apply her advice to new as well as enduring aspects of publicity campaigns.

Horowitz, Shel. *Marketing Without Megabucks: How to Sell Anything on a Shoestring.* AWM, Dept. JA–1. PO Box 1164, Northampton, MA 01061–1164; e-mail: info@frugalfun.com. <http://www.frugalfun.com>. 1993 with yearly updates.

The expertise encapsulated here is applicable to written work. Horowitz focuses on publicity, advertising, direct mail and establishing yourself as an expert.

Jenkins, Jerrold R., with Mardi Link. *Inside the Bestsellers.* Rhodes & Easton, 121 East Front Street, 4th Floor, Traverse City, MI 49684; 616–933–0445; e-mail: jenkins.group@smallpress.com. <http://www.smallpress.com>. 1997.

Inside 18 Bestsellers from Self- and Small Publishers would have been a more accurate title for this upbeat collection of stories. It will silence any doubts you may have about the importance of marketing, marketing and more marketing.

Jerome, John. *The Writing Trade: A Year in the Life.* Lyons & Burford, 31 West 21st Street, New York, NY 10010. Reprint edition, 1995.

Jerome, who earns his living as "a competent but essentially invisible writer," shares his experiences in this frank and winning month-by-month account.

Karasik, Paul. *How to Make It Big in the Seminar Business.* McGraw-Hill, 1221 Avenue of the Americas, New York, NY 10020. 1992.

For certain kinds of books, including books on business and personal growth, seminars spur sales. Setting them up is lots of work, but Karasik's tutelage is knowledgeable and well organized.

Klepper, Michael M., with Robert E. Gunther. *I'd Rather Die Than Give a Speech.* Citadel Press, 120 Enterprise Avenue, Secaucus, NJ 07094. 1995.

If public speaking figures in your promotion plans, this book should be helpful whether you dread it or not. Detailed, easy to follow and engaging.

❖ **Kremer, John.** *1001 Ways to Market Your Books, for authors and publishers.* Open Horizons Publishing Co., 209 South Main Street, #200, PO Box 205, Fairfield, IA 52556–0205; 800–796–6130 or 515–472–6130; fax: 515–472–1560; e-mail: JohnKremer@aol.com. <http://www.bookmarket.com>. Updated periodically.

With the inspiration and information offered here, any writer will be better able to attract readers.

❖ **Levine, Mark L.** *Negotiating A Book Contract: A Guide for Authors, Agents and Lawyers.* Moyer Bell, Kymbolde Way, Wakefield, RI 02879. 1988.

Mark Levine leads you step by step through clauses common in book contracts, explaining what you should try to delete, add or otherwise alter. Intelligent, intelligible advice.

Levinson, Jay Conrad. *Guerrilla Marketing Weapons: 100 Affordable Marketing Methods of Maximizing Profits from Your Small Business.* Plume/Penguin, 375 Hudson Street, New York, NY 10014. 1990.

Ideas in here will work for writing as well as widgets, and there are plenty of them.

❖ Maass, Donald. *The Career Novelist: A Literary Agent Offers Strategies for Success.*
See "A Foot in the Door Resources."

McCormack, Thomas. *The Fiction Editor, the Novel, and the Novelist.* St. Martin's Press, 175 Fifth Avenue, New York, NY 10010. Reissue edition, 1995.
What to hope for from your editor if you write fiction. And if you get less than you hoped for, tools you can use to make your book better.

McIntyre, Catherine V. *Writing Effective News Releases . . . How to Get Free Publicity for Yourself, Your Business, or Your Organization.* Piccadilly Books, PO Box 25203, Colorado Springs, CO 80936. 1992.
A generous array of examples, with detailed commentary.

Miles, Betty. *Planning Successful School Visits: Guidelines for Authors and Illustrators.* The Authors Guild, Inc., 330 West 42nd Street, New York, NY 10036; 212–563–5904; fax: 212–564–8363; e-mail: staff@authorsguild.org. 1994.
Miles, who co-chairs the Children's Book Committee of The Authors Guild, offers admirably thorough advice.

Moyer, Page Emory. *The ABC's of a Really Good Speech.* Circle Press, 38 The Circle, East Hampton, NY 11937. 1990.
Intelligent pointers. Writers who'd like to connect with readers through talks can use this to learn basic technique and build confidence.

Mulvany, Nancy C. *Indexing Books.* University of Chicago Press, 5801 South Ellis Avenue, Chicago, IL 60637. 1994.
You couldn't ask for a clearer, more comprehensive introduction. A book you'll want to study if you're planning to do your own index, or even considering that.

❖ Norwick, Kenneth P., and Jerry Simon Chasen. *The Rights of Authors, Artists, and Other Creative People.* Southern Illinois University Press, PO Box 3697, Carbondale, IL 62902–3697. 1992.
The best way to avoid legal problems and safeguard legal rights is to understand how the law actually works, and you will when you've read this book. Highly recommended. (Also see the other legal guides listed throughout "Resources.")

O'Connor, Richard F. X. *How to Market You and Your Book: The Ultimate Insider's Guide to Get Your Book Published With Maximum Sales.* Coeur de Lion Books, PO Box 90128, Santa Barbara, CA 93190. 1996.

O'Connor, whose career included jobs with major book publishers and retailers, agrees that authors have to get involved with marketing and offers his tips here.

❖ O'Keefe, Steve. *Publicity on the Internet: Creating Successful Publicity Campaigns on the Internet and the Commercial Online Services.* John Wiley & Sons, 605 Third Avenue, New York, NY 10158. <http://www.olympus.net/okeefe/PIO/>. 1997.

A remarkable overview. Clear and comprehensive enough for beginners to understand and use, and organized so that those with experience on the Net can quickly meet their ongoing needs for information.

❖ Parker, Roger C. *Looking Good in Print.* Ventana Press, PO Box 13964, Durham, NC 27709–3964. 1996.

The illustrations, which are wonderful, will help you grasp and appreciate design options for any kind of print production, not just desktop publishing. And together with the lively text, they'll also let you create effective promotional materials. See "The Self-Publishing Option Resources."

Poets & Writers Magazine.
See "A Foot in the Door Resources."

The Professions of Authorship: Essays in Honor of Matthew J. Bruccoli. Edited by Richard Layman and Joel Myerson. University of South Carolina Press, 937 Assembly Street, Carolina Plaza, 8th Floor, Columbia, SC 29208. 1997.

Retrospective and scholarly pieces, plus a few with a contemporary focus and one—on Emerson's income from books—that's fascinating in light of contemporary authors' earnings.

Publishing Research Quarterly. Rutgers University, Building 4051, New Brunswick, NJ 08903; 908–445–2280; fax: 908–445–3138. <http://www.transactionpub.com>. Published quarterly.

Readable—indeed, often well-written—scholarly pieces on topics such as "The Brave New Web" and "Monitoring the Health of North America's Small and Mid-Sized Book Publishers Since 1990."

Pushcart's Complete Rotten Reviews and Rejections: A History of Insult, a Solace to Writers. Edited by Bill Henderson and André Bernard. Pushcart Press, PO Box 380, Wainscott, NY 11975. 1998.

Are reviewers dumping on you? Are you worried that they might? Look here to see the terrible things they said about William Faulkner, John Milton, Saul Bellow, Jane Austen and a host of others who proved them wrong.

Quill. Society of Professional Journalists, PO Box 77, Greencastle, IN 46135–0077; 317–653–3333; e-mail: quillnet@link2000.net. Published monthly.

News and views for journalists.

Ring, Frances. *A Western Harvest: The Gatherings of an Editor.* John Daniel & Company, PO Box 21922, Santa Barbara, CA 93121; 800–662–8351. 1991.

As editor of *Westways,* Ring worked with Wallace Stegner, M. F. K. Fisher and a galaxy of other writers. This volume offers samples of their work along with backstage back-and-forth about editing and being edited.

Roan, Carol. *Speak Easy: A Guide to Successful Performances, Presentations, Speeches, and Lectures.* Starrhill Press, PO Box 551, Montgomery, AL 36101. 1995.

Friendly, practical and savvy guidance on how to be an effective public speaker even if you've never done it before and never wanted to.

Sabah, Joe. *How to Get on Radio Talk Shows All Across America without Leaving Your Home or Office.* Pacesetter Publications, PO Box 101975, Denver, CO 80250; e-mail: jsabah@aol.com or talkshows@aol.com. <http://members.aol.com/talkshows/>. 1997.

Good tips inextricably intertwined with pitches for various products Sabah sells. The book can be ordered with an audiotape and with a diskette you may find handy, although other ways of targeting talk-show hosts or approaching hundreds of them will cost you less.

Schwartz, Evan I. *Webonomics: Nine Essential Principles for Growing Your Business on the World Wide Web.* Broadway Books, 1540 Broadway, New York, NY 10036. <http://www.webonomics.com>. 1997.

Schwartz, who's written for *Wired* and *Business Week,* aims to cover the "production, distribution, and consumption of goods, services, and ideas" on the Internet.

Sensible Solutions' Judith Appelbaum and Florence Janovic. *The Writer's Workbook: A Full and Friendly Guide to Boosting Your Book's Sales.* **Pushcart Press, PO Box 380, Wainscott, NY 11975. 1991.**

A companion volume to the book you now have in your hands, this is a collection of tips and worksheets for people who are working on trade books.

Slezak, Ellen. *The Book Group Book: A Thoughtful Guide to Forming and Enjoying a Stimulating Book Discussion Group.* **Chicago Review Press, 814 North Franklin Street, Chicago, IL 60610. Second edition, 1995.**

The subtitle tells you what these essays offer readers. If you're an accomplished writer, and especially if you're an accomplished novelist, you can also use them to figure out ways of getting groups to discuss (and therefore promote) your work.

Stone, Bob. *Successful Direct Marketing Methods.* **NTC Business Books, 4255 West Touhy Avenue, Lincolnwood, IL 60646–1975; 800–323–4900. Updated periodically.**

By now a classic, Bob Stone's thorough and practical guide contemplates more sophisticated campaigns than you're likely to mount, but the principles and many of the tactics should prove useful.

Stone, Bob, and John Wyman. *Successful Telemarketing.* **NTC Business Books, 4255 West Touhy Avenue, Lincolnwood, IL 60646–1975; 800–323–4900. Second edition, 1993.**

Like the authors (high-level executives at Young & Rubicam and AT&T), the examples come from the big leagues. The advice, however, is applicable to small-scale operations as well.

Vitale, Joe. *CyberWriting: How to Promote Your Product or Service Online (without being flamed).* **Amacom, 1601 Broadway, New York, NY 10019. <http://www.bookfair.com/welcome/cyberwriter/new>. 1997.**

Nuts-and-bolts tips along with examples and resources.

Weiner, Richard. *Professional's Guide to Publicity.* **Public Relations Publishing Company, 437 Madison Avenue, New York, NY 10022. Third edition, 1982.**

A venerable instruction manual from a pro, with plenty of tips and examples.

West, James L.W. III. *American Authors and the Literary Marketplace since 1900.* University of Pennsylvania Press, 13th Floor, Blockley Hall, 423 Guardian Drive, Philadelphia, PA 19104–6097. 1988.

Professor West's study offers fascinating perspectives on the publishing process then and now.

Yudkin, Marcia. *6 Steps to Free Publicity and dozens of other ways to win free media attention for you or your business.* Plume/Penguin, 375 Hudson Street, New York, NY 10014. 1994.

Free is not the point. Effective is the point. This is a much richer book than the title indicates; in fact, it's chock full of good ideas.

Tools

Akers, Charlene. *First & Foremost: A Guide to Northern California's Independent Bookstores.* Heyday Books, PO Box 9145, Berkeley, CA 94709. 1996.

A lively introduction to roughly 300 bookstores, including many that host presentations by writers.

ALC (American List Counsel) List Connection. <http://www.amlist.com>.

Not just information about its mailing lists, but also a valuable page of "How-to articles for successful mailings."

American Bookseller. American Booksellers Association, 828 South Broadway, Tarrytown, NY 10591; 800–637–0037. <http://www.ambook.org/bookweb/>. Published monthly.

The magazine of the American Booksellers Association can let you see how booksellers think and what they're thinking about.

American Book Trade Directory. R.R. Bowker, 121 Chanlon Road, New Providence, NJ 07974; 888–BOWKER2; fax: 908–464–3553; e-mail: info@bowker.com. <http://www.bowker.com>. Updated periodically.

An alphabetical listing, by state (or Canadian province) and city, of more than 25,000 book outlets in North America, plus listings of wholesalers, distributors and jobbers who provide conduits to readers. Useful for identifying stores where your work should sell well. Try your library for a copy; use the bookselling category index, and pay particular attention to large wholesalers and small bookstore chains.

American Library Directory. R.R. Bowker, 121 Chanlon Road, New Providence, NJ 07974; 888–BOWKER2; fax: 908–464–3553; e-mail: info@bowker.com. <http://www.bowker.com>. Updated periodically.

More than 36,000 public, academic, government and special libraries are listed here by state and Canadian province and by city.

American Wholesalers and Distributors Directory. Gale Research, Inc., 835 Penobscot Building, Detroit, MI 48226–4094; 800–877–4253; fax: 800–414–5043. <http://www.gale.com>. Updated periodically.

A good tool for identifying companies that carry products compatible with your book and reach people who should want it.

ASJA Contracts Watch.
See "A Foot in the Door Resources."

Bacon's MediaSource. Bacon's Information, Inc., 332 South Michigan Avenue, Chicago, IL 60604; 800–621–0561. Updated annually.

Comprehensive database software that covers more than 40,000 print and broadcast media outlets, and has various bells and whistles for efficient list building, maintenance and the like.

Bacon's Publicity Checker. Bacon's Information, Inc., 332 South Michigan Avenue, Chicago, IL 60604; 800–621–0561. Updated annually.

Covering magazines in one volume and newspapers in another, the *Publicity Checker* is a good tool for preparing lists of reviewers and press release recipients.

Bacon's Radio/TV/Cable Directory. Bacon's Information, Inc., 332 South Michigan Avenue, Chicago, IL 60604; 800–621–0561. Updated annually.

These usefully annotated listings cover more than 10,000 radio stations and more than 2,500 commercial and non-commercial cable systems and television stations in two volumes. See "The Self-Publishing Option Resources" for other Bacon's products and services.

BISAC Subsidiary Rights Payment Advice Form and suggested contract clause, 160 Fifth Avenue, New York, NY 10010; 212–929–1393; fax: 212–929–7542. <http://www.bisg.org/>.

When you're going to be signing with a big book publisher, get the clause about the form into your contract; it can increase your chances of actually getting sub-rights royalties you're entitled to.

Bobby. <http://www.cast.org/bobby/>.
Use this program (originally designed to help make Web pages accessible to people with disabilities) to find out why your Web page looks great on Explorer and lousy on Netscape and what you can do to get it displayed correctly on various Web browsers.

BookWire. <http://www.bookwire.com>.
An excellent starting point for finding publishing information, BookWire provides a categorized listing of more than 3,000 publishing-related resources, a calendar of book events, links to review publications, and even a book publishing FAQ, among other things. You can submit your site to the BookWire Index by using the online submission form.

BookZone. <http://bookzone.com/bookzone/>.
In addition to its virtual bookshop, BookZone's attractions include BookPoint, a searchable listing of U.S. bookstores by state, city and/or zip that can bring up a city street map pinpointing the exact location of a selected store, and a directory of links to about 1,000 book-related Internet sites. E-mail them to have your site listed.

***Brands and Their Companies.* Gale Research, Inc., 835 Penobscot Building, Detroit, MI 48226–4094; 800–877–4253; fax: 800–414–5043. <http://www.gale.com>. Updated periodically.**
Have you identified a product or two or three or four or more that you might tie in with to boost your sales? Check here to see who makes it and distributes it.

BRS Radio Directory. <http://www.radio-directory.com/>.
BRS Radio Consultants provides a free comprehensive directory and analysis of radio stations on the Web, broken down into useful categories (e.g., Call Letters, Webcasters, Radio by State, Radio Formats, Public Stations, International).

Buyer's Index. <http://www.buyersindex.com/>.
More than 5,000 mail-order catalogs and Web shopping sites that might carry your book and let you reach target markets directly.

The Catalog Site. <http://www.catalogsite.com>.
Search this site's database of hundreds of free mail order catalogs by name or keyword for possible special sales opportunities, and go over the catalog reviews. Listings link to each catalog's Web site where possible.

Chase's Calendar of Events.
See "A Foot in the Door Resources."

Checkdomain.com. <http://www.checkdomain.com>.
Come here to find out if the domain name you want for your site has already been taken. It also contains a list of domains for countries other than the U.S.

CMG Mailing List Catalog. **CMG Information Services, 187 Ballardville Street, Suite B110, PO Box 7000, Wilmington, MA 01887; 800–677–7959.**
The College Marketing Group catalog, which is free, will lead you to lists of professors who teach specific courses, lists of library decision-makers and lists of individuals who buy books in a variety of specified subject areas.

College Press Network Index.
<http://www.cpnet.com/news/news.html>.
An index of online college newspapers both in the U.S. and abroad.

Contemporary Authors. **Gale Research, Inc., 835 Penobscot Building, Detroit, MI 48226–4094; 800–877–4253; fax: 800–414–5043. <http://www.gale.com>. Updated periodically.**
A good place to get yourself listed and to find addresses of writers you'd like to get blurbs from.

Crawford, Tad. *Business and Legal Forms for Authors and Self-Publishers.* **Allworth Press, 10 East 23rd Street, Suite 400, New York, NY 10010; 212–777–8395. Revised edition, 1996.**
The title says it. Allworth has several other books of interest to writers, so you might want to send for its catalog.

Cyberhound's® Guide to Associations and Nonprofit Organizations on the Internet. **Gale Research, Inc., 835 Penobscot Building, Detroit, MI 48226–4094; 800–877–4253; fax: 800–414–5043. <http://www.gale.com>. 1997.**

Site visits should help you tailor your approach to each group that might publicize and/or sell your material.

A Directory of American Poets and Fiction Writers. Poets & Writers, Inc., 72 Spring Street, New York, NY 10012; 212–226–3586. <http://www.pw.org>. Updated periodically.

If you'd like to contact particular novelists and/or poets for pre-publication comments, here's affordable information on addresses and phone numbers.

The Directory of Mail Order Catalogs. Edited by Richard Gottlieb. Grey House Publishing, Pocket Knife Square, Lakeville, CT 06039. Updated periodically.

Thousands of companies that sell products of every sort via printed materials are listed here. Get hold of the directory at your library to see which of them might do well with your book.

Directory of Public Relations Agencies and Resources on the WWW. <http://www.impulse-research.com/impulse/welcome.html>.

Along with its searchable worldwide directory, this site offers links to resources and organizations useful for Internet publicity.

Directory of Special Libraries and Information Centers. Gale Research, Inc., 835 Penobscot Building, Detroit, MI 48226–4094; 800–877–4253; fax: 800–414–5043. <http://www.gale.com>. Updated periodically.

Using the subject index, you can construct your own mailing list of libraries that should be especially receptive to your book.

Dogpile: A Multi-Engine Search Tool.
See "Getting the Words Right Resources."

Ecola Newsstand.
See "A Foot in the Door Resources."

Editor & Publisher Syndicate Directory Section. Editor & Publisher, 11 West 19th Street, New York, NY 10011; 212–675–4380; e-mail: edpub@mediainfo.com. <http://www.mediainfo.com>. 1996.

The subject index is useful and the ads are even more informative.

EditPros Index of Marketing Resources.
<http://www.editpros.com/resource.html>.

Diverse writing, marketing communication, and reference Internet resources.

E-mail:MEDIA. **<http://www.gugerell.co.at/gugerell/media/index.htm>.**
Downloadable and browsable lists of e-mail addresses for media people around the world, especially those in Europe, Australia, Canada and the U.S. Links lead to many other sites useful for getting in touch with media via the Web.

❖ *Encyclopedia of Associations.* **Gale Research, Inc., 835 Penobscot Building, Detroit, MI 48226–4094; 800–877–4253; fax: 800–414–5043.** **<http://www.gale.com>. Updated periodically.**
A first-class promotion tool whether you're being published or doing the publishing yourself, this is a conduit to nearly 23,000 groups committed to all sorts of causes and activities. Get it at your library and use the keyword index to zero in on the people who will welcome news of your book and help you spread the word about it.

EventSource. **<http://www.eventsource.com>.**
Information on upcoming trade events worldwide in your field.

EXPOguide. **<http://www.expoguide.com>.**
Target trade shows, conferences and exhibitions related to your work by date or location or alphabetically.

1st International Calendar of Annual Days, Weeks, Years and Decades. **<http://www.aarknet.com/affiliates/days.htm>.**
A listing by date of special events worldwide; useful for marketing tie-ins.

Freestats. **<http://www.freestats.com>**
If you display Freestat's banner at your Web site, this counter/stats service will tell you not only how many hits any given page of yours is getting, but also how many unique visitors it gets each day and month, what country they're from, and how they found your site (e.g., the search terms they used).

Gale Directory of Publications and Broadcast Media. **Gale Research, Inc., 835 Penobscot Building, Detroit, MI 48226–4094; 800–877–4253; fax: 800–414–5043.** **<http://www.gale.com>. Updated periodically.**
Thousands of newspapers, magazines, radio and TV stations and

cable stations are listed here and indexed so that it's easy to pinpoint special-interest market segments. Your library should have a set.

Grants and Awards Available to American Writers. PEN American Center, 568 Broadway, New York, NY 10012; 212–334–1660; fax: 212–334–2181. **Updated periodically.**

See "Money Resources," and if you spot a way to become a winner, try it out. Both the credentials and the funds should come in handy at any stage of a writing project or a writing career.

GuestFinder. <http://www.guestfinder.com/>.

Designed to make it easy for media to find guests, speakers, spokespersons, experts and interviewees of all kinds. Visit the site for information on getting yourself listed.

Inference Find.

See "Getting the Words Right Resources."

InfoSpace—The Ultimate Directory. <http://www.infospace.com/>.

An all-in-one reference that's searchable for everything from individuals' phone numbers and e-mails, to fax numbers for government executives and businesses.

Jonesreport. <http://www.bit-wise.com/jonesreport/jonesrpt/calevent.htm>.

A Calendar Events page lists special days six months in advance, along with ideas on how to use them for marketing.

❖ **"J" World Dates Archive. <http://www.dailyglobe.com/day2day.html>.**

This searchable and browsable Comprehensive Calendar of Birthdays, Holidays, Historical Events, and Fun Dates is a great source for news pegs.

Kiefer, Marie. *Book Publishing Resource Guide*. Ad-Lib Publications, 51½ West Adams, Fairfield, IA 52556; 800–669–0773 or 515–472–6617; fax: 515–472–3186; e-mail: Adlib100@aol.com. 1996.

An indispensable "directory of key contacts for marketing and promoting books" with more than 7,500 listings you can use in supplementing your publisher's marketing moves. This affordable book is considerably less expensive than *Literary Market Place* and, in this context, more useful.

Kremer, John. *Celebrate Today!*
See "A Foot in the Door Resources."

❖ **Liszt, the mailing list directory.** <http://www.liszt.com/>.
Great for finding that niche list, out of the 70,000 listed here, whose members exchange interesting ideas on your topic(s) and just might be the perfect market for your work.

Literary Market Place. **R.R. Bowker, 121 Chanlon Road, New Providence, NJ 07974; 888–BOWKER2; fax: 908–464–3553; e-mail: info@bowker.com. <http://www.bowker.com>. Updated annually.**
Like *Book Publishing Resource Guide* (above), *LMP* can help you add to and reinforce whatever efforts your publisher plans to make on your behalf. See especially "Book Review & Index Journals & Services," "Radio & Television Publicity" and "Public Relations Services."

Major Authors and Illustrators for Children and Young Adults. **Gale Research, Inc., 835 Penobscot Building, Detroit, MI 48226–4094; 800–877–4253; fax: 800–414–5043. <http://www.gale.com>. Updated periodically.**
Good hunting grounds for people who might provide blurbs.

Mediafinder. <http://www.mediafinder.com/>.
A search engine dedicated to print media and catalogs (whether or not they're on the Web). The Mailing Lists category is particularly useful for finding publications with targeted rentable lists.

Midwest Book Review. <http://www.execpc.com/~mbr/bookwatch/>.
An enormous index of Internet resources, categorized by subject (e.g., Publishers and Bookstores, The Arts, Media, Libraries and Universities, Writing and Publishing, Business and Finance).

The MIT List of Radio Stations on the Internet.
<http://wmbr.mit.edu/stations/list.html>.
More than 3,000 radio stations in the U.S., Canada and abroad are included. The U.S. stations are organized alphabetically, and by frequency, state and format.

National Directory of Catalogs. **Oxbridge Communications (dist. by Gale), 150 Fifth Avenue, Suite 302, New York, NY 10011; 212–741–0231; fax: 212–633–2938; e-mail: info@oxbridge.com. <http://www.mediafinder.com>. Updated periodically.**

Entries, which cover some 7,000 catalogs, are grouped under 78 product headings.

NetMechanic Link Check.
<http://www.netmechanic.com/link_check.htm>.
Because links are so important for building traffic and increasing content value, you'll want to make sure all yours always work. Use this free service to test the status of each one periodically.

NPR. <http://www.npr.org>.
The place to go for information on NPR programs and listings of local member stations, some with Web links.

Palder, Edward L. *The Catalog of Catalogs: The Complete Mail Order Directory.* **Woodbine House, 6510 Bells Mill Road, Bethesda, MD 20817. Updated periodically.**
An affordable introduction to thousands of special-interest mail-order operations. Look under the subject(s) your work treats to find catalogs that might sell it to potential readers.

Parrot Media Network. <http://www.parrotmedia.com/pmn.html>.
Regularly updated online directories of TV, radio and cable stations and newspapers. Bare-bones information is available for free (company name, call letters, rank, city and state), and more complete listings are available by paid subscription.

Power Media Selects: The Nation's Most Influential Media Elite. **Edited by Alan Caruba. Broadcast Interview Source, 2233 Wisconsin Avenue NW, Washington, DC 20007; 202–333–4904. Eleventh edition, 1997.**
A selective directory covering periodicals, radio and TV. Annotations are knowledgeable and colorful.

Publishing Trends.
See "A Foot in the Door Resources."

Radio Guide USA. <http://www.radioguide.com/>.
Contains format guides, a listing of the top 100 markets, DJ profiles, news and an interesting collection of radio station and music-related links.

Radio Online. <http://www.radio-online.com>.
Although much of the information here is available by paid regis-

tration only, access is free to an e-mail directory of people in broadcasting, links to radio stations on the Web and an events/promotional calendar.

❖ **RadioSpace. <http://www.radiospace.com/index.html>.**
The Radio Programs and Personalities section is divided by category and each entry links to the show's Web site. Although it's not comprehensive, RadioSpace is a great starting point for targeting shows you might get on.

Radio-TV Interview Report. **Bradley Communications Corp., 135 East Plumstead, Lansdowne, PA 19050–8206; 800–989–1400. <http://www.cadvision.com/Wordstorm/word1.html>. Published roughly 3x/month.**
The *Report,* a collection of ads, goes to thousands of people who might book you on radio, as well as to hundreds of TV talk-show producers and selected newspaper feature editors. Rates are reasonable; results are mixed.

Reading Group Choices: Selections for Lively Book Discussions. **Paz & Associates, 2106 20th Avenue South, Nashville, TN 37212; e-mail: dpaz@pazbookbiz.com. <http://www.pazbookbiz.com>. 1996.**
Wearing your writer (rather than your reader) hat, you can glean insights from these write-ups on ways to get your book included among the chosen.

Reference.com. <http://www.reference.com>.
Searchable directories let you browse more than 150,000 newsgroups, mailing lists and Web forums. In many cases, you can browse the postings as well, and if you're a registered user (no charge) you can post to newsgroups that Reference.com subscribes to.

Research Centers Directory. **Gale Research, Inc., 835 Penobscot Building, Detroit, MI 48226–4094; 800–877–4253; fax: 800–414–5043. <http://www.gale.com>. Updated periodically.**
Use the subject index to identify facilities that may want to order your book and/or help you spread the word about it. More than 14,000 research units are covered.

Ross, Marilyn. *National Directory of Newspaper Op-Ed Pages.*
See "A Foot in the Door Resources."

Saal, Rollene. *The New York Public Library Guide to Reading Groups.*
Crown, 201 East 50th Street, New York, NY 10022.
<http://www.randomhouse.com>. 1995.
   Though this is intended for people who want to start and sustain
reading groups, it can also help you tailor approaches to these groups
that might get them to focus on a book by you.

SavvySearch.
   See "Getting the Words Right Resources."

**Screen Actors Guild, 5757 Wilshire Boulevard, Los Angeles, CA
90036–3635; 213–954–1600.**
   If you've identified an actor who figures to love your work, ask the
Guild for contact information on the actor's agent or manager.

Search Engine Watch.
   See "Getting the Words Right Resources."

Standard Periodical Directory. **Oxbridge Communications (dist. by
Gale), 150 Fifth Avenue, Suite 302, New York, NY 10011;
212–741–0231; fax: 212–633–2938; e-mail: info@oxbridge.com.**
<http://www.mediafinder.com>. **Updated periodically.**
   Target special-interest publications listed here for reviews and other
print publicity.

Star Guide. **Axiom Information Resources, PO Box 8015, Ann Arbor,
MI 48107. 1997.**
   Addresses for movie stars, sports celebrities, politicians, astronauts
and more.

Subtext: The Book Business in Perspective. **Open Book Publishing, 90
Holmes Avenue, PO Box 2228, Darien, CT 06820; 203–316–8008;
fax: 203–975–8469; e-mail: Odasan@aol.com. Published biweekly.**
   Stephanie Oda's newsletter is geared to, and priced for, people inside
the big book publishing houses, but its short takes on people and
events can be useful to writers too.

Tile.net/Lists. <http://tile.net/listserv/>.
   Dedicated solely to LISTSERV discussion groups on the Internet—a
mere 11,000 or so. You can search here by keyword or browse the listing alphabetically by list description, name, subject, host country or
sponsor organization.

Trade Show Central. <http://www.tscentral.com/>.
Information on trade shows, exhibit services, conferences and seminars for a wide variety of industries (including publishing and broadcasting/media) via online searchable databases and links to related resources.

Ulrich's International Periodicals Directory. R.R. Bowker, 121 Chanlon Road, New Providence, NJ 07974; 888–BOWKER2; fax: 908–464–3553; e-mail: info@bowker.com. <http://www.bowker.com>. **Updated periodically.**
Enough periodicals are listed here to make your head spin. Available in libraries.

The Ultimate Black Book. **Compiled by Godfrey Harris and Kenneth L. Harris.**
See "Getting the Words Right Resources."

U.S. Census Bureau. <http://www.census.gov/>.
The Bureau's online library lets you search for demographic and assorted other information.

❖ **WebStep Top 100.** <http://www.mmgco.com/top100.html>.
A list of 100 top Internet directories and search engines, rated with two, three or four stars, that will list your site free. Filling out the different forms takes time but lets you satisfy each site's special requirements. Start with the ones that have four stars.

Weiner, Richard. *Webster's New World Dictionary of Media and Communications.* **Macmillan, 1633 Broadway, New York, NY 10019.** <http://www.all.links.com/dictionary>. **Revised and updated edition, 1996.**
With this affordable, original volume, you'll not only understand what publishing and media pros are talking about; you'll speak their language. Weiner is an authoritative award-winning PR practitioner.

Williams, Jane. *The Authentic Jane Williams Home School Market Guide.* **Bluestocking Press, PO Box 2030, Shingle Springs, CA 95682–2030; 800–959–8586 or 916–621–1123. 1997.**
A sizable, well-indexed directory prefaced by helpful advice on how to get the most from it.

The Writer's Directory. St. James Press/Gale Research, Inc., 835 Penobscot Building, Detroit, MI 48226–4094; 800–877–4253; fax: 800–414–5043. <http://www.gale.com>. Twelfth edition, 1995.
Useful for getting in touch with people who might provide blurbs.

❖ **The WWW Virtual Library.**
See "Getting the Words Right Resources."

People, Places and Programs

American Society of Journalists and Authors, 1501 Broadway, Suite 302, New York, NY 10036; 212–997–0947; fax: 212–768–7414; e-mail: asja@compuserve.com. <http://www.asja.org>.
Many ASJA members write for magazines. The group has meetings and a newsletter as well as the Dial-a-Writer Referral Service (see "Money Resources").

The Association for Women in Communications, 7 Commerce Center, 1244 Ritchie Highway, Suite 6, Arnold, MD 21012–1887; 410–544–7442; fax: 410–544–4640; e-mail: womcom@aol.com. <http://www.womcom.org>.
Membership benefits include a newsletter and an assortment of discounts as well as chances to network and learn at chapter meetings and the annual conference.

❖ **The Authors Guild, Inc.,** 330 West 42nd Street, New York, NY 10036; 212–563–5904; fax: 212–564–8363; e-mail: staff@authorsguild.org.
It's well worth joining this group of 6,500 professional writers and getting in as early in your career as you can, so request application forms. The Guild and its top-notch staff give writers power to deal with publishers by providing surveys of financial terms, seminars on current problems and opportunities for writers, a newsletter that disseminates solid, useful information, access to insurance, and sample forms, including model contracts.

The Authors Registry, 330 West 42nd Street, 29th Floor, New York, NY 10036; 212–563–6920; e-mail: registry@interport.net. <http://www.webcom.com/registry/main.html>.

A rights payment system that collects money from publishers, database producers and reprint services and distributes the funds to authors whose works are being used. Be sure you're included. The Web site provides the easiest way to sign up.

Authors Unlimited, 31 East 32nd Street, Suite 300, New York, NY 10016; 212–481–8484; fax: 212–481–9582.

Founded by Arlynn Greenbaum, an experienced book publicist, this is a speakers' bureau for authors who can give useful and/or entertaining talks to a variety of audiences. Write to find out about the selection process and the registration fee.

BISAC, 160 Fifth Avenue, New York, NY 10010; 212–929–1393; fax: 212–929–7542. <http://www.bisg.org/>.

The Book Industry Systems Advisory Committee, which performs many valuable services for book people, has a Subsidiary Rights Payment Advice Form that your publisher should be using.

"Book Trade & Allied Associations," *Literary Market Place.*

Listings here should lead you to groups you might join. See also "Getting the Words Right Resources," "A Foot in the Door Resources" and "The Self-Publishing Option Resources."

International Women's Writing Guild.

See "Getting the Words Right Resources."

National Society of Newspaper Columnists, PO Box 1203, Keller, TX 76244; e-mail: nsnc@flash.net. <http://www.columnists.com>.

A peppy newsletter, a convention and access to "the world's only web site packed with cybersonic columnar experience" are among the benefits NSNC offers.

The National Writers Association, 1450 South Havana, Suite 424, Aurora, CO 80012; 303–751–7844.

If you'd like to link up with other writers in your area, why not see if there's a chapter of this group nearby?

National Writers Union, 873 Broadway, Suite 203, New York, NY 10003; 212–254–0279.

Unlike other writers groups, this one is "a labor union" with an interest in collective bargaining, grievance resolution and boycotts.

PEN American Center, 568 Broadway, New York, NY 10012; 212–334–1660; fax: 212–334–2181.

Known for its social conscience and its excellent grants and awards directory (see above and in "Money Resources"), PEN has more than 100 centers around the world. Editors and translators, as well as professional writers, are members.

PEN Center USA West, 672 S. Lafayette Park Place, Suite 41, Los Angeles, CA 90057; 213–365–8500; fax: 213–365–9616.

PEN's West Coast U.S. group runs programs, gives awards and has a mentorship project designed to enhance the careers of "emerging writers from underserved communities."

Planned Television Arts, 301 East 57th Street, New York, NY 10022; 212–593–5820; fax: 212–715–1666; e-mail: ptActive@aol.com.

Now part of Ruder*Finn, PTA has lots of experience booking authors on radio and TV.

Poets & Writers.

See "Getting the Words Right Resources."

Poets House, 72 Spring Street, 2nd Floor, New York, NY 10012; 212–431–7920; fax: 212–431–8131.

Poets and poetry lovers gather here for readings, workshops and celebrations. The group has an admirable library too.

Public Relations Society of America Information Center, 33 Irving Place, 3rd Floor, New York, NY 10003; 212–995–2230.

A large collection of materials for professional public relations people; open to non-members for a modest fee. Call ahead to make an appointment.

Royalty Review Service, 317 Madison Avenue, Suite 807, New York, NY 10017; 212–557–2692; fax: 212–557–2697; e-mail: royalty@aol.com.

RRS understands how royalty statements work (and don't work). If their initial review of your records indicates you're missing money, they'll go after it for you on a contingent-fee basis.

Sensible Solutions, Inc., 271 Madison Avenue, Suite 1007, New York, NY 10016; 212–687–1761; fax: 212–867–8641; e-mail: Sensibly@aol.com. <http://www.happilypublished.com>.

Founded because readers of *How to Get Happily Published* asked for advice tailored to their particular books, Sensible Solutions is a consulting firm run by Judith Appelbaum and Florence Janovic. They confer with clients and then prepare target marketing plans designed to boost books' sales without big budgets.

Sisters in Crime, PO Box 442124, Lawrence, KS 66044–8933; 913–842–1325; e-mail: sistersincrime@juno.com.

Well worth joining if you write mysteries and want them to sell better. The group's brochure will acquaint you with its useful publications as well as its purposes and services.

Society of Children's Book Writers and Illustrators.

See "A Foot in the Door Resources."

Women's National Book Association, 160 Fifth Avenue, New York, NY 10010; 212–675–7805; fax: 212–989–7542; e-mail: skpassoc@internetmci.com. <http://www.bookbuzz.com>.

Also open to men, WNBA has members who are writers, people in publishing, educators, librarians, artists and booksellers. Send for information on the group's get-togethers and publications.

The Self-Publishing Option
Resources

O ne of the best ways for self-publishers to get help is by talking with other publishers, particularly smaller ones. Look below and in the local Yellow Pages for leads to those in your area. Other avenues to advice and assistance are also described below. For additional guidance, check back through the previous "Resources" sections. See especially "A Foot in the Door Resources" (since the directories that help writers find publishers also help publishers find people who'll publicize their work and/or buy rights to it) and "The Sale and Its Sequels Resources" (since the ingredients for success through established publishing companies are very similar to the ingredients for success as a self-publisher).

Advice, Analysis and Reportage

Adler, Elizabeth W. *Everyone's Guide to Successful Publications: How to Produce Powerful Brochures, Newsletters, Flyers, and Business Communications, Start to Finish.* Peachpit Press, 1249 Eighth Street, Berkeley, CA 94710; 800–283–9444 or 510–524–2178; fax: 510–524–2221; e-mail: orders@peachpit.com. <http://www.peachpit.com>. 1993.

Adler believes in integrating writing, design and marketing and covers all of those subjects, plus printing. Lots of useful checklists make this oversized volume especially valuable.

❖ **Barker, Malcolm E.** *Book design & production for the small publisher.* **Londonborn Publications, PO Box 77246, San Francisco, CA 94107–0246. 1990.**

A book that gives pleasure along with knowledge. The design is exemplary, and the tone unusually attractive. You get the feeling Barker doesn't just know his stuff; he's really rooting for you to grasp it too.

Beach, Mark. *Getting It Printed: How to Work with Printers and Graphic Arts Services to Assure Quality, Stay on Schedule, and Control Costs.* **North Light Books/Writer's Digest, 1507 Dana Avenue, Cincinnati, OH 45207; 513–531–2690; fax: 513–531–7107. Revised and updated edition, 1993.**

A clear, detailed primer that's applicable to books, although it doesn't often focus on them. Use it to see what your options are and to get help in exercising the ones that make sense for your project.

Bell, Patricia J. *The Prepublishing Handbook: What you should know before you publish your first book.* **Cat's-paw Press, 9561 Woodridge Circle, Eden Prairie, MN 55347.** **<http://www.cats-pawpress.com/print/>. 1992.**

Pat Bell calls this a "whether-to" book but it has good "how-to" material as well. Read it carefully if you think you might want to self-publish so you'll know what you're getting into.

Bielenberg, Tom, and Allan Kornblum. *From Doughnuts to Champagne.* **CLMP Monograph, Council of Literary Magazines and Presses, 154 Christopher Street, Suite 3C, New York, NY 10014–2839; 212–741–9110; fax: 212–741–9112. 1994.**

Tips from a bookseller and a publisher active on the literary scene.

Bly, Robert W. *The Copywriter's Handbook: A Step-by-Step Guide to Writing Copy That Sells.* See "The Sale and Its Sequels Resources."

❖ **Bly, Robert W.** *Targeted Public Relations: How to Get Thousands of Dollars of Free Publicity For Your Product, Service, Organization, or Idea.* **Henry Holt & Company, 115 West 18th Street, New York, NY 10011. 1993.**

A longer subtitle—*And How to Make That Publicity Generate Sales*—
would give an even better idea of how much this manual has to offer.
The publicity Bly explains is the best kind to get for most of what's
published.

Book, Albert C., and C. Dennis Schick. *Fundamentals of Copy & Layout.* **NTC Business Books, 4255 West Touhy Avenue, Lincolnwood,
IL 60646–1975; 800–323–4900. Third edition, 1996.**
Written for people who create ads (by no means a book's best selling
tool); useful for producing flyers and mailing pieces as well (which figure to work better) and full of instructive examples.

❖ **Book Marketing Update. Open Horizons Publishing Co., 209 South
Main Street, #200, PO Box 205, Fairfield, IA 52556–0205;
800–796–6130 or 515–472–6130; fax: 515–472–1560; e-mail:
JohnKremer@aol.com. <http://www.bookmarket.com>. Published
10x/year.**
John Kremer's newsletter is a steady source of new leads and ideas.

❖ **Cardoza, Avery.** *The Complete Guide to Successful Publishing.* **Cardoza Publishing, PO Box 1500, Cooper Station, New York, NY
10276. 1995.**
Practical start-to-finish guidance on publishing other people's books
or your own. Cardoza, a publisher himself, does a fine job of presenting
information, options and examples.

Crispell, Diane. *The Insider's Guide to Demographic Know-How:
Everything You Need to Find, Analyze, and Use Information About
Your Customers.* **American Demographics Press, 108 North Cayuga
Street, Ithaca, NY 14850. Third edition, 1993.**
Use the introductory essays when you're figuring out what sort of
market research to do, and consult the Sources sections when it's time
to go after your data.

Cyr, Donald G., and Douglas A. Gray. *Marketing Your Product: A
planning guide for small business.* **Self-Counsel Press, 1704 North
State Street, Bellingham, WA 98225; e-mail: selfcoun@pinc.com.
1994.**
The authors, who consult and give seminars, include worksheets in
this practical introductory handbook.

Daly, Charles P., Patrick Henry, and Ellen Ryder. *The Magazine Publishing Industry.* Allyn & Bacon, 160 Gould Street, Needham Heights, MA 02194. <http://www.abacon.com>. 1997.
History and how-to.

Dillehay, George. *Reader Surveys: Getting to Know Your Audience.* CLMP Monograph, Council of Literary Magazines and Presses, 154 Christopher Street, Suite 3C, New York, NY 10014–2839; 212–741–9110; fax: 212–741–9112. 1994.
Nuts-and-bolts guidance geared to literary publishers. Dillehay's background includes jobs at *Granta* and *The New York Review of Books.*

Doty, Betty. *Publish Your Own Handbound Books.* The Bookery, 6899 Riata Drive, Redding, CA 96002. 1980.
Both an instruction manual and a kit for producing one small book (for starters), this engaging and encouraging self-published work gives you the chance to control one more phase of the publishing process.

Editor & Publisher, 11 West 19th Street, New York, NY 10011; 212–675–4380; e-mail: edpub@mediainfo.com. <http://www.mediainfo.com>.
"The only independent weekly journal of newspapering," and a good magazine to get if you publish a paper.

Editor & Publisher International Year Book.
See "A Foot in the Door Resources."

Fletcher, Tana, and Julia Rockler. *Getting Publicity: The Very Best Book for Your Small Business.*
See "The Sale and Its Sequels Resources."

Folio: The Magazine for Magazine Management. Cowles Business Media, Inc., 470 Park Avenue South, New York, NY 10016–6819; 212–683–3540; e-mail: Cowlesnews@aol.com. Published 19x/year.
A magazine for people who publish and edit periodicals, with some articles and news items that will interest book publishers too.

Follett, Robert. *Financial Feasibility in Book Publishing.* Para Publishing, PO Box 8206-R, Santa Barbara, CA 93118–8206; 800–PARA-PUB; e-mail: Orders@ParaPublishing.com. <http://www.ParaPublishing.com/>. Second edition, 1997.

Experienced and articulate, Follett gives practical, easy-to-follow advice that should let you figure out whether publishing any given book makes economic sense.

Frasier, Lynne Ann. *The Small Business Legal Guide.* **Sourcebooks, Inc., 121 North Washington Street, Suite 2, Naperville, IL 60540. 1996.**
Designed for people who are just starting their own businesses, this covers a lot of ground well and with verve.

Frugé, August. *A Skeptic Among Scholars.* **University of California Press, 2120 Berkeley Way, Berkeley, CA 94720. 1993.**
A behind-the-scenes history of the University of California Press which sheds light on how scholarly publishing really works and reveals quite a bit about other kinds of publishing too.

Gatta, Kevin, Gusty Lange, and Marilyn Lyons. *Foundations of Graphic Design.* **Davis Publications, PO Box 15015, 50 Portland Street, Worcester, MA 01615–0015. 1991.**
Filled with helpful illustrations and exercises, this is a textbook for beginners. As you read, bear in mind that computers now perform many of the tasks designers used to have to do by hand.

Glenn, Peggy. *Publicity for Books and Authors.*
See "The Sale and Its Sequels Resources."

Gold, Jerome. *Publishing Lives: Interviews With Independent Book Publishers in the Pacific Northwest and British Columbia.* **Black Heron Press, PO Box 95676, Seattle, WA 98145. 1996.**
Some of the country's most colorful small publishers tell their stories in these 30 interviews from the early '90s. "Sentiment and opinion are interwoven with fact," Gold notes, so look here for drama and passion and inspiration more than for guidance.

Graham, Gordon. *As I Was Saying: Essays on the International Book Business.* **Hans Zell Publishers/R.R. Bowker, 121 Chanlon Road, New Providence, NJ 07974; 888–BOWKER2; fax: 908–464–3553; e-mail: info@bowker.com. <http://www.bowker.com>. 1994.**
Drawing on speeches and articles he created during his long and distinguished publishing career, Graham believes that "there is a cohesive worldwide book community." Even if you're a beginner, this collection can make you feel at home in it.

Greco, Albert N. *The Book Publishing Industry.* Allyn & Bacon, 160 Gould Street, Needham Heights, MA 02194. <http://www.abacon.com>. 1997.

A detailed overview that focuses on book publishing as a business and a cultural force, with emphasis on how big firms do things.

Heine, Art and Jean. *Book $elling 101: A Marketing Primer for Authors and Publishers.* J-Mart Press, PO Box 8884, Virginia Beach, VA 23450–8884. <http://www.bookworld.com/bookselling101/>. 1995.

Art and Jean Heine know and show that smooth author-publisher teamwork makes for success. A handy hands-on manual.

Hodgson, Richard S. *The Greatest Direct Mail Sales Letters of All Time.* Dartnell Books, 4660 North Ravenswood Avenue, Chicago, IL 60640–4595. 1995.

Hodgson, a direct mail ace, analyzes many different kinds of mailing pieces so you can see why they worked and how to create your own. A diskette with 93 examples on it is tucked into the book.

"How to Submit Your Books to Book-of-the-Month Club." Book-of-the-Month Club, Inc., Time-Life Building, 1271 Avenue of the Americas, New York, NY 10020–2686; 212–522–4200.

If you're interested in approaching one or more of the eight BOMC clubs (and you certainly should be), call or write to get this sheet of instructions. Be sure to identify yourself as a publisher, not an author.

Hubbard, J. T. W. *Magazine Editing for Professionals.* Syracuse University Press, 1600 Jamesville Avenue, Syracuse, NY 13244–5160. Second and revised edition, 1989.

Detailed, well-illustrated advice on managerial and editorial matters.

❖ Huenefeld, John. *The Huenefeld Guide to Book Publishing.* The Huenefeld Company, Inc., PO Box 665, Bedford, MA 01730–0665; 617–275–1070; fax: 617–275–1713. Revised fifth edition, 1993.

John Huenefeld has been helping small publishers manage their operations for a good long time through consulting services and seminars (see below), through his newsletter and through this sizable volume, which discusses everything from starting a book-publishing venture to selling one.

The Huenefeld Report, The Huenefeld Company, Inc., PO Box 665, Bedford, MA 01730–0665; 617–275–1070; fax: 617–275–1713. Published fortnightly.

Huenefeld's newsletter is virtually unique as a source of information and ideas on running a "modest-sized book publishing" company. Write for information and a sample copy.

❖ *Independent Publisher.*
See "A Foot in the Door Resources."

International Book Publishing: An Encyclopedia. **Edited by Philip G. Altbach and Edith S. Hoshino. Garland Publishing, 717 Fifth Avenue, 25th Floor, New York, NY 10022. 1995.**

Essays on aspects of publishing around the world, some firmly grounded in fact, some more a matter of opinion and most by distinguished and knowledgeable practitioners.

Jenkins, Jerrold R., with Mardi Link. *Inside the Bestsellers.*
See "The Sale and Its Sequels Resources."

Jenkins, Jerrold R., and Anne M. Stanton. *Publish to Win: Smart Strategies to Sell More Books.* **Rhodes & Easton, 121 East Front Street, 4th Floor, Traverse City, MI 49684; 616–933–0445; e-mail: jenkins.group@smallpress.com. <http://www.smallpress.com>. 1997.**

Generally sound, useful, upbeat advice on producing and selling books in a variety of channels. Keep in mind, though, that pointers on dealing with agents and major publishers are riddled with misinformation.

Journal of Scholarly Publishing. **University of Toronto Press, Journals Department, 5201 Dufferin Street, North York, Ontario, Canada M3H 5T8. Published quarterly.**

Consistently interesting and well-edited, this journal has new ideas, new information and new perspectives to offer publishers whether they're scholarly or not.

Judd, Karen. *Copyediting: A Practical Guide.*
See "Money Resources."

❖ **Kamoroff, Bernard B.** *Small-Time Operator: How to Start Your Own Small Business, Keep Your Books, Pay Your Taxes, and Stay Out of*

Trouble. Bell Springs Publishing, PO Box 1240, Willits, CA 95490; 707–459–6372. Updated periodically.

A self-publishing success story, Kamoroff's manual provides excellent guidance on managing financial affairs.

Kanellos, Nicolás. *Textbook Adoptions: A Promising Market for Literary Presses.* CLMP Monograph, Council of Literary Magazines and Presses, 154 Christopher Street, Suite 3C, New York, NY 10014–2839; 212–741–9110; fax: 212–741–9112. 1994.

A useful introduction.

Kavka, Dorothy, and Dan Heise. *The Successful Self-Publisher: Produce and Market Your Own Best Seller.* Evanston Publishing, 4848 Brownsboro Center Arcade, Louisville, KY 40207; 800–594–5190 or 502–899–1919; fax: 502–896–0246. 1996.

Although you shouldn't count on having a bestseller, you can rely on the promise of this book's sub-subtitle: *Basic Step-by-Step Techniques for Success in Designing, Typesetting, Printing and Selling a Book.* Thorough and easy to follow.

Kramer, Felix, and Maggie Lovaas. *Desktop Publishing Success: How to Start and Run a Desktop Publishing Business.* Irwin/Kramer Communications, PO Box 844, Cathedral Station, New York, NY 10025. <http://www.nlightning.com/dtpsabout.html>. 1991.

A well-organized, energizing, practical guide. Ignore the dated material on equipment.

Kremer, John. *Book Publicity Kit: How to Write a News Release, Get Reviews, Schedule Interviews, and Get On-Going National Publicity for Books and Other Products.* Open Horizons Publishing Co., 209 South Main Street, #200, PO Box 205, Fairfield, IA 52556–0205; 800–796–6130 or 515–472–6130; fax: 515–472–1560; e-mail: JohnKremer@aol.com. <http://www.bookmarket.com>. 1997.

This "Do-It-Yourself Marketing Kit" reproduces 187 promotional pieces and comments briefly on them in a separate section.

❖ Kremer, John. *1001 Ways to Market Your Books for Authors and Publishers.* Open Horizons Publishing Co., 209 South Main Street, #200, PO Box 205, Fairfield, IA 52556–0205; 800–796–6130 or 515–472–6130; fax: 515–472–1560; e-mail: JohnKremer@aol.com. <http://www.bookmarket.com>. Updated periodically.

One good idea after another, dealing with all aspects of marketing, including editorial and production matters. Kremer's bimonthly newsletter, *Book Marketing Update,* complements the advice here and in his other books, listed elsewhere in this section.

Landen, Hal. *Marketing With Video: How to Create a Winning Video for Your Small Business or Non-Profit.* **Oak Tree Press, RD 1, PO Box 378, Slate Hill, NY 10973; 914–355–1400. 1996.**

Mastering the process may not be a wise use of your time and money, but understanding it will help you hire and work with professionals when and if videos seem important to your work. Landen paints a detailed picture.

Laughing Bear Newsletter, **PO Box 613322, Dallas, TX 75261–3322; 817–283–6303; e-mail: laughingbr@aol.com. <http://members.aol.com/laughingbr/lbp.htm>.**

Tom Person's friendly monthly focuses on the small press universe. You can get it by sending an SASE with 52 cents postage or via the Web site, which includes a free list of libraries that deal with small press books.

Levinson, Jay Conrad. *Guerrilla Marketing Weapons: 100 Affordable Marketing Methods for Maximizing Profits from Your Small Business.* **Plume/Penguin, 375 Hudson Street, New York, NY 10014. 1990.**

Great for people who have lots of energy and relatively little money to invest in marketing. Levinson is also the author of other Guerrilla Marketing books, including *Guerrilla Marketing* and *Guerrilla Marketing Attack.*

Li, David H. *All-by-Yourself Self-Publishing.* **Premier Publishing Company, PO Box 341267, Bethesda, MD 20827; 301–469–7051; e-mail: davidli@erols.com. 1996.**

Thoughtful and thorough, Li uses his own experiences to explain in detail how to publish books and periodicals with practically no outside help.

McVay, Barry L. *Getting Started in Federal Contracting: A Guide Through the Federal Procurement Maze.* **Panoptic Enterprises, PO Box 11220, Burke, VA 22009–1220; 800–594–4766 or 703–451–5953. Fourth edition, 1996.**

Brisk straight talk from a former Department of Defense contracting officer about getting the government as a customer. Panoptic Enterprises, run by Barry and Vivina McVay, also offers consulting services.

Mulvany, Nancy C. *Indexing Books.*
See "The Sale and Its Sequels Resources."

The New York Times Manual of Style and Usage. **Edited by Lewis Jordan. Times Books/Random House, 201 East 50th Street, New York, NY 10022. <http://www.randomhouse.com>. 1982.**
A standard reference work. Entries are arranged alphabetically rather than topically.

❖ **O'Keefe, Steve.** *Publicity on the Internet: Creating Successful Publicity Campaigns on the Internet and the Commercial Online Services.*
See "The Sale and Its Sequels Resources."

Ortman, Mark. *A Simple Guide to Self-Publishing: A time and money-saving handbook to printing, distributing, and promoting your own book.* **Wise Owl Books, 1225 East Sunset Drive, Suite 373, Bellingham, WA 98226–3529; 360–671–5858; e-mail: owlbooks@aol.com. Second edition, 1996.**
A short course in the basics, with leads to other information you'll need.

❖ **Parker, Roger C.** *Looking Good in Print.* **Ventana Press, PO Box 13964, Durham, NC 27709–3964. 1996.**
Once you've got your desktop publishing software up and running, consult Parker's excellent book-and-CD-Rom set for ways to use it to best advantage.

Perle, E. Gabriel, and John Taylor Williams. *The Publishing Law Handbook.* **Aspen Law & Business, 270 Sylvan Avenue, Englewood Cliffs, NJ 07632. Second edition, 1992.**
Your lawyer should, and probably will, be familiar with this hefty, handily organized volume, and its discussions will be understandable to you. It's expensive, so you may want to try nearby libraries for a copy when you need information on specific legal issues.

Phillips, Michael, and Salli Rasberry. *Marketing without Advertising.* **Nolo Press, 950 Parker Street, Berkeley, CA 94710. <http://www.nolo.com>. 1997.**
Designed for small businesses but adaptable for books and periodicals.

Absorb the appealing, intelligent thesis (success stems from running a wonderful operation) and latch onto the practical pointers and checklists.

Picard, Robert G., and Jeffrey H. Brody. *The Newspaper Publishing Industry.* **Allyn & Bacon, 160 Gould Street, Needham Heights, MA 02194. <http://www.abacon.com>. 1996.**
A broad overview, with due attention to small and specialized papers, plus information about how this business works and well-founded views on what the future holds for it.

❖ **PMA List. <http://www.pma-online.org/>.**
E-mail info@pma-online.org for subscription information.
Small and self-publishers share an awe-inspiring range of experience through this extremely active e-mail list. If you subscribe, budget plenty of time to read and file the valuable posts. As you'll see, the ratio of substance to silliness is remarkably good.

❖ **Poynter, Dan.** *Book Fairs: An Exhibiting Guide for Publishers.* **Para Publishing, PO Box 8206-R, Santa Barbara, CA 93118–8206; 800–PARAPUB; e-mail: Orders@ParaPublishing.com. <http://www.ParaPublishing.com/>. Updated periodically.**
A knowledgeable guide that answers the essential questions about promoting and selling books through exhibits. See below for other Poynter products and services.

Poynter, Dan. *Book Marketing: A New Approach.* **Para Publishing, PO Box 8206-R, Santa Barbara, CA 93118–8206; 800–PARAPUB; e-mail: Orders@ParaPublishing.com. <http://www.ParaPublishing.com/>. 1997.**
A Special Report on the nitty-gritty of selling to bookstores, libraries, sub-rights buyers and "non-traditional" markets.

❖ **Poynter, Dan.** *The Self-Publishing Manual.* **Para Publishing, PO Box 8206-R, Santa Barbara, CA 93118–8206; 800–PARAPUB; e-mail: Orders@ParaPublishing.com. <http://www.ParaPublishing.com/>. Updated periodically.**
Still the leader. This book has launched thousands of self-publishing ventures. Read it just as soon as you decide to go ahead with yours.

Printer's Ink. **<http://www.tshore.com/lib/pi/picont.html>.**
Thomson-Shore Printing's free quarterly newsletter on book manu-

facturing with information on new technologies, paper information, tips on how to prepare your book for printing, etc. Read it online, download it in Adobe Acrobat, or get on the 20,000+ mailing list to receive the hard-copy version.

Publish, 501 Second Street, San Francisco, CA 94107–1455. <http://www.publish.com>. Published monthly.
A desktop publishers' periodical with an annual buyers' guide.

The Publisher Notes, **c/o Melvett Chambers, PO Box 8475, Denver, CO 80202; 303–321–2955; e-mail: Melvettc@msn.com. Published bimonthly.**
News items and other short pieces for beginners.

Publishing Research Quarterly. **Transaction Publishers, Rutgers University, Building 4051, New Brunswick, NJ 08903; 908–445–2280; fax: 908–445–3138. <http://www.transactionpub.com>. Published quarterly.**
Scholars and others who've done some digging for hard data about the book world report their findings here.

❖ *The Publish-It-Yourself Handbook: Literary Tradition and How-To.* **Edited by Bill Henderson. Pushcart Press, PO Box 380, Wainscott, NY 11975. Fourth edition, 1998.**
By now a classic, this collection of spirited essays by self-publishers and their supporters should serve to embolden authors considering the self-publishing option and to entertain and inform readers of all sorts.

Radke, Linda Foster. *The Economical Guide to Self-Publishing: How to Produce and Market Your Book on a Budget.* **Five Star Publications, 4696 West Tyson Street, Chandler, AZ 85226–2903; e-mail: info@fivestarsupport.com. <http://www.fivestarsupport.com>. 1996.**
Speaking from experience, Radke covers the whole publishing process with special attention to deploying dollars.

Raugust, Karen. *The Licensing Business Handbook.* **EPM Communications, 160 Mercer Street, 3rd Floor, New York, NY 10012–3212; 212–941–0099; fax: 212–941–1622; e-mail: epmcommun@aol.com. Second edition, 1997.**
Get hold of this book at your library or send for the brochure about it if licensing holds promise for your work.

Reynolds, Don, Jr. *Crackerjack Positioning: Niche Marketing Strategy for the Entrepreneur.* Atwood Publishing, 5103 South Sheridan, Suite 524, Tulsa, OK 74145; 918–459–0110. 1993.

Easy to absorb and fun to read, the lessons Reynolds distills from experience are likely to stick with you. Though they're geared to whole companies, they can serve for books or lines of books as well.

❖ Ross, Tom and Marilyn. *The Complete Guide to Self-Publishing.* Writer's Digest Books, 1507 Dana Avenue, Cincinnati, OH 45207; 513–531–2690; fax: 513–531–7107. 1994.

Another excellent comprehensive guide. Examples are interesting, and detailed, specific advice is clear.

Ross, Marilyn and Tom. *How to Make Big Profits Publishing City & Regional Books: A Guide for Entrepreneurs, Writers and Publishers.* Communication Creativity, PO Box 909, 425 Cedar Street, Buena Vista, CO 81211–0909; 800–331–8355. 1987.

Ringing changes on their *Complete Guide to Self-Publishing* (see above), Marilyn and Tom Ross provide an array of examples here that's wondrous to behold. Obviously, lots of people now realize that it's easier to publish for limited geographical markets than for the widely dispersed (and probably mythical) general reader.

Ross, Marilyn and Tom. *Selling Books as Premiums & Incentives.* Communication Creativity, PO Box 909, 425 Cedar Street, Buena Vista, CO 81211–0909; 800–331–8355. 1997.

A high-priced pamphlet about the basic moves toward making bulk sales to businesses and organizations.

Salisbury, Linda and Jim. *Smart Self-Publishing: An author's guide to producing a marketable book.* Tabby House, 4429 Shady Lane, Charlotte Harbor, FL 33980–3024; e-mail: Publisher@TabbyHouse.com. <http://www.tabbyhouse.com/publish/>. Second edition, 1997.

The Salisburys, who also offer book production services, cover the basics smoothly here.

Schwartz, Evan I. *Webonomics: Nine Essential Principles for Growing Your Business on the World Wide Web.* See "The Sale and Its Sequels Resources."

❖ Shelton, Connie. *Publish Your Own Novel.* Columbine Books, PO Box 456, Angel Fire, NM 87710; 800–996–9783. 1996.

Actually, every self-publisher can profit from this good solid book, although the leads in the appendices pertain mostly to fiction. Shelton is the author of the Charlie Parker mysteries.

Small Publisher, c/o Nigel Maxey, PO Box 1620, Pineville, WV 24874; 304–732–8195.

How-to and human-interest pieces appear in this bimonthly paper along with ads that are sometimes hard to distinguish from editorial content.

Steinberg, Jacob. *I Never Had a Best-Seller: The Story of a Small Publisher.* Hippocrene Books, 171 Madison Avenue, New York, NY 10016. 1993.

Steinberg isn't complaining. He's describing a different sort of publishing house, a niche business like so many successful small companies. It's an engaging and revelatory account.

Stone, Bob. *Successful Direct Marketing Methods.*
Stone, Bob, and John Wyman. *Successful Telemarketing.*
See "The Sale and Its Sequels Resources."

Strong, William S. *The Copyright Book: A Practical Guide.* The MIT Press, 55 Hayward Street, Cambridge, MA 02142. Fourth edition, 1992.

A thorough, orderly introduction to copyright by a lawyer whose specialty it is. Semi-annual updates are available by subscription.

Walter, Russ. *The Secret Guide to Computers,* c/o Russ Walters, 22 Ashland Street, #2, Somerville, MA 02144–3202; 617–666–2666. Updated periodically.

Part buyer's guide, part user's guide, amazingly comprehensive and engagingly antic.

Wheildon, Colin. *Type & Layout: How typography and design can get your message across—or get in your way.* Strathmoor Press, 2550 Ninth Street, Suite 1040, Berkeley, CA 94710–2516; e-mail: info@strathmoor.com. 1995.

Admirable for its clarity and a standout among design guides because it's based on research. Helpful for book design, periodical design, promotion piece design, whatever.

Williams, Robin. *The Non-Designers Design Book: Design and Typographic Principles for the Visual Novice.* Peachpit Press, 1249 Eighth Street, Berkeley, CA 94710; 800–283–9444 or 510–524–2178; fax: 510–524–2221; e-mail: orders@peachpit.com. <http://www.peachpit.com>. 1994.

Excellent examples and a breezy style make the principles easy to grasp and apply.

Williams, Thomas A. *Kitchen-Table Publisher: How to Start, Manage and Profit from Your Own Homebased Publishing Company (Using Your Desktop Computer).*

See "Money Resources."

Tools

ALC (American List Counsel) List Connection.
See "The Sale and Its Sequels Resources."

American Bookseller.
See "The Sale and Its Sequels Resources."

American Book Trade Directory. R.R. Bowker, 121 Chanlon Road, New Providence, NJ 07974; 888–BOWKER2; fax: 908–464–3553; e-mail: info@bowker.com. <http://www.bowker.com>. Updated periodically.

The listings here will let you target bookstores—and large and small bookstore chains—where your work figures to sell well. Available in libraries.

American Library Directory. R.R. Bowker, 121 Chanlon Road, New Providence, NJ 07974; 888–BOWKER2; fax: 908–464–3553; e-mail: info@bowker.com. <http://www.bowker.com>. Updated periodically.

As above, a fine tool for targeting. Some libraries may have the online version along with the bound book.

Basement Full of Books. <http://www.sff.net/bfob/>.
A searchable directory of "Books Available By Mail Directly from Their Authors." Listings are free.

BISAC Subsidiary Rights Payment Advice Form and suggested contract clause, 160 Fifth Avenue, New York, NY 10010; 212–929–1393; fax: 212–929–7542. <http://www.bisg.org/>.

Get the clause about the form into any contract with a big book publisher to increase your chances of actually getting sub-rights royalties you're entitled to.

Bobby.

See "The Sale and Its Sequels Resources."

"Book Manufacturing," *Literary Market Place.*

Turn to this resource listing of service providers for everything you need to make your book a reality: indexers, proofers, designers, typesetters, prepress and printing firms, paper mills, binders, etc.

"Book Review & Index Journals & Services," *Literary Market Place.*

A useful checklist when the time comes to start sending out review copies.

BookWire.

See "The Sale and Its Sequels Resources."

BookZone.

See "The Sale and Its Sequels Resources."

Bowker Catalog. R.R. Bowker, 121 Chanlon Road, New Providence, NJ 07974; 888–BOWKER2; fax: 908–464–3553; e-mail: info@bowker.com. <http://www.bowker.com>.

Like its counterpart from Gale (see below), this free catalog should stimulate your thinking about promotional possibilities.

Brands and Their Companies.

Good leads for special sales. See "The Sale and Its Sequels Resources."

BRS Radio Directory.

See "The Sale and Its Sequels Resources."

Buyer's Index.

See "The Sale and Its Sequels Resources."

The Catalog Site.

See "The Sale and Its Sequels Resources."

Checkdomain.com.
See "The Sale and Its Sequels Resources."

The Chicago Manual of Style. **University of Chicago Press, 5801 South Ellis Avenue, Chicago, IL 60637. 14th edition, 1993.**
Billed as "the essential guide for writers, editors, and publishers," this is the aristocrat of style manuals and a favorite with many academics.

College Press Network Index.
See "The Sale and Its Sequels Resources."

Copyright Clearance Center Online. <http://www.copyright.com/>.
Come here to get the latest in copyright news and resources, access your account and/or search one of CCC's catalogs to see if a work has been registered.

Crawford, Tad. *Business and Legal Forms for Authors and Self-Publishers.* **Allworth Press, 10 East 23rd Street, Suite 400, New York, NY 10010; 212–777–8395. Revised edition, 1996.**
Why reinvent the wheel when this affordable book is available?

Cyberhound's® Guide to Associations and Nonprofit Organizations on the Internet.
See "The Sale and Its Sequels Resources."

The Directory of Mail Order Catalogs.
See "The Sale and Its Sequels Resources."

Directory of Public Relations Agencies and Resources on the WWW.
See "The Sale and Its Sequels Resources."

Doty, Betty, and Rebecca Meredith. *Hey Look . . . I Made a Book!* **Ten Speed Press, PO Box 7123, Berkeley, CA 94707. 1992.**
With this friendly little guide, you can actually create a bound book (or several, for that matter) and have quite a good time doing it.

Dustbooks, PO Box 100, Paradise, CA 95967; 800–477–6110; e-mail: len@dustbooks.com. <http://www.dustbooks.com>.
Get your publications listed in the Dustbooks Small Press Information Library (which includes *The International Directory of Little Magazines and Small Presses*), and use these volumes to identify small publishers in your area who might be willing to give you advice and moral support.

"Editorial Services," *Literary Market Place.*

A list you can use to find editorial aid nearby. Be sure to get samples, check references and compare prices before you make a deal.

EditPros Index of Marketing Resources.

See "The Sale and Its Sequels Resources."

E-mail: MEDIA.

See "The Sale and Its Sequels Resources."

❖ *Encyclopedia of Associations.*

A stellar source of information about people who will want your work. See "The Sale and Its Sequels Resources."

1st International Calendar of Annual Days, Weeks, Years and Decades.

See "The Sale and Its Sequels Resources."

Flash Magazine. **BlackLightning Publishing, Riddle Pond Road, West Topsham, VT 05086; 800–252–2599; fax: 802–439–6463; e-mail: sales@flashmag.com. <http://www.flashweb.com>.**

A monthly periodical about publishing equipment and techniques.

Freelance Editorial Association Yellow Pages and Code of Fair Practice. **Freelance Editorial Association, PO Box 380835, Cambridge, MA 02238–0835; 617–643–8626. Updated periodically.**

A directory of professionals for hire—including copy editors, developmental editors, production specialists and fact checkers—plus guidance on how to work with them.

Freestats.

See "The Sale and Its Sequels Resources."

Gale Research Catalog. **Gale Research, Inc., 835 Penobscot Building, Detroit, MI 48226–4094; 800–877–4253; fax: 800–414–5043. <http://www.gale.com>.**

First-rate stimulation when you need ideas about getting in touch with readers. Write to request a copy.

Gebbie Press All-in-One Directory. **Gebbie Press, PO Box 1000, New Paltz, NY 12561; 914–255–7560. Updated periodically.**

Bare-bones information on periodicals, radio and TV stations and news syndicates nationwide. Ignore the advice about using job titles rather than names in addresses.

International Literary Market Place. R.R. Bowker, 121 Chanlon Road, New Providence, NJ 07974; 888–BOWKER2; fax: 908–464–3553; e-mail: info@bowker.com. <http://www.bowker.com>. Updated periodically.

Listings include publishers, booksellers, libraries, book clubs, literary agents and organizations in 170 countries outside the United States. Go through the book at your library if your work might sell overseas.

The Internet Promotions Megalist. <http://www.2020tech.com/submit.html>.

Here you can get your site submitted to and listed with the right places for promotional purposes: Links to Sites That Distribute Your Site to Other Sites, Sites That List Your URL for Free, Reciprocal Link Services, and others.

Jonesreport.
See "The Sale and Its Sequels Resources."

❖ **"J" World Dates Archive.**
See "The Sale and Its Sequels Resources."

Kiefer, Marie. *Book Publishing Resource Guide*. Ad-Lib Publications, 51½ West Adams, Fairfield, IA 52556; 800–669–0773 or 515–472–6617; fax: 515–472–3186; e-mail: Adlib100@aol.com. 1996.

Created by people who know how publishing really works, this directory provides information on wholesalers, retailers, catalogers, sales reps, publicity and marketing services, reviewers, radio and television shows and on and on.

❖ **Kiefer, Marie. *Directory of Printers*. Ad-Lib Publications, 51½ West Adams, Fairfield, IA 52556; 800–669–0773 or 515–472–6617; fax: 515–472–3186; e-mail: Adlib100@aol.com. 1994.**

An extremely useful, intelligently indexed directory that gives you information about more than 700 companies along with information on how to deal with them.

Kiefer, Marie. *The Top 200 News, Talk and Magazine Shows*. Ad-Lib Publications, 51½ West Adams, Fairfield, IA 52556; 800–669–0773

or 515–472–6617; fax: 515–472–3186; e-mail: Adlib100@aol.com. 1996.

Shows with "some sort of national audience" are listed here.

Library Review Media.

See the "Book Review & Index Journals & Services" section of *LMP*, especially the entries for *Booklist*, *The Bulletin of the Center for Children's Books*, *Choice*, *The Horn Book Magazine*, *Library Journal*, *School Library Journal* and *VOYA*, and be sure to include those that are appropriate for your book(s) on your review-copy list.

❖ **Liszt, the mailing list directory.**

See "The Sale and Its Sequels Resources."

❖ *Literary Market Place.* **R.R. Bowker, 121 Chanlon Road, New Providence, NJ 07974; 888–BOWKER2; fax: 908–464–3553; e-mail: info@bowker.com. <http://www.bowker.com>. Updated annually.**

Like *Book Publishing Resource Guide* (above), *LMP* is replete with useful information. Since it's more expensive and also more likely to be available in libraries, you'd be smart to use it there.

Logos: The Journal of the World Book Community. **Whurr Publishers/Thomas Slatner & Co., 1127 Kennedy Boulevard, North Bergen, NJ 07047–1839; 201–865–6662. Published quarterly.**

Logos publishes pieces by book industry insiders from many nations.

Magazine and Newsletter Editors' Resource List.

See "Getting the Words Right Resources."

Mailing lists.

See *Book Publishing Resource Guide* and *Literary Market Place*, above, and Standard Rate and Data Service, below.

Mediafinder.

See "The Sale and Its Sequels Resources."

Midwest Book Review.

See "The Sale and Its Sequels Resources" and be sure to submit your book for review.

The MIT List of Radio Stations on the Internet.

See "The Sale and Its Sequels Resources."

Multicultural Publishing and Education Council.
<http://www.mpec.org>.
MPEC's site includes useful links to multicultural book publishers and distributors, as well as membership information.

National Endowment for the Arts. <http://arts.endow.gov/>.
National Endowment for the Humanities.
<http://www.neh.fed.us/>.
Visit these sites to get information on and links to funding and grant resources and projects, NEA- and NEH-related news and the like.

NetMechanic Link Check.
See "The Sale and Its Sequels Resources."

New Marketing Opportunities. **Edited by Sophia Tarila.**
See "A Foot in the Door Resources."

"Open Horizons Catalog." Open Horizons Publishing Co., 209 South Main Street, #200, PO Box 205, Fairfield, IA 52556–0205; 800–796–6130 or 515–472–6130; fax: 515–472–1560; e-mail: JohnKremer@aol.com. <http://www.bookmarket.com>.
The list you can use to get whatever John Kremer products you need at various points throughout the publication process.

Palder, Edward L. *The Catalog of Catalogs: The Complete Mail Order Directory.* **Woodbine House, 6510 Bells Mill Road, Bethesda, MD 20817. Updated periodically.**
An affordable guide you can use to identify and approach mail-order operations suitable for your subject.

Parrot Media Network.
See "The Sale and Its Sequels Resources."

Poynter, Dan, and Charles Kent. *Publishing Contracts: Sample Agreements for Book Publishers on Disk.* **Para Publishing, PO Box 8206-R, Santa Barbara, CA 93118–8206; 800–PARAPUB; e-mail: Orders@ParaPublishing.com. <http://www.ParaPublishing.com/>. 1995.**
Changeable at will on your computer and meant to be used in conjunction with professional advice on your particular situation, these forms pertain to several different kinds of deals.

The Publicity Process. **Edited by Christine Friesleben Goff. Iowa State University Press, 2121 South State Avenue, Ames, IA 50010; 800–862–6657. Third edition, 1989.**

Thoughtful essays by Iowa State faculty members on both the theoretical and the practical aspects of publicity.

Publishers, Distributors & Wholesalers of the United States. **R.R. Bowker, 121 Chanlon Road, New Providence, NJ 07974; 888–BOWKER2; fax: 908–464–3553; e-mail: info@bowker.com. <http://www.bowker.com>. Updated periodically.**

Available in print and online via libraries.

Publishers Weekly, **249 West 17th Street, New York, NY 10011; 212–463–6758; fax: 212–463–6631. <http://www.bookwire.com/pw>.**

If you have arranged to distribute your book to stores around the country, send a review copy to *PW* at least three months before its official publication date. Check the masthead at the beginning of the magazine to find the proper editor, and be sure to include information about your distribution setup along with other background data in your covering letter. *PW* is also a window on publishing events and trends; a subscription will keep you up to date, and if you can sell one of the magazine's departmental editors on a story idea, you'll boost your book's chances in bookstores.

Publishing Agreements: A Book of Precedents. **Edited by Charles Clark. New Amsterdam Books, 101 Main Street, Franklin, NY 13775. Third edition, 1989.**

Clark is an English lawyer turned editor and publisher. His compendium of contracts includes a book club rights agreement, an electronic publishing agreement, a translator's agreement and much more.

Radio Guide USA.

See "The Sale and Its Sequels Resources."

Radio Online.

See "The Sale and Its Sequels Resources."

❖ **RadioSpace.**

See "The Sale and Its Sequels Resources."

Radio-TV Interview Report.

See "The Sale and Its Sequels Resources."

Rank This! <http://www.rankthis.com>.
Determine where your site ranks with eight of the major search engines, how to improve it to increase traffic, and who your competition is.

Reference.com.
See "The Sale and Its Sequels Resources."

Search Engine Watch.
See "Getting the Words Right Resources."

Smart Business Supersite. <http://www.smartbiz.com/>.
A good general business site, specializing in "how-to" information on the Internet. Its "Business on the 'Net" page includes a useful collection of articles, tips, resources and links.

Smith, Peggy. *Mark My Words: Instruction and Practice in Proofreading.* **EEI Press, 66 Canal Center Plaza, Suite 200, Alexandria, VA 22314–5507; 800–683–8380 or 703–683–0683; fax: 703–683–4915; e-mail: info@eeicom.com. <http://www.eeicom.com>. Revised edition, 1993.**
Any typo, any misspelling, any grammatical glitch sends a signal to your readers that maybe you're not to be trusted. With this practical manual, you can avoid conveying that impression by learning to catch mistakes and to communicate clearly with the people who are supposed to correct them.

Smith, Ronald Ted. *Book Publishing Encyclopedia.* **BookWorld, 1933 Whitfield Park Loop, Sarasota, FL 34243; e-mail: bookworld@gnn.com. <http://www.bookworld.com>. Second edition, 1996.**
Don't expect a tome. This is more like one distributor's collected wit and wisdom, organized alphabetically. Smith heads BookWorld.

❖ *Stock Photo Deskbook: Your Instant Key to Over 180 Million Images.* **The Photographic Arts Center, 163 Amsterdam Avenue, New York, NY 10023. Updated periodically.**
Would pictures of Africa, carousels, honeymoons or nursing homes enhance your text? Would pictures of anything else? Chances are, you can find them by using the Subject Matter Index in this guide to "existing images." Entries include fax numbers as well as phone numbers,

and some of the artwork you're interested in may be quite inexpensive, or even free.

Talab, R. S. *Commonsense Copyright: A Guide to the New Technologies.* McFarland & Company, Inc., Publishers, PO Box 611, Jefferson, NC 28640. 1986.

Especially useful if what you're publishing is a collection of previously published work and/or if non-print media figure in your publishing plans.

Theobald, Mary Miley. *Museum Store Management.* AltaMira Press, 1630 North Main Street, Suite 367, Walnut Creek, CA 94596; 510–938–7243; fax: 510–933–9720. 1991.

If museums would be good places to sell the products you produce, get hold of this guide. Absorbing advice for the people who run the stores will give you a big head start on framing your approaches to them.

Tile.net/Lists.
See "The Sale and Its Sequels Resources."

Trade Show Central.
See "The Sale and Its Sequels Resources."

Trade Shows Worldwide. Gale Research, Inc., 835 Penobscot Building, Detroit, MI 48226–4094; 800–877–4253; fax: 800–414–5043. <http://www.gale.com>. Updated periodically.

Trade shows are useful not only for actually selling books (if exhibitors' costs are not prohibitively high) but also for learning your way around an industry with a view toward eventually using the promotion, publicity and sales possibilities it offers.

U.S. Census Bureau.
See "The Sale and Its Sequels Resources."

The Video Source Book. Gale Research, Inc., 835 Penobscot Building, Detroit, MI 48226–4094; 800–877–4253; fax: 800–414–5043. <http://www.gale.com>. Updated periodically.

Among the more than 145,000 programs covered here, you may find leads to people who'd be interested in making videos based on your book(s). See the subject index for starters.

❖ **WebStep Top 100.**
See "The Sale and Its Sequels Resources."

H. W. Wilson Catalog. H. W. Wilson Company, 950 University Avenue, Bronx, NY 10452; 800–367–6770. <http://www.hwwilson.com>.

Reference books by the dozens, some of which may be grist for your mill.

Working Press of the Nation. R.R. Bowker, 121 Chanlon Road, New Providence, NJ 07974; 888–BOWKER2; fax: 908–464–3553; e-mail: info@bowker.com. <http://www.bowker.com>. Updated periodically.

The subject indexes and the amount of information included in each listing make this three-volume set valuable. Explore it at your library for leads to receptive people in radio and TV as well as in periodical publishing.

People, Places and Programs

About Books, Inc., PO Box 1500, 425 Cedar Street, Buena Vista, CO 81211; 800–331–8355 or 719–395–2459; fax: 719–395–8374.

Tom and Marilyn Ross offer consulting services, books, tapes, seminars and a catalog of publishing resources you can use to order their books and plenty of others.

Allworth Press, 10 East 23rd Street, Suite 400, New York, NY 10010; 212–777–8395.

Tad Crawford started Allworth to provide "practical information to creative professionals." Check his catalog to see which books meet your needs.

ARRI, 58 Leigh Avenue, Princeton, NJ 08542; 609–924–1330; fax: 609–921–8203; e-mail: arrisend@aol.com.

Arri Sendzimir copyedits and formats manuscripts on disks and outputs pages ready for the printer.

The Authors Guild, Inc., 330 West 42nd Street, New York, NY 10036; 212–563–5904; fax: 212–564–8363; e-mail: staff@authorsguild.org.

When and if you decide to publish other people's work as well as your own, ask for a copy of the Guild's model trade book contract and consider basing your contract on it. After all, who has better reason to be fair to authors than a self-publisher?

The Authors Registry.
See "The Sale and Its Sequels Resources."

Bacon's Information, Inc., 332 South Michigan Avenue, Chicago, IL 60604; 800–621–0561.
Bacon's has mailing services and a clipping service plus its well-known media directories (see "The Sale and Its Sequels Resources").

Bar Codes.
These machine-readable IDs streamline sales for booksellers and bolster your image as a serious, professional publisher in every retailer's eyes. See BISAC, Fotel and *Book Publishing Resource Guide* below.

Malcolm E. Barker Consulting Services, PO Box 77246, San Francisco, CA 94107–0246; 415–485–5433.
Barker, of the much (and deservedly) praised *Book design & production for the small publisher* (see above), offers guidance in person as well as in print.

Henry Berry, PO Box 176, Southport, CT 06490; 203–332–7629; e-mail: henryberry@aol.com.
A stalwart of the small press community, Berry consults on many phases of the publishing process and offers free preliminary consults by phone or mail.

BISAC (Book Industry Systems Advisory Committee), 160 Fifth Avenue, New York, NY 10010; 212–929–1393; fax: 212–929–7542. <http://www.bisg.org/>.
BISAC develops and disseminates formats and forms that improve book ordering and distribution processes. Visit its area on the BISG Web site to learn more, and be sure to order and use its subject categories on your book covers.

BISG (Book Industry Study Group), 160 Fifth Avenue, New York, NY 10010; 212–929–1393; fax: 212–929–7542. <http://www.bisg.org/>.
Publishers, booksellers, manufacturers, librarians and others who work with books come together through BISG to gather and disseminate data about the book business.

The Book Printers, 110 Second Avenue South, Building A1, Pacheco, CA 94553–5502; 510–676–2571; fax: 510–676–2923.

Run by Kathleen and Ervin Slaski, this firm does short runs: 100–2,000 copies. Send for the "Printing with The Book Printers" pamphlet; it presents a good deal of sensible advice as it explains and exemplifies the company's capabilities.

Bookwrights, 2255 Westover Drive, Charlottesville, VA 22901; 804–823–8223; e-mail: mayapriya@bookwrights.com. <http://www.mindspring.com/~bookwrights/>.

Bookwrights handles design (including cover design) and production (including help with ISBNs and other industry identifiers) from disk or manuscript to bound books.

Cataloging-in-Publication Division, Library of Congress, Washington, DC 20540.

Send for the "PCN Publishers Manual" and for the form called "Request for Preassignment of Library of Congress Catalog Card Number" well in advance of publication.

The Combined Book Exhibit, 277 White Street, Buchanan, NY 10511; 914–739–7500; fax: 914–739–7575; e-mail: cbe@computer.net. <http://www.combinedbook.com>.

CBE displays books at industry conferences and conventions. Its Web site includes a useful informational list of distributors and wholesalers with addresses, phone and fax numbers, e-mails, Internet links where possible, and, coming soon, each company's specialty.

Consortium House, 139 Wittenberg Road, Bearsville, NY 12409; 914–679–8867; fax: 914–679–9248; e-mail: eugenegs@aol.com or chpub@aol.com.

A consulting company that specializes in business and product development for publishers. It's run by Gene Schwartz, an active, influential and respected participant in many publishing-related activities.

Copyright Office, Library of Congress, Washington, DC 20559–6000; 24-hour hotline for ordering application forms: 202–707–9100. <http://www.loc.gov/copyright>.

You'll want the "Copyright Basics" pamphlet (Circular 1) and Form TX—the application for copyright registration for a nondramatic literary work—as early as possible. (If you need applications for other kinds of creative work, the Copyright Office will supply them too.)

Council of Literary Magazines and Presses, 154 Christopher Street, Suite 3C, New York, NY 10014–2839; 212–741–9110; fax: 212–741–9112.

Formerly CCLM (the Coordinating Council of Literary Magazines), CLMP is dedicated to preserving, supporting and promoting literary periodicals and presses.

Crane Duplicating, 17 Shad Hole Road, PO Box 99, Dennisport, MA 02639; 508–760–1601; fax: 508–760–1544. <http://www.graphicillusions.com>.

Those "bound galleys" that reviewers like can come from printers who produce early copies with unadorned covers, or you can get them from a specialized company like this one or Sterling-Pierce (below). Because Cranes has been making bound galleys for decades, their name has become shorthand for the product.

Cypress House, 155 Cypress Street, Fort Bragg, CA 95437, 707–964–9520; fax: 707–964–7531; e-mail: 75104.1375@compuserve.com.

Editorial, design, production and marketing services are available from Cypress House. Send for its pamphlet, which will give you an excellent sense of the people you'd be working with and the mix of jobs you might hire them to handle.

Desktop Miracles, 4951 Airport Parkway, Suite 640, Addison, TX 75248; 972–788–0008; fax: 972–788–0014; e-mail: btkerrig@desktopmiracles.com. <http://www.desktopmiracles.com>.

Editorial and production services for printed materials and Internet sites.

Distributors.

See *Book Publishing Resource Guide* and *Literary Market Place,* above, for listings of distributors, and consult the *Resource Guide* and the *Subject Guide to Books in Print* to find publishers who might function as distributors for you because they issue books like yours.

Editorial Freelancers Association, 71 West 23rd Street, Suite 1504, New York, NY 10010; 212–929–5400; fax: 212–929–5439.

If you call the Editorial Freelancers Job Phone (see "People, Places and Programs" in "Money Resources") to describe the services you need, you'll hear from experienced people who want the work. As you would with any job applicant, ask for samples and check references.

EEI, 66 Canal Center Plaza, Suite 200, Alexandria, VA 22314–5507; 800–683–8380 or 703–683–0683; fax: 703–683–4915; e-mail: info@eeicom.com. <http://www.eeicom.com>.

In addition to its helpful books (see above and below), EEI provides helpful people to do editorial and production tasks as needed, and training programs to help you do selected tasks better.

Evanston Publishing, 4848 Brownsboro Center Arcade, Louisville, KY 40207; 800–594–5190 or 502–899–1919; fax: 502–896–0246.

Evanston can handle any part or all parts of the publishing process from editing through printing.

Fithian Press, PO Box 1525, Santa Barbara, CA 93102–1525; 800–662–8351.

"Creative co-publishing"—the author pays for production in exchange for a royalty of 50–70% of the net receipts. The brochure offers details.

Fotel, Inc., 41 West Home Avenue, Villa Park, IL 60181; 630–834–4920.

This company produces bar codes for publishers large and small.

Global Interprint, 2447 Petaluma Boulevard North, Petaluma, CA 94952; 707–765–6116; fax: 707–765–6018.

An experienced print broker (which means they'll select and supervise the printing process for you), Interprint specializes in complex projects.

Indexers.

If your book is nonfiction and you'd like to maximize library sales, make sure it has a good index. Leads are available through the Editorial Freelancers Association (see above) and through the American Society of Indexers (see *Literary Market Place*).

International Titles/Harry Smith, 931 East 56th Street, Austin, TX 78751–1724; 512–451–2221; fax: 512–467–1330; e-mail: leint@eden.com.

An exhibit service that could represent your titles at library and book trade conferences and conventions.

Internet Publicity Services. <http://www.olympus.net/okeefe/PIO/>.
The author of *Publicity on the Internet* (see above) promotes books and
authors through this company. Check out the information here, which
also links to its useful companion site, Internet Publicity Resources.

**Interpub, PO Box 50123, Eugene, OR 97405; 541–342–6901; e-mail:
cliffmar@efn.org.**
Cliff Martin's company offers special-sales services, among other
things. Send for details.

**ISBN Agency, R.R. Bowker, 121 Chanlon Road, New Providence,
NJ 07974; 888–BOWKER2; fax: 908–464–3553; e-mail:
info@bowker.com. <http://www.bowker.com>.**
Every book you plan to do needs an ISBN to be salable in normal
channels. Send for the forms as soon as you've settled on a title.

**ISSN (International Standard Serial Number), Library of Congress
National Serials Data Program, Washington, DC 20540;
202–707–6452. <http://lcweb.loc.gov/issn/>.**
The periodical world's equivalent of the ISBN.

**The Jenkins Group, 121 East Front Street, 4th Floor, Traverse City,
MI 49684; 616–933–0445; e-mail: jenkins.group@smallpress.com.
<http://www.smallpress.com>.**
Publishers of *Independent Publisher* (which runs reviews as well as
how-to pieces) and *Publishing Entrepreneur* (which is a bit thin on substance), Jerry Jenkins' latest company also offers (and hypes) seminars,
publishing services and books about publishing.

**Kramer Communications, 259 University Avenue, Suite 204, Palo
Alto, CA 94301; 650–321–6444; e-mail: felix@nlightning.com.
<http://www.nlightning.com/dtpsabout.html>.**
Felix Kramer, co-author of *Desktop Publishing Success* (see above),
provides "start-to-finish" desktop publishing services, including training for those who want to do as much as possible themselves.

**John Kremer, Book Marketing Consultant, 209 South Main Street,
#200, PO Box 205, Fairfield, IA 52556–0205; 800–796–6130 or
515–472–6130; fax: 515–472–1560; e-mail: JohnKremer@aol.com.
<http://www.bookmarket.com>.**
Advice of the sort you'll find in Kremer's books (above) is available
from Kremer in person by the hour, day or project.

Jeffrey Lant Associates, PO Box 38–2767, Cambridge, MA 02238; 617–547–6372; e-mail: drjlant@worldprofit.com. <http://www.worldprofit.com/>.

Lant favors "unabashed" self-promotion, as his "Sure-Fire Business Success Catalog" will show you. Depending on your personality and the nature of your work, his ideas and products may appeal or repel.

MAS Sales Enterprises, 341 East 33rd Street, Suite 1R, New York, NY 10016; 212–213–3696; fax: 212–545–7990; e-mail: MASales@aol.com.

Myra Sincoff's company specializes in reaching "nontraditional" markets for books, including corporations, catalogs and associations.

Museum Store Association, 501 South Cherry Street, Suite 460, Denver, CO 80222–1325; 303–329–6968; fax: 303–329–6134.

If what you're publishing is perfect for museum shops, you may want to join this association, so you can get and use its directory of members.

NAPRA (New Age Publishing & Retailing Alliance), PO Box 9, 6 Eastsound Square, Eastsound, WA 98245–0009; 360–376–2702; fax: 360–376–2704; e-mail: napra@pacificrim.net.

A good group to join if you publish for the "New Age" market.

National Association of Desktop Publishers, 460 Old Boston Street, Topsfield, MA 01983; 800–874–4113 or 508–887–7900.

Membership brings you a journal, a newsletter, a directory of courses and assorted other benefits.

National Association of Independent Publishers, PO Box 430, Highland City, FL 33846–0430; 941–648–4420; e-mail: NAIP@aol.com.

Headed by Betsy Lampé, NAIP welcomes "everyone on all levels of publishing, writing, etc." and supplies useful information partly through its *Publisher's Report* newsletter, which members get and others can subscribe to.

Panoptic Enterprises, PO Box 11220, Burke, VA 22009–1220; 800–594–4766 or 703–451–5953.

Advice on contracting with the federal government from a company run by Vivina and Barry McVay (see McVay's *Getting Started in Federal Contracting*, above).

❖ **Para Publishing, PO Box 8206-R, Santa Barbara, CA 93118–8206; 800–PARAPUB; e-mail: Orders@ParaPublishing.com. <http://www.ParaPublishing.com/>.**

Dan Poynter's Para Publishing supplies an ever-expanding collection of clever, practical products and services for self-publishers, including "Special Reports" on book marketing, reviews, publicity and direct mail (to name a few) and a variety of workshops (some high on a hill overlooking the Pacific Ocean). Send for detailed information.

Peachpit Press, 1249 Eighth Street, Berkeley, CA 94710; 800–283–9444 or 510–524–2178; fax: 510–524–2221; e-mail: orders@peachpit.com. <http://www.peachpit.com>.

Peachpit specializes in books that help people use computers to advantage. Send for the catalog.

Poets & Writers, Inc.

See "Getting the Words Right Resources."

Poets House.

See "The Sale and Its Sequels Resources."

Printing by Design, 70 East 93rd Street, New York, NY 10128; 212–831–8520; fax: 212–348–3599.

Marion Morey can handle design and printing for you, whether you're doing books or periodicals or promotional materials or all of the above.

❖ **Publishers Marketing Association, 627 Aviation Way, Manhattan Beach, CA 90266; 310–372–2732; fax: 310–374–3342; e-mail: PMAonline@aol.com. <http://pma-online.org/>.**

The best association of and for small publishers, PMA issues a newsletter, offers co-op and Internet marketing opportunities, runs programs including a Publishing University, and hosts a remarkably informative e-mail list, among other things.

Quality Books, Inc., 1003 West Pines Road, Oregon, IL 61061; 815–732–4450; fax: 815–732–4499.

Quality Books distributes adult nonfiction from small publishers to libraries. They're selective; call or write to get more information about the various services they offer and to find out how to submit a copy of your book for consideration.

Deborah A. Rust Design, 219 East 5th Street, New York, NY 10003; 212–254–8649.
One-stop shopping for cover design, interior design and the production steps before printing. Rust does periodicals as well as books.

Sensible Solutions, Inc., 271 Madison Avenue, Suite 1007, New York, NY 10016; 212–687–1761; fax: 212–867–8641; e-mail: Sensibly@aol.com. <http://www.happilypublished.com>.
The consulting firm that grew out of *How to Get Happily Published*, Sensible Solutions handles marketing for self-publishers, among others. See "The Sale and Its Sequels Resources."

SPAN (Small Publishers Association of North America), PO Box 1306, 425 Cedar Street, Buena Vista, CO 81211–1306; 719–395–4790; fax: 719–395–8374; e-mail: SPAN@span-assn.org. <http://www.SPANnet.org>.
Run by Marilyn and Tom Ross (see above), SPAN publishes a newsletter and often gears products and services to self-publishers.

SPAWN (Small Publishers, Artists and Writers Network), PO Box 2653, Ventura, CA 93002–2653; 805–643–2403; e-mail: execdir@spawn.org. <http://www.spawn.org>.
Offers information, news and opportunities for anyone interested in writing and publishing. Check out its online resources and newsletter at its Web site.

Standard Rate and Data Service, 1700 Higgins Road, Des Plaines, IL 60018–5605; 800–851–7737 or 847–375–5000; fax: 847–375–5001. <http://www.srds.com>.
SRDS products are designed to give people the facts they need to place ads intelligently in periodicals, on the air and online. You'll want their catalog if your plans include an ad campaign.

Stanford Professional Publishing Course. Stanford Alumni Association, Bowman Alumni House, Stanford, CA 94305–4005; 800–621–3022 or 415–725–6259; fax: 415–725–7510. <http://sunsite.stanford.org/SOLAR/publishing.courses/>.
An established, intensive 13-day program for "book and magazine publishing professionals who are hungry for new ideas."

Sterling-Pierce Co., 422 Atlantic Avenue, East Rockaway, NY 11518; 516–593–1170; fax: 516–593–1401.
A popular source for bound galleys.

The Town House Press, 552 Weathersfield, Fearrington Post, Pittsboro, NC 27312; 800–525–5470.

Alvin Schultzberg, who runs The Town House Press, will handle all aspects of production, including design, for small editions, and he can also steer you toward help with sales and publicity.

Traverse Bay Display and Packaging, 4366 Deerwood Drive, Traverse City, MI 49686–3810; 800–240–9802; fax: 616–938–3296; e-mail: tbdp@traverse.com.

A source for "dumps," those little cardboard containers used for displaying books. Send for the brochure and assess your chances of getting the necessary counterspace or floorspace before you order.

Unique Books, 5010 Kamper Avenue, St. Louis, MO 63139; 314–776–6695; fax: 314–776–0841.

Another company that distributes books from smaller publishers to libraries. See Quality Books, above.

University of Chicago Publishing Program. The University of Chicago, Graham School of General Studies, 5835 Kimbark Avenue, Chicago, IL 60637; 773–702–1724; fax: 773–702–6814.

Courses for developing a variety of publishing skills, including a week-long seminar on "The Business of Publishing."

Volunteer Lawyers for the Arts.

See "Money Resources."

Wholesalers.

See *Book Publishing Resource Guide* and *Literary Market Place,* and pay special attention to the national giants, Baker & Taylor and Ingram.

Women's National Book Association.

See "The Sale and Its Sequels Resources," and call to find out if there's a nearby WNBA chapter you might join.

Money Resources

To earn more money from writing, first figure out how to recycle material for multiple markets; then use the resources in previous sections to attract as many different buyers as you can. To win money, save money, supplement your income and stretch the dollars you have, see the resources listed below.

Advice, Analysis and Reportage

Bly, Robert W. *The Copywriter's Handbook: A Step-by-Step Guide to Writing Copy That Sells.* Henry Holt & Company, 115 West 18th Street, New York, NY 10011. 1990.

A good-size chunk of this manual by a pro explains how to sell copywriting skills.

Brabec, Barbara. *Homemade Money.* Betterway Books/Writer's Digest, 1507 Dana Avenue, Cincinnati, OH 45207; 513–531–2690; fax: 513–531–7107. Fifth revised edition, 1997.

Sales in six figures testify to the value of the advice in here.

Brenner, Robert C. *Pricing Guide for Desktop Services.* Brenner Information Group, 9340 Carmel Mountain, Suite C, San Diego, CA 92129–2161. Fourth edition, 1996.

If your production skills have gotten good enough to sell, you'll want to consult this thoughtful, detailed manual.

Byers, Judy. *Words on Tape: How to Create Profitable Spoken Word Audio on Cassettes and CDs.* Audio Cassette Producers, 1660 South Albion, Suite 309, Denver, CO 80222; 303–751–1198; fax: 303–751–5655; e-mail: HowToAudio@aol.com. <http://www.AudioCP.com>. 1997.

Lively and knowledgeable guidance filled with interesting facts and figures ("expect to sell one audiobook for each 10 books sold," for instance).

Chelekis, George. *The Action Guide to Government Grants, Loans, and Giveaways.* Perigee Books/Putnam, 200 Madison Avenue, New York, NY 10016. <http://www.putnam.com>. 1993.

Chekelis provides advice (on how to write grant proposals and business proposals, for instance) along with lists of funding sources of various sorts, including foundation grants for the arts.

Crawford, Tad, and Tony Lyons. *The Writer's Legal Guide.* Allworth Press, 10 East 23rd Street, Suite 400, New York, NY 10010; 212–777–8395. Revised edition, 1996.

Crawford, a lawyer-writer, offers some good guidance on money matters including taxes.

Dailey, Gene. *Secrets of a Successful Entrepreneur: How to Start and Succeed at Running Your Own Business.* K&A Publications, 4847 Hopyard Road, Suite 3201B, Pleasanton, CA 94588. 1994.

See especially the chapters on raising money and financial strategies, and take advantage of the many useful worksheets.

Davidson, Jeffrey P. *Marketing for the Home-Based Business.* Bob Adams, Inc., 260 Center Street, Holbrook, MA 02343; 617–767–8100. 1990.

Pointers on a range of subjects, from stationery to client relations.

The Editorial Eye.

See "Getting the Words Right Resources."

Edwards, Paul and Sarah. *Working from Home: Everything You Need to Know about Living and Working Under the Same Roof.* Putnam, 200 Madison Avenue, New York, NY 10016. <http://www.putnam.com>. Fourth edition, 1994.

A useful commonsense guide on setting up and managing any kind of home-based business.

Ensign, Paulette. *How to write and market booklets for CA$H.* Organizing Solutions, 12675 Camino Mira Del Mar, #179, San Diego, CA 92130; 619–481–0890; fax: 619–793–0880; e-mail: 75031.2606@compuserve.com. 1996.

Step-by-step guidance in a pricey spiral-bound package about creating booklets like those Ensign produces for herself and her clients. "Over 400,000 copies sold without spending a penny of advertising," the cover line says.

Evans, Rupert. *Book-on-Demand Publishing.* BlackLightning Publishing, Riddle Pond Road, West Topsham, VT 05086; 800–252–2599; fax: 802–439–6463; e-mail: info@BlackLightning.com. <http://www.flashweb.com/flash/>. 1995.

How to produce bound books—in quantities from 1 to 1,000 for yourself and/or for others—and how to figure out whether you want to.

Flash Compendium. **BlackLightning Publishing, Riddle Pond Road, West Topsham, VT 05086; 800–252–2599; fax: 802–439–6463; e-mail: info@BlackLightning.com. <http://www.flashweb.com/flash/>. 1992.**

Practical pieces on design and production compiled from back issues of *The Flash*—"a small, eclectic newsletter" about aspects of "the revolution in business enabled by personal computers and laser printers."

Glenn, Peggy. *Word Processing Profits at Home.* Aames-Allen Publishing, 18281 Gothard Street, #105, Huntington Beach, CA 92648–1205. Second edition, 1993.

How to set up and run a word-processing business, by someone who's done it.

Hadley, Joyce. *Part-Time Careers: For anyone who wants more than just a job—but less than a 40-hour week!* Career Press, PO Box 687, Three Tice Road, Franklin Lakes, NJ 07417; 800–CAREER–1. 1993.

Lots of ideas and a good little list of places to find more information.

Irwin, D. Kelly. *Start a Business without Borrowing.* Emerald Ink Publishing, 7141 Office City Drive, Suite 220, Houston, TX 77087; 800–324–5663 or 713–643–9945; e-mail: emerald@emeraldink.com. <http://www.emeraldink.com>. 1995.

As a bank loan officer, Irwin reports, he saw all too many people who didn't understand that starting a successful business takes months, if not years, of hard, focused work. His manual is designed to get that work done.

Judd, Karen. *Copyediting: A Practical Guide.* **Crisp Publications, 1200 Hamilton Court, Menlo Park, CA 94025; 415–323–6100. Second edition, 1990.**

A helpful primer despite its outdated coverage of computers in the writing and production processes.

❖ **Kamoroff, Bernard.** *Small-Time Operator: How to Start Your Own Small Business, Keep Your Books, Pay Your Taxes, and Stay Out of Trouble!* **Bell Springs Publishing, PO Box 1240, Willits, CA 95490; 707–459–6372. Updated periodically.**

Kamoroff has years of experience as a financial adviser and tax accountant for small businesses and years of experience running small businesses of his own. This very popular guide covers everything from getting started (figuring out how much money you need and then getting your hands on it) to bookkeeping to the legal and financial technicalities of partnerships, payrolls and, yes, taxes. Bell Springs has other books about small businesses too; ask for the brochure.

❖ **Kopelman, Alexander.** *National Writers Union Guide to Freelance Rates & Standard Practice.* **National Writers Union, 873 Broadway, Suite 203, New York, NY 10003; 212–254–0279. 1995.**

Specific facts, figures and tips about deals with all sorts of companies that might be customers for your work.

Kramer, Felix, and Maggie Lovaas. *Desktop Publishing Success: How to Start and Run a Desktop Publishing Business.* **Kramer Communications, 259 University Avenue, Suite 204, Palo Alto, CA 94301; 650–321–6444; e-mail: felix@nlightning.com. <http://www.nlightning.com/dtpsabout.html>. 1991.**

Remarkably thorough, readable and friendly, this is a book you'll want to buy if you're thinking of cashing in on desktop expertise. Both authors are experienced enough to really know what they're talking about and generous enough to tell you what you need to know to compete with them.

Levinson, Jay Conrad. *Guerrilla Marketing Weapons.*

See "The Self-Publishing Option Resources."

Parker, Lucy V. *How to Open and Operate a Home-Based Writing Business.* The Globe Pequot Press, 6 Business Park Road, PO Box 833, Old Saybrook, CT 06475–0833; 800–304–4562. 1994.

Parker takes you step by step through a process she herself has negotiated. Case studies and worksheets add to the value of her advice.

Rogers, Trumbull. *Editorial Freelancing: A Practical Guide.* Aletheia Publications, 38–15 Corporal Kennedy Street, Bayside, NY 11361. 1995.

Rogers knows what he's talking about, and if you're interested in selling your editorial skills, you'd be smart to listen.

Sanders, Scott Russell. *Writing from the Center.* Indiana University Press, 601 North Morton Street, Bloomington, IN 47404–3797; 800–842–6796 or 812–855–4203. 1995.

See the chapter on "The Writer in the University" if you're considering teaching as a way to make some money. Sanders, a professor of English at Indiana U., is the author of several books. This one focuses on relationships between writing and "home territory."

Sanow, Arnold, and J. Daniel McComas. *Marketing Boot Camp: 85 Profit-Packed Tools, Techniques & Strategies To Boost Your Bottom Line . . . NOW!* Kendall/Hunt Publishing, 4050 Westmark Drive, Dubuque, IA 52002. 1994.

Lacing their prose with buzz words, checklists, sidebars and attention-getting typefaces, the authors present an "automated database marketing system" designed to build "lasting relationships with your key audiences."

Sharpe, Leslie T., and Irene Gunther. *Editing Fact and Fiction: A Concise Guide to Book Editing.* Cambridge University Press, 40 West 20th Street, New York, NY 10011–4211. 1994.

Useful whether you're selling your editorial skills or honing them for your own use, or both.

Shaw, Eva. *Ghostwriting: How to Get Into the Business.* Marlowe & Company, 632 Broadway, 7th Floor, New York, NY 10012. 1991.

Drawing on her own fund of experience, Shaw explains the whole process of ghostwriting—not just how to get into the business, as the subtitle says, but how to structure and price your services as a literary ghost and how to work with the source of your material.

❖ **Shaw, Lisa.** *How to Make Money Publishing from Home: Everything You Need to Know to Successfully Publish Books, Newsletters, Greeting Cards, Zines, and Software.* **Prima Publishing, 3875 Atherton Road, Rocklin, CA 95765. <http://www.primapublishing.com/>. 1997.**

An admirably practical guide. Based firmly on experience, Shaw's lively, detailed advice is accompanied by sample business and marketing plans.

Shaw, Lisa. *1001 Ways to Market Yourself and Your Small Business.* **Perigree Books/Putnam, 200 Madison Avenue, New York, NY 10016. <http://www.putnam.com>. 1997.**

Tips to incorporate in your marketing plans and to use as stimulants for additional ideas.

Smith, Peggy. *Mark My Words: Instruction and Practice in Proofreading.* **EEI Press, 66 Canal Center Plaza, Suite 200, Alexandria, VA 22314–5507; 800–683–8380 or 703–683–0683; fax: 703–683–4915; e-mail: info@eeicom.com. <http://www.eeicom.com>. Revised edition, 1993.**

Those of you who like catching typos and other errors can upgrade proofreading skills through the exercises in here, and sell them when they're good and strong. Smith is also the author of *Letter Perfect: A Guide to Practical Proofreading* (see this section's "Tools") from EEI.

STET Again! More Tricks of the Trade for Publications People. **EEI Press, 66 Canal Center Plaza, Suite 200, Alexandria, VA 22314–5507; 800–683–8380 or 703–683–0683; fax: 703–683–4915; e-mail: info@eeicom.com. <http://www.eeicom.com>. 1996.**

A collection of articles from *The Editorial Eye* (see "Getting the Words Right Resources"), designed to keep editorial skills sharp.

Stoughton, Mary. *Substance & Style: Instruction and Practice in Copyediting.* **EEI Press, 66 Canal Center Plaza, Suite 200, Alexandria, VA 22314–5507; 800–683–8380 or 703–683–0683; fax: 703–683–4915; e-mail: info@eeicom.com. <http://www.eeicom.com>. Second edition, 1996.**

Primarily a book of exercises, *Substance & Style* also includes interesting short essays on topics such as "Is It Wrong to Tamper with a Quotation?" and "Fair Use and Copyright."

Today's $85,000 Freelance Writer. BSK Communications, 886 Oradell Avenue, PO Box 543, Oradell, NJ 07649; 800–797–9027; e-mail: bskcom@internexus.net. <http://www.tiac.net/users/bskcom>. Published bimonthly.

A magazine by and for self-employed commercial copywriters interested in improving performance and pay.

Woll, Thomas. *Publishing for Profit: Strategic Management for Smaller and Self-Publishers.* Fisher Books, 4239 West Ina Road, Suite 101, Tucson, AZ 85741; e-mail: fisherbook@aol.com. <http://www.fisherbooks.com/home.html>. 1998.

Woll, who runs Cross River Publishing Consultants in Katonah, NY, provides nuts-and-bolts advice about the business and financial aspects of publishing. Forms and illustrations help make his manual crystal clear.

Williams, Thomas A. *Kitchen-Table Publisher: How to Start, Manage and Profit from Your Own Homebased Publishing Company (Using Your Desktop Computer).* Venture Press, 9741 NW Seventh Circle, Suite 5–25, Plantation, FL 33324. 1997.

Detailed advice on relatively profitable kinds of publishing—like directories and ad compilations for shoppers, real-estate buyers and newcomers to a neighborhood.

Tools

Annual Register of Grant Support. R.R. Bowker, 121 Chanlon Road, New Providence, NJ 07974; 888–BOWKER2; fax: 908–464–3553; e-mail: info@bowker.com. <http://www.bowker.com>. Updated periodically.

More than 3,000 grants-giving organizations are listed here.

Awards, Honors & Prizes. Gale Research, Inc., 835 Penobscot Building, Detroit, MI 48226–4094; 800–877–4253; fax: 800–414–5043. <http://www.gale.com>. Updated periodically.

This is a two-volume general reference work about all kinds of awards in the United States and abroad. Its subject index will lead you to those for which you're eligible. Entries are sensibly annotated.

AwardWeb: Collections of Literary Award Information. <http://www.city-net.com/~lmann/awards/index.html>.

Links to international literary award pages, with an emphasis on science-fiction prizes.

Bower, Gail Hellund. *Artists and Writers Colonies: Retreats, Residences, and Respites for the Creative Mind.* **Blue Heron Publishing, 24450 Northwest Hansen Road, Hillsboro, OR 97124; 503–621–3911. 1995.**

A lengthy listing, with a good deal of useful information about every facility.

Bowker's Complete Video Directory. **R.R. Bowker, 121 Chanlon Road, New Providence, NJ 07974; 888–BOWKER2; fax: 908–464–3553; e-mail: info@bowker.com. <http://www.bowker.com>. Updated periodically.**

A useful compendium if you're scouting for people who might be interested in a video based on your print product.

The Foundation Center Catalog. **The Foundation Center, 79 Fifth Avenue, New York, NY 10003–3076; 212–620–4230. <http://www.fdncenter.org>.**

If the world of grants is new to you, start by ordering *The Foundation Center's User-Friendly Guide,* a helpful booklet, and/or by going to one of the Center's collections, browsing around and asking questions (see "People, Places and Programs," below). Then zero in on appropriate entries in *The Foundation Directory, The Foundation Grants Index, Foundation Grants to Individuals* and any of the specialized Foundation Center publications that fit your needs.

❖ *Grants and Awards Available to American Writers.* **PEN American Center, 568 Broadway, New York, NY 10012; 212–334–1660; fax: 212–334–2181. Updated periodically.**

An indispensable—and inexpensive—reference for writers in search of funds. Well worth perusing whether you write fiction, nonfiction, poetry, children's books, plays or all of the above.

Grant Seekers Guide: Foundations That Support Social & Economic Justice. **Edited by James McGrath Morris and Laura Adler. Moyer Bell, Kymbolde Way, Wakefield, RI 02879. Fourth revised edition, 1996.**

Meant primarily for "the overworked, underpaid, dedicated employee of one of the many small organizations seeking to bring about social change," this substantial, well-indexed guide should be useful to authors and publishers with that sort of agenda.

Hollywood Creative Directory, 3000 West Olympic Boulevard, Suite 2525, Santa Monica, CA 90404; 800–815–0503 or 310–315–4815; e-mail: hcd@hollyvision.com. <http://www.hollyvision.com>. **Published triannually.**

Look here for names, addresses, etc. of producers, studio and network executives and more. The Web site offers frequent updates and access to the company's related directories, including one that lists Hollywood agents and managers.

Iowa State University Press Journalism/Mass Communication Books Catalog. Iowa State University Press, 2121 South State Avenue, Ames, IA 50010; 800–862–6657.

The books listed here include several about writing and editing for periodicals and electronic media.

Lesko, Matthew. *Information U.S.A.* **Viking Penguin, 375 Hudson Street, New York, NY 10014. 1986.**

Good leads to state and federal funds. Be sure to check the lengthy index for the subject(s) your work covers.

Literary Market Place. **R.R. Bowker, 121 Chanlon Road, New Providence, NJ 07974; 888–BOWKER2; fax: 908–464–3553; e-mail: info@bowker.com. <http://www.bowker.com>. Updated annually.**

LMP comes in handy in two ways where money is concerned: It has lists that you can consult to find funding (see "Awards, Contests & Grants" and "Employment Agencies"), and it has lists that you can get on to earn fees, given relevant skills (see "Typing & Word Processing Services," "Electronic Publishing Consultants" and "Editorial Services," including its "Activity Index" subdivisions for copy-editing, ghost writing, indexing, line editing, proofreading, research, rewriting and special assignment writing).

Million Dollar Directory. **Dun's Marketing Services, a Division of Dun & Bradstreet, Three Sylvan Way, Parsippany, NJ 07054. Updated periodically.**

Businesses often need writers—to prepare annual reports, speeches, feature stories, newsletters and manuals. Try using the geographic and industry classification indexes in this multivolume work to zero in on companies that might hire you. Entries cover more than 160,000 U.S. businesses with net worths over $500,000.

My Big Sourcebook: For People Who Work with Words or Pictures.
Written by the staff of EEI Communications. EEI Press, 66 Canal
Center Plaza, Suite 200, Alexandria, VA 22314–5507;
800–683–8380 or 703–683–0683; fax: 703–683–4915; e-mail:
info@eeicom.com. <http://www.eeicom.com>. 1996.

Nearly 400 pages of annotated listings cover books, periodicals,
courses, groups, awards and electronic resources that can be helpful to
professional communicators.

National Endowment for the Arts.
National Endowment for the Humanities.

See "The Self-Publishing Option Resources"

Research Centers Directory. Gale Research, Inc., 835 Penobscot
Building, Detroit, MI 48226–4094; 800–877–4253; fax:
800–414–5043. <http://www.gale.com>. Updated periodically.

By affiliating with institutions, individuals can become eligible for
some grants offered to non-profit groups. To find the centers most
likely to take you under their wing, look up your project's subject in
the directory's index and then study the description of each group listed
under that heading.

Smith, Peggy. *Letter Perfect: A Guide to Practical Proofreading.* EEI
Press, 66 Canal Center Plaza, Suite 200, Alexandria, VA
22314–5507; 800–683–8380 or 703–683–0683; fax: 703–683–4915;
e-mail: info@eeicom.com. <http://www.eeicom.com>. 1995.

The title says it.

Thomas Register of American Manufacturers. Thomas Publishing
Company, 5 Penn Plaza, New York, NY 10001; 800–699–9822 or
212–290–7277. <http://www.thomasregister.com>. Updated
periodically.

A great source of leads to companies that might buy your work
in bulk. The *Thomas Register,* a 26-volume set, is available in
libraries.

Words on Cassette. R.R. Bowker, 121 Chanlon Road, New Providence, NJ 07974; 888–BOWKER2; fax: 908–464–3553; e-mail:
info@bowker.com. <http://www.bowker.com>. Updated periodically.

Look here for leads to producers and distributors who might be
interested in the audio version of your work.

Writer's Digest Catalog.
See "A Foot in the Door Resources."

"Writer's Profit Catalog™," 22 East Quakenbush Avenue, 3rd Floor, Dumont, NJ 07628; 201–385–1220.
Bob Bly, author of *Secrets of a Freelance Writer: How to Make $85,000 a Year; Technical Writing: Structure, Standards, and Style* and several other titles designed to boost writers' revenues, offers them all via this catalog. He's created an audiotape program too—"The High-Profit Writer."

❖ **Write Time.**
See "A Foot in the Door Resources"

People, Places and Programs

American Book Producers Association, 160 Fifth Avenue, New York, NY 10010; 800–209–4575 or 212–645–2368; fax: 212–989–7542.
If you have enough expertise and writing credits to work for a book packager, or if you think you'd like to become one, get in touch with this group. Its members think up and produce all sorts of titles.

Associated Writing Programs. Tallwood House, Mailstop 1E3, George Mason University, Fairfax, VA 22030; 703–993–4301; fax: 703–993–4302; e-mail: awp@gmu.edu.
<http://web.gmu.edu/departments/awp/>.
For a small membership fee, the creative writer can take advantage of a number of income-generating programs sponsored by AWP, including a placement service.

Audio Cassette Producers, 1660 South Albion, Suite 309, Denver, CO 80222; 303–751–1198; fax: 303–751–5655; e-mail: HowToAudio@aol.com. <http://www.AudioCP.com>.
Judy Byers' company handles audio production from concept through packaged product.

Authors Unlimited, 31 East 32nd Street, Suite 300, New York, NY 10016; 212–481–8484; fax: 212–481–9582.
Arlynn Greenbaum, who runs this speakers' bureau, is selective, of course, but if you're a good speaker with a good track record, get in touch.

Council of Literary Magazines and Presses, 154 Christopher Street, Suite 3C, New York, NY 10014–2839; 212–741–9110; fax: 212–741–9112.

Contact the Council of Literary Magazines and Presses if fine writing is what you aim to publish. Originally the Coordinating Council of Literary Magazines, CLMP offers financial and moral support.

Dial-a-Writer Referral Service, American Society of Journalists and Authors, 1501 Broadway, Suite 302, New York, NY 10036; 212–398–1934; fax: 212–768–7414; e-mail: asja@compuserve.com. <http://www.asja.org>.

Some people ask the Dial-a-Writer referral service to find them collaborators and ghosts. A writer who pays the price of admission to the ASJA can see who candidates are, what they want and whether any of their projects is attractive, financially and otherwise.

Editorial Freelancers Association, 71 West 23rd Street, Suite 1504, New York, NY 10010; 212–929–5400; fax: 212–929–5439.

Members have access to information about job opportunities through a telephone bulletin board. The EFA also offers a newsletter, a directory and insurance at group rates, plus educational and supportive meetings.

EEI, 66 Canal Center Plaza, Suite 200, Alexandria, VA 22314–5507; 800–683–8380 or 703–683–0683; fax: 703–683–4915; e-mail: info@eeicom.com. <http://www.eeicom.com>.

The magnificent *New York Public Library Writer's Guide to Style and Usage* and other valuable titles created by EEI are described above. If you sell writing and/or editing services, check out additional offerings in the EEI Press catalog and training brochures.

The Foundation Center, 79 Fifth Avenue, New York, NY 10003–3076, 212–620–4230; 1001 Connecticut Avenue, NW, Suite 938, Washington, DC 20036, 202–331–1400; Hurt Building, Suite 150, 50 Hurt Plaza, Atlanta, GA 30303–2914, 404–880–0094; 312 Sutter Street, San Francisco, CA 94108, 415–397–0902; 1356 Hanna Building, 1422 Euclid Avenue, Cleveland, OH 44115, 216–861–1934. <http://www.fdncenter.org>.

With national offices in New York and Washington, DC, field offices in Atlanta, San Francisco and Cleveland and cooperating collections in libraries throughout the United States and abroad, the Foundation Center is a splendid source of information about thousands of foundations that offer grants to individuals and groups. See "Tools," above, for information on the Center's publications.

Freelance Editorial Association, PO Box 380835, Cambridge, MA 02238–0835;781–643–8626.
<http://www.tiac.net/users/freelance/index.htm>.
   "A nationwide nonprofit organization, run by volunteers, that works to promote the interests of editorial freelancers."

International Association of Business Communicators, One Hallidie Plaza, Suite 600, San Francisco, CA 94102; 800–776–4222; fax: 415–362–8762.
   Are you working part-time for big business to pay the bills, or thinking of doing that? If so, consider joining IABC. It offers seminars, a job hotline, a speakers bureau and excellent opportunities to network through local chapters.

The National Association of Independent Publishers Representatives, 111 East 14th Street, Suite 157, New York, NY 10003; 888–624–7779; e-mail: naipr@aol.com.
   If you're getting to the point where you'll be publishing several titles a year, send for information on NAIPR, a group of roughly 300 reps. Their pamphlet "Selling on Commission: Guidelines for Publishers" provides an overview.

National Endowment for the Arts.
   See "The Self-Publishing Option Resources"

Poets & Writers, Inc., 72 Spring Street, New York, NY 10012; 212–226–3586. <http://www.pw.org>.
   Through their publications and referral services, Poets & Writers can boost the income as well as the spirits of people who write fiction and poetry.

State Councils for the Arts.
   The best way to find out whether your state has an arts council is by writing your governor's office. If it does, ask for full information about the council's programs.

U.S. Government.
   Federal agencies engaged in all sorts of activities have libraries and

issue press releases about where funds are going and what they've been earmarked for. There's grist for sales and promotion plans when and if money is allocated to a particular region for study of the particular subject you've written about, so ask to be put on the mailing lists of agencies whose bailiwicks are relevant to your writing/publishing efforts. And find out if they have special-interest libraries that might buy your book.

Volunteer Lawyers for the Arts, 1 East 53rd Street, 6th Floor, New York, NY 10022 and other locations (see below); 212–319–2787. VLA Art Law Hotline: 212–319–2910.

Founded in New York to provide legal services for artists who can't afford lawyers' fees, Volunteer Lawyers for the Arts has affiliates across the continent: in California (San Francisco, Los Angeles and La Jolla), Colorado (Denver), Connecticut (Hartford), the District of Columbia, Florida (Clearwater, Fort Lauderdale, Miami and Tallahassee), Georgia (Atlanta), Illinois (Chicago), Iowa (Cedar Rapids and Dubuque), Kentucky (Lexington and Louisville), Louisiana (New Orleans), Maine (Augusta), Maryland (Baltimore), Massachusetts (Amherst and Boston), Minnesota (Minneapolis), Missouri (St. Louis), Montana (Missoula), New Jersey (Trenton), New York (Albany, Buffalo, Huntington and Poughkeepsie, as well as New York City), North Carolina (Raleigh), Ohio (Cleveland and Toledo), Oklahoma (Oklahoma City), Ontario (Toronto), Pennsylvania (Philadelphia), Rhode Island (Narragansett), South Carolina (Greenville), Tennessee (Nashville), Texas (Austin and Houston), Utah (Salt Lake City) and Washington (Seattle). Write or call the affiliate nearest you to find out about services and costs, or send $10 to the NYC office for the group's directory.

Women in Communications, 10605 Judicial Drive, Suite A–4, Fairfax, VA 22030–5167; 703–359–9000.

Job hotlines and programs that hone professional skills are just two of the benefits Women in Communications offers members. Contact national headquarters for information on nearby chapters.

Writers Groups.

Like IABC and Women in Communications, The Authors Guild, PEN and several other writers groups help writers save money, by offering medical insurance at group rates, for example. See entries in "The Sale and Its Sequels Resources" and be sure to find out how groups you belong to can make your dollars stretch.

Index

About the Author

Judith Appelbaum—who's been a columnist and reviewer for *The New York Times Book Review,* an editor of *Harper's* and the managing editor of *Publishers Weekly*—is managing director of Sensible Solutions, Inc., the New York book marketing firm. Winner of the Publishers Marketing Association Benjamin Franklin Award for Lifetime Achievement, she serves on the faculty of the Publishing Institute at the University of Denver and is a leader in industry efforts to improve royalty payments for the benefit of authors and publishers alike.